An Apollo 11 Memoir

BY

RICHARD STACHURSKI

Copyright © 2013 Richard Stachurski
All rights reserved.
ISBN: 1482527650
ISBN-13: 9781482527650
Library of Congress Control Number: 2013902941
CreateSpace Independent Publishing Platform,
North Charleston, South Carolina

Below Tranquility Base

An Apollo 11 *Memoir*
by
Richard Stachurski

FOR THE MEN AND WOMEN OF THE
APOLLO MANNED SPACE FLIGHT
NETWORK WHO MADE THIS
MISSION POSSIBLE

CONTENTS

Photo/Illustration Credits	IX
Preface	1
Cast of Characters	3
Part I Rehearsal	7
Chapter One	9
Chapter Two	17
Chapter Three	25
Part II Dress Rehearsal	35
Chapter Four	37
Chapter Five	43
Chapter Six	51
Chapter Seven	61
Part III An Unlikely Actor	71
Chapter Eight	73
Chapter Nine	79
Chapter Ten	85
Chapter Eleven	91
Chapter Twelve	97
Chapter Thirteen	103

Chapter Fourteen	115
Chapter Fifteen	127
Chapter Sixteen	135
Part IV Beginner's Call	141
Chapter Seventeen	143
Part V Curtain Time	151
Chapter Eighteen	153
Chapter Nineteen	171
Chapter Twenty	193
Chapter Twenty-One	207
Chapter Twenty-Two	229
Chapter Twenty-Three	263
Part VI Curtain Call	293
Chapter Twenty-Four	295
End Note	299
Appendix A—The Manned Space Flight Network	301
Appendix B—Saturn V Launch Vehicle	313
Appendix C—Command and Service Module	319
Appendix D—Lunar Module	327
Appendix E—Abbreviations and Acronyms	331
About The Author	333

PHOTO/ILLUSTRATION CREDITS

Figure 1: The layout of the third floor of the Mission Control Center. (NASA illustration)

Figure 2: The *Apollo 11* control room console positions. (NASA illustration)

Figure 3: The *Apollo 9* Orange Team. (NASA photo)

Figure 4: The author, Major John Monkvic with his signature sunglasses, and George Egan, who is partially visible nearest the camera. (Screen shot from a NASA documentary film)

Figure 5: Flight Director Gene Kranz and his White Team. (NASA photo courtesy of George Ojalehto)

Figure 6: A beaming Chris Kraft celebrates the safe recovery of *Apollo 11*. (NASA photo)

Figure 7: Up against the ceiling of the Mission Control Room: the infamous *Apollo 11* mission plaque. (NASA photo)

Figure A-1: The 210-foot Goldstone Mars antenna that tracked *Apollo 11* down to the lunar surface. (NASA photo)

Figure A-2: The worldwide *Apollo* Manned Space Flight Network. (NASA illustration)

Figure A-3: The tracking ship *Vanguard*. (US Navy photo)

Figure A-4: A cutaway view of the ARIA. (NASA illustration)

Figure B-1: The Saturn V launch vehicle and *Apollo* spacecraft. (NASA illustration)

Figure B-2: The Saturn third stage and the *Apollo* spacecraft. (NASA illustration)

Figure B-3: The Mobile Service Structure being moved away from the launchpad. (NASA photo)
Figure C-1: Apollo Command and Service Modules and Launch Escape System. (NASA illustration)
Figure C-2: Command Module. (NASA illustration)
Figure C-3: Antenna locations. (NASA illustration)
Figure D-1: Lunar Module. (NASA illustration)

PREFACE

Did you ever have a job that you would pay to do? I did. No, really, it's true. Did I tell my boss that? No, I did not. What was this dream job, and how did I, of all people, come to have it? How well did I do the job? Those are all good questions. This book is meant to answer them.

It began about three years ago with the discovery of four handwritten notebooks found in the bottom of a box full of *Apollo* memorabilia. At the time, my instinct was to leave them in their quiet hiding place. I was fully engaged in researching a book on a totally different subject. However, I took the first notebook and read a portion of it to my writers' group, the Saturday Literature Saloon. The members made it clear, immediately and forcibly, that if I didn't stop what I was doing and get started on a memoir based on the notebooks they would "vote me off the island." This book is the result. I am indebted to Nancy Cisneros, who patiently edited my attempts at meaningful prose.

CAST OF CHARACTERS

CALL SIGN	POSITION
AFD	Assistant Flight Director—Assists the flight director and acts for him in his absence.
BOOSTER	Booster Systems Engineer—Monitors and evaluates performance of Saturn V propulsion systems during pre-launch and ascent. The booster systems engineer can send an abort command to the spacecraft.
CAPCOM	Capsule Communicator—Provides the communications interface between the space vehicle crew and the flight controllers.
COMPUTER M&O	Computer Maintenance and Operations—Part of the team responsible for the configuration and operation of the mission operations computer (MOC); reports to the computer supervisor.
COMPUTER SUP	Computer Supervisor—Oversees operation of the mission operations computer (MOC) at the Mission Control Center in Houston. The MOC receives telemetry and tracking data, computes position and maneuver data, monitors space vehicle status, and generates displays for the flight controllers.

COMM CONTROL	Communications Controller—Responsible for long-line communications between Houston and the worldwide tracking network.
COMM TECH	Air-to-Ground Communications Technician—Responsible for maintaining continuous, high-quality communications with the flight crew whenever the spacecraft is in view of a tracking station.
CONTROL	Lunar Module Guidance, Control, and Propulsion Officer—Responsible for the propulsion, guidance and navigation, and control systems of the Lunar Module.
CPC	Communications Processor Controller—Team leader responsible for operation of the computers that receive data from the tracking network and route it within the Mission Control Center.
CVTS	Space Vehicle Test Supervisor (Kennedy Space Center)—Test conductor for the Saturn V launch vehicle.
DISPLAY	Display Technician—Oversees the group and individual display systems that supply mission controllers with vehicle and crew status data.
EECOM	Command and Service Module (CSM) Electrical, Environmental, and Consumables Manager—Monitors CSM electrical power generation, distribution, and consumption. Also responsible for cabin structural integrity, temperature, pressure, and lighting.
FAO	Flight Activities Officer—Keeps track of progress against the mission flight plan, and develops and coordinates revised plans as mission progress requires.
FLIGHT	Flight Director—Responsible for conduct of the mission from the time the launch vehicle lifts clear of the Launch Umbilical Tower at Kennedy Space Center until mission recovery.
FIDO	Flight Dynamics Officer—Specialist in launch and descent trajectories and orbital parameters.

GNC	Guidance, Navigation, and Control Officer—Responsible for Command and Service Module (CSM) propulsion, attitude control, and navigation systems.
GODDARD VOICE	Goddard Voice Control Technician (Goddard Space Flight Center)—Works with the Houston communications control technician to configure and maintain tracking network voice communications.
GUIDO	Guidance Officer—Navigation and guidance software specialist.
HOUSTON TM	Houston Telemetry Technician—Maintains and operates the telemetry ground stations that receive and distribute space vehicle telemetry.
INCO	Instrumentation and Communications Systems Officer—Responsible for Command and Service Module (CSM) communications.
NETWORK	Network Controller—Exercises operational control of the worldwide network of tracking stations, ships, and aircraft that provides spacecraft tracking data, and relays spacecraft telemetry and voice communications to the Mission Control Center.
O&P	Operations and Procedures Officer—Responsible to the flight director for interpretation and implementation of the mission rules.
PAO	Public Affairs Officer—Releases information on mission progress.
RETRO	Retrofire Officer—Plans trajectories for a safe return to Earth from any point in the mission profile, including required retrofire times.

RSO	Range Safety Officer (Air Force Eastern Test Range)—Represents the air force commander responsible for the operation of the Eastern Test Range. Has the authority to order the remote destruction of the Saturn launch vehicle if it shows signs of being out of control during launch and crosses preset abort limits designed to protect populated areas.
RTC	Real-Time Command Controller—Monitors and maintains the capability to uplink commands to the *Apollo* spacecraft.
SIMSUP	Simulation Supervisor—Leader of the team that conducts integrated training exercises for flight crews and flight controllers.
SRO	Supervisor of Range Operations—The air force agent responsible for the overall conduct of operations on the Air Force Eastern Test Range, a chain of shore- and sea-based launch and tracking sites, including launch pads at Cape Canaveral Air Force Station and John F. Kennedy Space Center.
SURGEON	Medical Officer—Monitors the health of the flight crew members and responds to in-flight health concerns.
TELCOM	Lunar Module Telemetry, Electrical, Extra Vehicular Activity Mobility Unit Officer—Monitors Lunar Module electrical and environmental systems and the functioning of the lunar extravehicular activity spacesuits.
TIC	Telemetry Instrumentation Controller—Monitors and maintains the flow of telemetry data from the tracking stations to the Houston Mission Control Center.
TRACK	Tracking Controller—Responsible for the quality of tracking data transmitted from remote stations to Houston. Prepares the Site Configuration Message, which contains instructions on how a tracking station is to set up its systems for the next space vehicle viewing period.

PART I
REHEARSAL

CHAPTER ONE

Midsummer dawn on the coastal plains of Texas is not very different from the hot, humid afternoons. The air that moves through the window as I drive chills momentarily, but doesn't really cool. It carries the sound of frogs from the bayou that runs parallel to the road. Its black waters are invisible in the early light, but it's there, with its brilliant egrets and squat, ugly cottonmouth snakes. Spanish moss hangs from great black oak columns and glints gray-green in my headlights. The morning air carries not only sound, but a smell of dense, rotting vegetation. The jungles of Ceylon must smell this way, but the odor doesn't belong here on the white-striped concrete of Bay Area Boulevard as I head west in the general direction of a town called Clear Lake City.

The road to the small town of Webster doesn't spend all of its time in the bayou thickets. Instead as you cross Horsepen Slough you detect a sudden lessening of the forest cover. On the right, across open fields, the silhouettes of tract houses rise up out of the darkness. On the left, you can make out the shapes of larger, multistoried buildings. Those larger outlines mark my destination, but I can't get there from here at this hour of the morning, at least not directly. The buildings are surrounded by a six-foot-high chain-link fence. The secondary gates that allow access are closed. I have to head for the main gate, running the red light as I turn left from Bay Area Boulevard onto El Camino Real. No one is around to give a damn about red lights at this hour of the morning—a thought that makes me wonder what I'm doing here myself. That notion escalates to the larger question of why I am here at all. I disallow that thought and it fades, but not without a struggle.

I head south on El Camino, the main artery of Clear Lake City, a sprawling, bedroom suburb that didn't exist in 1961. Now, in the midsummer of 1969, the Dickinson Shopping Center supports the residents of the single-story, brick-faced homes that line streets with names like Seafoam Road and Buccaneer Lane. Along the east side of El Camino, shiny new two-story office buildings house NASA support contractors like Philco-Ford and Grumman. About a mile south of these office buildings, just past the volunteer fire department, El Camino intersects what once had been sleepy Farm to Market Road 528. I turn left onto what is now NASA Road One, a broad boulevard lined with office buildings, hotels, motels, restaurants, and the ubiquitous fast-food outlets.

From the top floor of one of the hotels, the black, all-seeing eye of CBS peers out of a white background at a cluster of buildings across the highway. Those buildings are my early morning destination—NASA's Manned Spacecraft Center. The view from that hotel is probably very familiar to you even if you have never, ever traveled south of Philadelphia. It has served as the background for hundreds of hours of news reports and interviews read or conducted by the always avuncular Walter Cronkite and his colleagues. This morning, as has been the case in many of those news reports, you can see a random pattern of lights burning on various floors of the buildings that make up the NASA complex.

Sentences like, "The lights burn brightly here in Houston tonight as NASA specialists concentrate on diagnosing and fixing the problems with the triple-decker cogitator circuitry," delivered with appropriate solemnity, always provided a neat lead-in or cutoff for the CBS newscasts. In fact, the lights that were on as those grave words were spoken were probably on for the same reason they're on now. The night people, the cleanup crews, always supervised by large black women wearing yellow rubber gloves and aquamarine pedal pushers, are moving from office to office in the buildings that can have a single story to as many as nine, like in Building 2. That's where the director of flight operations, Christopher Kraft, presides.

As I turn left off NASA Road One toward the center's main gate, I switch off my headlights so that the guard can see the security pass on the windshield of my battered VW. Instead of waving me through as I expected, he raises his hand for me to stop. At this hour I'm even shorter on original thoughts than usual, so I fall back on the not-so-creative, *Oh fuck, what now?*

"Could I see your badge, sir? Special check this morning," says the voice above the roof of my car.

After I fumble for the badge in my pocket and hand it to the guard, he compares the face in the picture to the sleepy collection of features framed by the car window. That can't be a real treat—the head on the badge has big ears and GI eyeglasses, topped by brown crew-cut hair. The head in the window looks even worse, layered over as it is with a thick coat of tired.

Satisfied, the guard hands back the badge.

"Thank you, sir. Have a nice day."

"I think it may be way too early for that to happen."

The man must be used to these hours—he's so goddamn cheerful. Somewhat less cheerful, I slide the badge into my shirt pocket with my left hand as my right pushes the gear shift toward first.

After getting by the gate guard, I head straight down the length of 2nd Street, a broad thoroughfare that runs along the western edge of the main complex of center buildings. The entire center covers about 1,600 acres on the edge of Clear Lake, a small saltwater extension of Galveston Bay. Most of the major buildings are confined to a smaller area, leaving much of the acreage to field grasses and trees. The buildings themselves, mostly dark now except for random rectangles of yellow light, are constructed of a light-tan stone that is nearly white in sunlight and contrasts sharply with the large, darkly tinted windows. The architecture is institutional but still manages to be very nearly attractive, resembling a modern college campus, with a large quadrangle at the center of the complex and walkways that go from point to point in the most indirect way possible. Unlike Cape Kennedy where the Erector Set steel towers make the center's function clear, it would be hard to guess what goes on here if it were not for an occasional roof decorated with an array of antennas. Much to the dismay of some tourists, there's not much to see in the way of impressive hardware. The most critical activities go on inside—inside buildings, inside electrical circuits, inside people's heads—and the most important buildings have no windows that might hint at their inner purpose.

The buildings don't have names. They have numbers. Building 47 flickers by on the right. I know it's time to turn right onto Avenue C. Half a block later, I turn right again into an asphalt parking lot rendered grayish-green by the glare of mercury vapor streetlamps illuminating the space between night and day. The lot is nearly empty. The darting gray moths far outnumber the cars. On the left, the single-story cafeteria building is dark. On my right is a two-story windowless structure, featureless outside, but with insides looking like a scene from Chaplin's *Modern Times*. Engine generators and motor generators whose health is charted on a garish illuminated status panel seem to fill every square foot of floor space. Their power feeds half of the hybrid structure directly ahead of me. The left half of that building, Building 30, is a two-story office wing not unlike many others on the site. My own office is there (or at least my desk is there in a room shared with three others), but the real business of Building 30 is carried on in the right wing—a three-story windowless structure whose contours mimic the shape of its computer inhabitants. A two-story structure connects the two wings. Viewed from the air, the three structures have the shape of an H. The lobby of the building is in the crossbar of the H. I pick a parking space close to the walkway that leads between the wings toward the lobby. Finding a close spot will be a problem later in the day. Right now, convenient parking is, as nearly as I can tell, the one and only fringe benefit of arriving in the gray light of dawn. I pull into a space two steps from the sidewalk and shut down the VW—ignition off with the right hand, lights off with the left, brake on with the right, left hand to the door, and right hand to my briefcase.

Somehow neither the slam of the car door nor the sounds of my steps sound very crisp in the humid Gulf Coast morning—a condition of the atmosphere or a state of mind? I go up two steps and start along the walkway, empty lit offices on my left and the solid aggregate wall of the Mission Operations Wing on my right. W. C. Fields peers incongruously from his poster perch on a white wall in one of the office spaces. The walk is short. A rush of conditioned air escapes as I open the lobby door.

The sound of the door attracts the attention of the security guard on duty at the desk on the right side of the lobby. He stirs and looks up sleepily. A broad grin appears on his black face, and he speaks his greeting in a slightly mocking drawl, "Well, looks like somebody else has pulled some prime duty time today! What's goin' on at this hour?"

"Not much is going on yet, Mr. Jones, but we're going to pull the building together and run some launch simulations later on this morning," I reply, using the formal title because I don't know the man's first name. It occurs to me that this lack of knowledge is strange. I see the man often enough and enjoy our exchanges. We have discovered that we were at one time stationed at the same northern air force base, he as an air policeman and I as a missile launch officer. This connection adds a special flavor to our conversations at these odd hours, but somehow the problem of first names is never solved. It won't get solved this morning either. I have too many other things to worry about.

Mr. Jones's desk sits at the entrance to a short hallway leading from the brightly lit lobby into the windowless Operations Wing.

"Y'all do all of the right things today, ya hear!" is Jones's parting comment as I go past his desk.

"You bet," I reply over my shoulder as I head in the general direction of the half-windowed doors of the main computer complex. About twenty feet short of those doors another hall joins the first hall from the left. I turn into that hall, which is lined with doors—elevators on each side, and restrooms at the end. It occurs to me that the stairs would provide some badly needed exercise. But at this hour, that notion never comes close to the action stage. Instead, I punch the elevator button and the blue doors slide open—not much competition for the elevators at this hour.

As the doors slide shut I push the button for the third floor. The elevator lurches into motion and starts an uneven ascent. "Everything is up to date in Space City," is the only comment I can muster as I think for the hundredth time about the really dumb bastards who decided to install these hydraulic motors instead of the normal electric motor–driven cable mechanisms. I guess the idea was to avoid installing big electric motors that might affect the functioning of the building's delicate electronic systems. Whatever the reason, the elevators spend more time out of service for maintenance than anything else in the building—a building crammed full of gee-whiz gadgets. One of my coworkers jokes that if we don't reach the Moon it will be because these elevators didn't get the right people to the control room.

Eventually, the elevator reaches the third floor after just two heart-stopping shudders. A left turn out of the elevator and three or four steps put me into one of the four hallways on this floor. The hallways form a square, which separates an outer ring of support rooms and cable connection cabinets from an inner core of equipment and control rooms. The floor I walk on is made up of three-foot-square panels mounted on steel frames that are removable to allow access to cable space under the floor. Miles and miles of wire covered by gray insulation are strung under the three floors of the building.

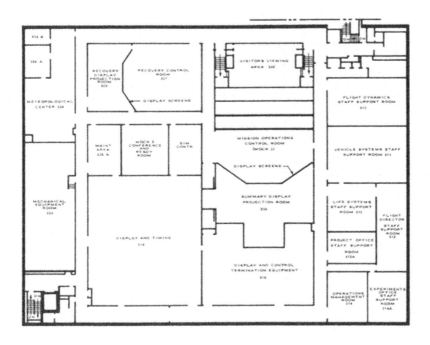

Figure 1: The layout of the third floor of the Mission Control Center. (NASA illustration)

About the time that I reach the coffee and snack machines lined up along the inboard side of the hall, an inhabitant of the electrical underworld appears in a black, rectangular hole left by a missing floor panel. The cable troll sports a gray crew cut. A brown work shirt and matching trousers work hard to cover the beer belly that overhangs his brown leather tool belt. You have to wonder how he gets around down there in that dark, cramped netherworld.

"Hey, NETWORK,[1] how come they got your ass in here at this hour?" he growls down the length of the corridor.

---

1   My communications call sign is NETWORK. The job title is Network Controller. Appendix A provides a description of the Apollo Manned Space Flight Network that I am supposed to control during the upcoming lunar landing mission.

"Well if it isn't Tom Swift and his Electric Grandmother! What are you doing feeding the building at this hour?" My question is a serious one. They may be doing something that I will need to know about in a couple of hours.

"Some dumbass in Recovery Control decided he needed some extra voice loops. Has to have them today—can't wait! What's so fuckin' important today?"

"Launch sims today, Dutch. Last practice session before the real thing. Everybody is getting a little nervous now that we're almost there. I don't know why those guys need them today. Maybe they're just getting spooked."

"There ain't nothing to be nervous about! I ain't nervous. Are you?"

"Dutch, I get nervous every time I think about you and your gang of cable thieves crawling around pulling out wires by the handful."

"Don't worry about us, NETWORK. We'll be done before launch day. Then it'll be your turn."

My reply is smothered by the appearance of a head around the corner and a shout reminding Dutch of the necessary connection between pulling cable and continued employment. I backtrack to my original destination, a gray door set back about four feet from the hall on the inboard side. Reaching for the door handle, I try to force my head into a higher gear. The room behind the doors is the third-floor Mission Operations Control Room—*Apollo 11* Mission Control. Time to quit screwing around and go to work.

CHAPTER TWO

The door opens into the right rear corner of the control room. The wall on my right as I enter runs the full length of the room. The flat plane of the wall is broken first by the large windows of the adjacent Recovery Control Room, then by double doors leading to another hallway, and finally by the windows of the Simulation Control Room. High up on the wall above the windows, standing out in multicolored contrast to the institutional gray walls, are plaques displaying the emblems worn by each of the *Gemini* flight crews. The custom of crew patches began on *Gemini V*. Each subsequent crew designed its own emblem bearing their names and the mission number. Only the *Gemini X* patch doesn't have the crew members' names on it (Young and Collins). The plaques, hung like heraldry-emblazoned shields in the great hall of some Norman castle, lent a kind of historical solemnity to a room less than ten years old. What with shining white space suits and fiery steeds from the Martin Company stables, the parallel doesn't seem to be too much of a stretch—I wonder if William the Conqueror was given to muttering the medieval equivalent of "Oh, shit!" when things didn't go quite right.

The decorations on the left wall of the corridor are functional—wall lockers used for storage by the people who work in the control room, and a small gray door that allows access to the control room lighting panels. The left wall extends no more than twenty-five feet from the entry door that I used, before it diminishes into a series of three steps that descend about five feet down to floor level. As you walk past these steps, the corridor gives way to the larger expanse of the control room itself. It becomes apparent that the steps are actually three tiers stretching across the rear of the room and providing amphitheater-like benches for three rows of consoles. A fourth row of consoles squats on the control room floor in front of the three gradually elevated rows. The entire front wall of the control room is covered by display devices—two plot-boards, one ten by twenty feet and another ten by ten feet, as well as three ten-by-ten projection TV screens.

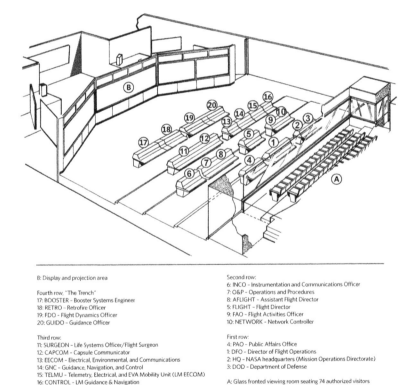

B: Display and projection area

Fourth row, "The Trench"
17: BOOSTER – Booster Systems Engineer
18: RETRO – Retrofire Officer
19: FDO – Flight Dynamics Officer
20: GUIDO – Guidance Officer

Third row:
11: SURGEON – Life Systems Officer/Flight Surgeon
12: CAPCOM – Capsule Communicator
13: EECOM – Electrical, Environmental, and Communications
14: GNC – Guidance, Navigation, and Control
15: TELMU – Telemetry, Electrical, and EVA Mobility Unit (LM EECOM)
16: CONTROL – LM Guidance & Navigation

Second row:
6: INCO – Instrumentation and Communications Officer
7: O&P – Operations and Procedures
8: AFLIGHT – Assistant Flight Director
5: FLIGHT – Flight Director
9: FAO – Flight Activities Officer
10: NETWORK – Network Controller

First row:
4: PAO – Public Affairs Office
1: DFO – Director of Flight Operations
2: HQ – NASA headquarters (Mission Operations Directorate)
3: DOD – Department of Defense

A: Glass fronted viewing room seating 74 authorized visitors

Figure 2: The *Apollo 11* control room console positions. (NASA illustration)

At the rear of the room, behind the rows of consoles, large windows reveal the tiered red seats of the viewing room—a theater-like arrangement that offers tour groups an unsurpassed view of genuine, steely-eyed rocket scientists laboring in this great hall of whiz-bang technology. In the opinion of some of the flight controllers, the monkey-house environment created by the glass panels does have its compensations—especially when the tour group is made up of Texas coeds who forget that they are sitting above us so that we can, perhaps, see more than they suspect.

At this hour, both the viewing room lights and the control room lights are turned up to their brightest setting. In this light, the control room carpet shows its age—ragged edges, tears at the corners, and random coffee stains. The four rows of light green consoles crouch like so many aluminum frogs. The expressions in their cathode-ray eyes range from dull black through sullen gray to bright, empty whiteness. At the front of the room, the large group displays are blank, showing only hundreds of square feet of matte black screen. Only the Greenwich Mean Time clock display mounted above one of the projection TV screens is active, its red digits rolling over to remind me that I had better get on with what I had come here to get on with.

Flickering white lights on the console communications panels give evidence that lines are in use. Somewhere in the building hardware or computer tests are being run and coordinated on the circuits marked by the busy white lights. The control room is stark and silent, almost drab in the bright light from the incandescent fixtures overhead—not at all the setting for great drama. Not now—but soon—the room will be transformed as the houselights are dimmed and the players come on stage to rehearse again the spectacle set to open on the sixteenth day of July, when three men set out for the Moon. This show will open out of town—a quarter of a million miles out of town.

It's time to start the transformation. The first order of business is coffee. I climb up two tiers to the console at the right end of the fourth row—the end nearest the short banister that separates the console tiers from the hall with the gray lockers. I collect the coffeepot and head off back to the utility room near the elevators to clean and refill it. Space exploration requires personal sacrifice.

Once the coffee is in the works, the next priority is a trip to the small gray door near the hall lockers. Behind the door, in a small pit-like room, are the rheostats for the control room lights. When you enter the room you can't see the lights you're trying to adjust. I have to squeeze my awkward six-foot-three-inch frame through the door two or three times before I find a satisfactory combination. With the light lowered, the mood of the control room begins to change. Shadows hide stains and frayed edges. The flashing lights of the communications panels and the bright cathode ray displays now add a sense of urgency and importance.

Eminently more dramatic, I think as I make my way back to my console. I pull up one of the gray plastic-and-chrome chairs as I think about the next steps in getting the set ready for today's rehearsal. I flip open the black three-ring binder containing the console log sheets and make the required entries—type of test, console position, date, and operator's name. Two time columns run down the left side of each sheet, one labeled GMT and the other T/GET. GMT stands for Greenwich Mean Time, the time at the prime meridian passing through the old Royal Observatory at Greenwich, England. Having everyone use the twenty-four-hour GMT or ZULU clock, as it is sometimes called, is meant to prevent a timetable Tower of Babel by providing a single reference for operations that extend across all of the Earth's time zones. The other column, T/GET, refers to two different times. A T time or, more often, a T minus time refers to the time remaining before some major event such as liftoff. I've read somewhere that up through the launch of the Explorer 2 satellite back in 1958, the term X minus time was used. I don't know why a change was made. But given that Explorer 2's launch vehicle failed and the satellite never reached orbit, the change may have been part of a search for better karma. Or maybe T just sounded less ominous than X.

In any case, we have T minus time and its counterpart GET, or ground elapsed time, which is just the time elapsed since mission liftoff. The GMT digital clock shows ten hours and twenty-eight minutes. To the right of that clock, a second clock shows a T minus time of one hour and thirty-two minutes, referenced to the start of today's launch simulation. I enter both times in the log with the note, "Console manned."

With the log initiated, I swivel my chair slightly to the right and lean over to open the bottom drawer in a two-drawer pedestal that sits under the shelf of the console. The drawers separate my operating position on the left half of the console from that of my assistant who is due on board a little later in the morning. Reaching toward the rear of the drawer, I gather up a fresh pad of notepaper, resisting the temptation to thumb through the ever-present *Playboy* magazine. No time for that.

I swivel around toward the rear of the room and retrieve another black binder from a small shelf formed by the next console tier. A label identifies the binder as the "Support Count Handbook," a most useful document filled with recipes for whatever operation you might like to run today. In fact, the book contains so-called support counts that give a time-phased scheme for preparing and integrating all of the elements required by a particular operation. There is, for instance, a count for tests involving Houston and the actual spacecraft on the launchpad. Another countdown, the one we are running today, integrates the Houston control and simulation elements with the Command and Service Module simulator at Cape Kennedy. Each countdown starts with the checkout of the most basic system elements and then progressively adds them together in an orderly sequence until they make an integrated whole, capable of supporting the planned operation—at least that's the theory. In practice, some damn thing always breaks, and then the count just helps you remember the pieces that need to be juggled to get to the right place at the required time.

Flipping the book open to the simulation support count, I list on my notepad all of the steps that should have been completed prior to my arrival—a device for finding out where I ought to be. I will have to talk to some people to see if that's where I really am, so I open my briefcase and extract the black coils of my headset. I clip the headset to the frame of my glasses on the left side, insert the earpiece, and position the slender microphone. With my left hand, I reach over and plug the headset jack into its receptacle on the edge of the console shelf, simultaneously depressing a white key on the communications panel labeled NETWORK. A slight pressure with my right foot on the transmit switch located on the floor under the console, and our simulated space spectacular is on the air.

"COMM CONTROL, NETWORK, my loop."

My first call is to the communications console position on the first floor. The communications controller is likely to be monitoring six or more voice channels. The words *my loop* tell him that I am calling on a circuit labeled NETWORK that is dedicated to my use for controlling center operations. My voice comes back to me so loudly in the empty control room that I wonder about the need for a headset.

"NETWORK, COMM CONTROL, if you don't knock that shit off, you'll wake somebody up down here," comes the reply, delivered in a monotone snarl.

It doesn't take any more than that to identify the midnight shift controller. Steve Richards, variously known as "Gramps" or the "Brain Surgeon," is a balding former master sergeant slightly older than most of the other technicians and controllers. That's not hard to do considering that the average age of the controllers working in the room will be about twenty-six when the full team comes on board. Richard's age, his gap-toothed buccaneer grin combined with more than the usual human allotment of cussedness, and a vocabulary that Norman Mailer would envy account for the "Gramps" sobriquet.

His second nickname was earned in a fleeting, unsuccessful encounter with Hollywood fame. As happened fairly frequently, a film crew was working in the control room on some space-related epic. A part of the script required the star, actor Hugh

O'Brian, to be filmed at the CAPCOM console. Richards and some others were rounded up to sit at the other consoles in the room to lend authenticity to the scene. He ended up at the SURGEON's console adjacent to the CAPCOM console. During a break in the shooting, O'Brian, who probably had no idea of the source or real-life role of the conscripted extras, turned to his left and politely asked Richards if he was actually a doctor. Without hesitation or the least trace of levity, Richards replied, "Yeah, I'm a fucking brain surgeon."

"Good morning to you, Mr. Richards. How's the count going?"

"Pretty good so far, NETWORK. All of the circuits are up and checked. The only problem was one of the Cape air-to-ground circuit checks. The level was low when COMM TECH ran his checks. Those clowns at the simulator said it was the line. We took it down and it checked out OK. They're checking the crew station at their end now—should be up pretty soon."

"Rog, COMM CONTROL. Everything else on schedule?"

"That's affirm, your Networkship. It's all yours."

"OK, Steve. Give me a shout if you see a telemetry cat show up. COMPUTER M&O will want to run some checks before the simulation starts."

"Roger that, NETWORK."

With the communications circuits up and checked, we're on our way to another rehearsal of another rehearsal. The communications links are checked out early in every count. They are the copper and steel nervous system that, during an actual mission, ties together the Manned Space Flight Network. The circuit paths for today's simulation are much simpler than those required for an actual mission. They connect the Command Module simulator at Cape Kennedy directly to Building 422 here on-site. For today's exercise, the simulation controllers will merge the spacecraft simulator data with counterfeit booster data, run it through some computers and switching gear to make it look like it came from a network tracking station, and pass it on to their "trainees" at the Cape and here in the control center.

The simulators at the Cape, where most of the crew training is done, don't look much like spacecraft from the outside. The interior of the simulator duplicates the crew compartment of the actual vehicle. The outside consists of a series of boxlike structures piled one on another. The structures contain the mechanisms needed to simulate various functions. The boxes that cover the windows, for example, provide a realistic view of the outside environment. Both the Command Module and the Lunar Module simulators look like a jumble of blocks teetering in a precarious pile. Astronaut John Young described the Command and Service Module simulator as looking like "the great train wreck."

During a familiarization and training trip to the Cape, Riley McCafferty, the knowledgeable and always cordial manager of the spacecraft simulator group, gave me ten minutes of instruction on how to drive a Lunar Module and then sent me off to make a simulated docking with the Command Module. The last thing I saw, before everything went dark, was the side of the Service Module coming at me at high speed.

A crew in training might spend hundreds of hours in the Lunar Module and Command and Service Module simulators, training on their own or in integrated linkups with Houston. During an integrated launch simulation such as today's, the simulation people use their magical powers to confuse, confound, and generally screw over the minds and egos of both crew members and flight controllers. The Simulation Supervisor (SIMSUP) and his band of sorcerers watch the consternation they create through the windows of their operations room located on the right-hand wall of the Mission Control Room. They go about their task with a near maniacal thoroughness, simulating hardware and software failures—sometimes even people failures.

CHAPTER THREE

"NETWORK, COMPUTER M&O, your loop."

"COMPUTER M&O, NETWORK, go ahead."

"Rog, NETWORK, COMPUTER SUP is in. He asked me to let you know that they're loading the machine now. We'll be ready in a couple of minutes."

"OK, let me know and we'll make a checkout run."

"Roger that, NETWORK."

With the simulators at the Cape and the simulation computers in Houston up and tied together by more than a thousand miles of cable, the mission computer on the first floor and the displays it drives throughout the building are the last props required for our electronic stage production.

"DISPLAY, NETWORK, my loop."

"Go, NETWORK."

"Did you copy COMPUTER M&O?"

"That's affirmative, NETWORK. We'll be ready when he is. Do you want some clocks?"

"Rog, give me a minus five minutes in the countdown clock and a simulation GMT of sixteen July one-three-two-seven. I'll give you a clock start time when we're ready."

"Copy, NETWORK, minus five and thirteen twenty-seven GMT."

Like just about everybody else in this room I have a crew of backroom experts who do most of the real work of getting flight-critical data to the flight controllers. Most of the back rooms are on the same floor as the Mission Control Room. In my case, the back room is on the first floor in the bowels of the building where a fifteen-man group called the Instrumentation Support Team works to make sure that the network communication, command, telemetry, and tracking systems function as required to support the mission plan. These are the people who will work with the mission computer team to check the quality of the data to make sure we're set for this day's run. A quick check shows at least one man on each console. That will do for a checkout.

I'm in the middle of a mental gathering of loose ends from earlier parts of the count when a voice edged with impatience intrudes.

"NETWORK, COMPUTER SUP, on three NETWORK."

Before I can reach to press the foot pedal and respond, the impatient voice tries again. "NETWORK, COMPUTER SUP, how do you read?"

"COMPUTER SUP, NETWORK, you're five-by, how me?"

"Five-by" is shorthand for "five-by-five," a numeric description of circuit quality meaning "loud and clear." A circuit that is weak but readable might be described as "two-by-three." Some of us favor the numerical descriptions.

"You're loud and clear, NETWORK. How about listening up and responding when you're called?"

It doesn't take long to mentally frame a reply. *And a good morning to you, Mr. Clayton, you miserable son of a bitch.* But it's too early in the day to take him on, and besides they have rules about that kind of crap on the circuits. My response is polite but edged with appropriate sarcasm.

"And a bright and shiny good morning to you, COMPUTER SUP."

"I don't know about the morning, NETWORK, but I hope we have a better day than yesterday," comes the ever-so-cordial reply.

"Have a better day! Not much chance, at least not with Mr. Clayton in charge of the computing machinery."

I speak the words without activating the transmit switch, looking forward—with just a measure of self-pity—to a tough morning. But then the thought of Elden Clayton presiding in all his empirical majesty over a room full of harassed controllers and submissive machines brings a faint grin. This Autocrat of the Tape Drives is a small man with delicate hands and features, topped by wavy red hair. He's an impeccable man, both in speech and dress, but his impeccability has a compulsive edge. To go along with his neatly tailored suit, which invariably features a folded handkerchief in the breast pocket, and his color-coordinated shirts and ties, Mr. Clayton possessed the unusual distinction of never, ever making a mistake—at least to hear him tell it. To defend that distinction, he makes free use of a devastating, unguided temper tipped with barbed sarcasm. In other circumstances, that temper, and his God-given infallibility, would classify Clayton as just another asshole to be avoided at all costs.

But these aren't other circumstances. COMPUTER SUP presides over the mission operations computer, an IBM 360. It is the machine that takes in tracking and telemetry data, figures out the health of the space vehicles, determines their present positions, calculates the maneuvers needed to get them to their next intended position, and drives the display systems that get the data to the flight controllers. The functions are so critical that one and sometimes two other machines are operated in parallel, as hot backups. So you can't write Mr. Clayton off. You have to catalog his quirks, track his eccentricities, and keep them in mind as you try to filter any real signal that might be concealed in his verbal noise.

"The operations computer is loaded, NETWORK. We can start a checkout run whenever you're ready."

Clayton's voice catches me in the act of mentally working him over and it takes me a second to pick a start time. "OK, COMPUTER SUP, can you make one-one-three-five?"

"Roger, NETWORK. Tell your people not to make display requests before I clear it."

"My people" know enough to wait until the computer is up and clearance is given before requesting data displays, so I go about my business neatly cutting off Clayton's last word.

"SIM COORD, NETWORK, your loop. Can you make one-one-three-five for a checkout run?"

A quick affirmative reply indicates that the training and simulation computers will be ready. To get the simulation data into the control center, the communications processor, a UNIVAC 490 computer, must be up and ready to route data to the mission computer. Another check confirms that the communications machine is alive and well on the first floor.

The start time has to be coordinated with the other consoles on the first floor, so I depress the white light marked NETWORK on my communications panel. There are dozens of voice circuits on each panel, and each controller might listen to half a dozen or more at any one time. To the uninitiated, it's got to sound like a cross between a hog auction and a Chinese fire drill. Identifying the circuit you're on when you transmit lets the controller at the other end know where to make his reply.

The NETWORK circuit is mine, and the people manning the first-floor consoles—command, telemetry, tracking, communications, and air-to-ground voice—monitor the loop at all times. At least that's the theory.

"RTC, NETWORK, on three NETWORK."

"N-N-NETWORK, RTC, go ahead." Glenn Spears, real-time command controller, comes up on the circuit.

To go along with his stutter, Spears has the shakiest pair of hands in the building. Rumpled hair, glasses perched low on his nose, and a paunch exaggerated by a sunken chest give him the look of a man fighting a losing battle with the Second Law of Thermodynamics. When you look at him you wonder what he could possibly be doing in this world of steely-eyed, no-sweat missile workers.

But when Spears sits down at his console it's like the old Clark-Kent-in-the-phone-booth trick. His hands still shake and his lower lip trembles, but all of the moving parts in his mind engage with a solid, barely audible click.

If you add up all of the moments of sheer terror, the job that Spears does is the most demanding one that our team is responsible for. If you are onboard the *Apollo* spacecraft, your only link with Earth is an invisible electromagnetic umbilical radiating from one of a series of tracking stations ringing the globe in a near equatorial belt. That beam of radio frequency energy provides you voice contact with the blue-and-white planet receding in the black sky. It gives you the data you need to find your way from the Earth to the Moon and back again. Without it you would drift forever in the blackness.

Except for the periods when you are between stations in Earth orbit or behind the Moon in lunar orbit, this electronic carrier beam is locked onto one of your vehicle's antennas like a searchlight tracking a nighttime intruder. Beginning hours before launch, hundreds of people maintain that fragile electronic thread until you return safely to Earth. And when the time comes to hand the spacecraft over from one probing beam to the next because the Earth's rotation is carrying the vehicle out of view of the current ground station, Glenn Spears's job is to see that the handover of the spacecraft from one ground station to the next is precise and orderly with only one carrier on at a time.

Mostly the handovers are routine, taking only a certain amount of timing. The handover times are specified in a Site Configuration Message that reaches each station at least thirty minutes before the station has acquisition of signal. For primary stations, stations scheduled to turn on their uplink carriers and establish two-way lock, the message specifies the vehicle, the uplink mode, and the handover times.

If everything is working normally, stations hand over at the specified times without a countdown from the RTC. But during critical mission phases, with several spacecraft to be tracked at the same time and vital data to be uplinked to a least one of them, ground station failures can and do happen. When they do, Spears has seconds to review available alternative ground stations and spacecraft priorities, and direct the rearrangement that keeps crews and vehicles safe and as close to the planned mission timeline as possible. Two carriers on at the same frequency turn the whole thing to worms. To prevent that, Spears counts the two tracking stations down to a split-second transfer of the electronic torch held out to the voyagers in space. Spears has mastered his trade. He sometimes makes mistakes during simulations. But simulations are the place for mistakes. In the real world, he doesn't make mistakes—and his hands never stop shaking.

"RTC, NETWORK, stand by for a checkout run at one-one-three-five and let me know when you have a good interface."

"R-R-Roger, NETWORK."

"TIC, NETWORK, did you copy?"

"That's affirm, NETWORK," comes the rapid reply from Wayne Boatman, the telemetry instrumentation controller. Boatman is a younger man than Spears, with dark wavy hair, professorial horn-rimmed glasses, and a barrel-chested, broad-shouldered look that suggests great physical strength. Boatman knows what he is supposed to know, and you can get at it with a minimum of flak. No problem there.

"TRACK, NETWORK, did you copy the start time?" No reply—silence. "TRACK, NETWORK, my loop." More silence. This time the transmission has a sharper inflection on its leading edge. "TRACK, NETWORK."

"Go ahead, NETWORK."

"TRACK, NETWORK, how do you read?" This last just to make sure the circuit is working the way it should.

"You're five-by, NETWORK."

The circuit is fine, no problem there.

"Did you copy the checkout run start time?"

"That's negative, NETWORK."

This is turning out to be a lot tougher than it ought to be.

"Can you support a one-one-three-five start?"

"Rog, NETWORK, we're always ready." The comeback is edged with sarcasm, but Don Webb is working the tracking console, so that's no real surprise. Webb is a small man with large barbed-wire eyebrows that he keeps twisted into a perpetual defensive snarl. He's pretty good at what he does if his ego doesn't get in the way—but most of the time it does. He ain't going to take no crap from nobody! Have to keep that in mind.

I hesitate just for a second before calling the next position. Sometimes the cattle-judging quality that clings to the kind of thinking I've just been doing slows me down a little. But usually I can pass through the awkward mental pause with the thought that those kinds of judgments come with the territory. And if I'm working them over, the people in the bowels of the building are returning the compliment. I hope I get a passing grade.

"COMM CONTROL, COMM TECH, did you copy?"

Steve Richards quickly replies, "We hear you, NETWORK."

Chet Brantley, the air-to-ground communications technician, follows with, "Roger, NETWORK."

Brantley, an older white-haired man with a never-failing courtesy in his voice, has a highly specialized job. He worries about one thing—voice communications with the spacecraft. Of all the circuits that reach from Houston to Europe, Australia, Africa, and ships and aircraft on and above the Atlantic, Pacific, and Indian Oceans, those that carry air-to-ground voice are always given priority over other data. Before each spacecraft pass, the air-to-ground communications technician contacts each ground station scheduled to support that pass. He runs checks with the station communications technician to make sure that the very high frequency and Unified S-band voice links are configured and working. He also makes sure that the circuits connecting the ground stations to Goddard Space Flight Center in Maryland and then on to Houston are five-by-five. Brantley's work is highly visible and tense. He is good at it.

With everyone accounted for, I check the GMT clock. It is seconds from rolling over to eleven thirty-five. As the zeroes come up in the seconds slot, the minute's digit "five" rolls into place and the countdown clock starts to move. Minus four minutes and fifty-nine seconds, fifty-eight...The simulated Greenwich clock begins to count up from thirteen twenty-seven toward the simulated launch time of thirteen thirty-two. The muscles along the backs of my legs contract ever so slightly. I become aware of the tendons running to the base of my skull. *No need for that now,* I tell myself, angry at the appearance of the telltale tension symptoms. How the hell can you sweat the practice for a practice?

As the clock moves past minus three minutes, Clayton reports that the mission computer is up. The background slides for the launch displays appear on the projection screens at the front of the room. Startlingly white rectangular coordinate grids, they transform the front of the room into the focal point of the rows of consoles that seem to stir in anticipation of the promised theatrics.

With the computer online, the console television displays are functional, driven by digital data that's supplied by the computer and converted into numbers, letters, and symbols by display equipment here on the third floor. Using thumbwheels and switches on my console, I call up the TV guide on my left display screen. It shows all of the channels in use and what they are being used for. I look for the display that gives the status of the telemetry data coming into the building and dial it up on another screen. A quick glance shows good data from all of the simulated space vehicles. My telemetry controller reports good input, and the command controller reports that his system is good. We just have to watch the clock now.

As the clock passes ten seconds, I start counting down to myself, a backward sequence of numbers in the best space-thriller tradition. As the countdown clock rolls over all zeros and starts to count up, I shift my attention from the clock to the large display just below it, expecting to see the trajectory plot moving up from the origin. Nothing moves!

"DISPLAY, NETWORK."

"Go ahead, NETWORK."

"What's the problem with the 10 by 20 and the 10 by 10?"

"Stand by and I'll check it."

"NETWORK, DISPLAY, we don't see any data to the plot-boards."

"Rog, DISPLAY."

It was time to start at the input and see why there was no output.

"TRACK, NETWORK, how does your tracking data look?"

"NETWORK, TRACK, everything looks good."

"COMPUTER SUP, NETWORK, my loop."

The ever-pleasant voice of Mr. Clayton comes snarling back, "Go ahead, NETWORK."

"We don't see any dynamic plot on the 10 by 20 or 10 by 10. Can you check your output?"

"NETWORK, COMPUTER SUP, I'll check my output after you check with DISPLAY to see what they screwed up."

I suspected that this would be a good day. Now I have no doubt whatsoever.

"I've already checked with DISPLAY, SUP. He doesn't see any data."

No response—dead silence. Fifteen seconds later the red lines that depict the launch trajectory of the Saturn V begin moving up from the lower left corners of the plot-boards.

"COMPUTER SUP, did you find a problem?" No response. "COMPUTER SUP, NETWORK, my loop," this time with irritation added for emphasis.

"NETWORK, COMPUTER M&O," comes the reply from the hardware type who works for Clayton and worries about what gets connected to what.

"Go ahead, babe. What did you find?"

"We had the data distribution switch in the wrong position—should be OK now."

"Looks good, M&O, thanks."

PART II
DRESS REHEARSAL

CHAPTER FOUR

The rehearsal for the rehearsal moves on toward its conclusion with a simulated spacecraft heading for a fictitious orbit. As the plot-boards continue to scribe position and velocity curves, various members of the cast begin to drift onstage.

First among them is my partner, George Egan. George is a dark-haired, bespectacled navy veteran from the Cajun country near New Orleans. He's not a NASA type, being employed by Philco-Ford, and is one of the few contractors working the front room—the control room. George works the right seat of our two-position console. He worries about everything in the "building," while I worry about everything outside the building—tracking stations, ships, aircraft, and the communications between them. When the "building" breaks, I keep the flight director off his ass while he works the problem. When something breaks outside, he returns the favor—a satisfactory symbiotic arrangement.

George's "Good Morning," competes with the sounds my headset is injecting into my ear and the clatter of his briefcase hitting the plastic sheet that covers the console. It always surprises me when I hear George speak. When a native of Louisiana speaks, I expect to hear a soft drawl or maybe a touch of Cajun French inflection. George's speech patterns run counter to my expectations. They are closer to the Ohio River than the lower Mississippi. Maybe he has been away from home too long.

Itinerant workers, like military and aerospace contractor types, tend to lose any accent they might once have had. They end up with neutral speech patterns that are hard to assign to any place in particular—part of the price you pay for mobility. George sounds like he has been away from home for a very long time.

"How's it going?" George continues as he starts into the routine of initiating a log and getting his headset on.

"Looks OK so far, the usual air-to-ground long-line bullshit, but everything is up right now. As soon as the crew gets into the simulator we should be ready to go."

George doesn't make any reply to my last transmission, giving me a slight nod as he slides his headset jack into the console receptacle and keys the mic to get a voice check with Communications Control. While George makes his check, I start to sort through my data book to get organized for the first simulation run. The data book is a loose-leaf notebook that serves as your memory when the real thing quits working. A lot of people use some device of this sort to collect useful bits of information and keep it handy.

This morning, because we are working launch simulations, I am looking for two items in particular. The first is an extract that I had prepared from the mission rules document. The flight mission rules contain a section for each important mission phase. In each section the rules list all of the conditions and equipment that you need for going ahead with that phase. The rules are written well before a mission, when you can quietly contemplate the consequences of a failure and decide where it leaves you. When the time of troubles is really upon you, the rules can be your best friend—summarizing complex fault tree analyses into the decision-making shorthand you need when you have seconds to respond to the question, "GO or NO-GO?" It is a good idea to look at the rules as often as you can before launch day carries you over the line between nervous anticipation and tense execution.

After leafing through a few pages, I find what I am looking for—several handwritten sheets covered with plastic loose-leaf sheet protectors. On the sheets, I had listed all of the Mission Control Center items that are considered mandatory for launch. *Mandatory* always struck me as an officious, inflexible description. But that's how the items are classified, despite the fact that at T minus ten seconds all "mandatory" items become "highly desirable." Given that these rules are meant to be decision aids, "sorta mandatory" wouldn't work, and so, in spite of my misgivings, the rules-makers went with the more definitive categorization. Included in this first list is a minimum set of internal communications, data displays, and telemetry and tracking processing capability needed to safely launch the mission.

Another set of plastic protectors contains copies of sheets taken directly from the mission rules. Each sheet displays a list of tracking stations that cover the launch along with a matrix that tells you if you are GO or NO-GO for launch when a particular system is lost at one of the ground tracking stations. There are five of these sheets covering launch azimuths from seventy-two degrees to one hundred and eight degrees. The *Apollo 11* launch window is four and a half hours long. If you launch on time, you launch on the seventy-two-degree heading. If not, the launch azimuth moves south as the launch time moves deeper into the four-and-a-half-hour time block. The azimuth variation helps to maintain the right relationship between the plane of the *Apollo* orbit and the position of the Moon when the spacecraft arrives. The seventy-two- and one-hundred-and-eight-degree limits are dictated by the air force range safety officer, who takes a dim view of dropping expended rocket boosters on unsuspecting Florida taxpayers.

Sets of rules like the ones I've just dug out apply to each job in the room. When the time comes to get up on the voice loop and tell the flight director you are GO for launch, you make that commitment on the basis of having the things that the rules say you have to have. When the time comes, you make a mental tally of what you have and what you don't have, and then you make your call.

With mission rules sheets located, I flip through the data book and locate the second set that I need, the Launch/Translunar Injection Work Schedule. George and I had gotten together with our team and made a schedule of everything we needed to do between T minus two hours and the translunar injection burn that started the crew on their way to the Moon. It pays to stay organized for the times when things begin to go wrong, and you have to stay focused on the essentials.

As I organize my organizers, the door on the right side of the control room opens and closes with a metallic clang. As I continue to study our work schedule, I hear footsteps cross the carpet and stop next to one of the consoles in the first row nearest the front of the room. The footsteps are followed by a startling crash as books and loose-leaf binders strike the quarter-inch-thick sheet of plastic that covers the console desk.

Dave Reed, our flight dynamics officer, or FIDO as he is called on the voice net, has arrived on the set. Reed is an escapee from somewhere in the Rocky Mountain west, maybe Montana or Wyoming. He has been with NASA for about five years. His blond crew-cut, square-jawed, all-American good looks and his fraternity house sense of humor make me think he has missed his calling. He should have been a Methodist minister, or a congressman, maybe even a CIA recruiter. Instead, if the rumors have any credibility, he is running for flight director, a position filled more than once by an upwardly mobile FIDO.

Reed's duty station is in the center of the first row of consoles, an area known as "the trench." That designation is in part the result of these four consoles being the lowest in the room, with the other three rows rising progressively upward behind them like metal parapets. I think too that the designation describes the kind of high-stress environment that its inhabitants live in. The flight dynamics officer worries about the spacecraft's flight path—where it is now, where it is likely to go, and how to get it to its destination. If there were just two bodies involved, the spacecraft and the Earth, that wouldn't present much of a problem. The mathematics of a two-body problem allows precise solutions and long-term predictions of a vehicle's path. But when you throw in the Moon and the action of other planets, the solutions are short term, requiring constant monitoring and updating. The flight dynamics officer's job involves a continuous process of receiving tracking data on present position, using it to update the predicted path of the spacecraft, and calculating the maneuvers required to reach the Moon and return to Earth.

The other combatants in the trench are the guidance officer (GUIDO), the retrofire officer (RETRO), and the booster systems engineer (BOOSTER). The guidance officer's job is to make sure that the onboard guidance packages are functioning properly and that updated position and trajectory information is transferred to the spacecraft's computers. The retrofire officer worries about how to get the crew back to Earth, not only at the end of a nominal mission, but also from any intermediate point, in the event that things get so screwed that the mission has to be terminated. The booster systems engineer monitors the three stages of the Saturn V, a huge, complex beast that works on the unsophisticated principle that more is better. In this case, 7.5 million pounds of thrust is more and therefore better, a direct application of the proverbial bigger hammer.

The booster systems engineer on this shift is Bill Brady, on loan to Houston from the NASA organization responsible for booster development, the Marshall Space Flight Center in Huntsville, Alabama. Brady, a tall man wearing horn-rimmed glasses, has a physique that reminds me of knots in a piece of string. He is unfailingly courteous and soft-spoken. He has an air of confidence that makes it clear that his reliability is equal to that of the great machine he tends—a machine sometimes referred to as "Brady's Bus."

At about the time that Brady drops his gear on the booster console, the checkout run comes to an uneventful conclusion. I check the quality of the data with my troops on the first floor. Everything looks good so I let John Blalock, the simulation supervisor (SIMSUP), know that we're ready to go on to the real rehearsal.

"Roger, NETWORK," he responds, "everything looks squared away. The crew has shown up and they should get in shortly. Don't call us, we'll call you."

"OK, babe, we'll stand by."

With all of that settled, I glance around at the coffeepot. The red light is on—fantastic—time for a cup before the next act. Pulling my plug, I tell George he's got it and start up the step clutching my nondescript, not-so-clean brown cup.

CHAPTER FIVE

By the time that I get through half a cup of coffee, the room has pretty much filled up. Down in the trench Will Presley, the guidance officer, is sorting out his paperwork for the day's runs. In the second row, below me and slightly to my left, Charlie Dumis, the Command and Service Module electrical, environmental, and consumables manager (EECOM), is trying to untangle the knots in his headset cord, and it looks like the cord is winning. Of all of the people in the room, Dumis is the most directly involved in the operation of the Command Module. He is responsible for the care and feeding of its major support systems.

To Charlie Dumis's left, directly in front of the flight director's console, Charlie Duke, the capsule communicator (CAPCOM), is rummaging through his briefcase. Duke's job as capsule communicator is to be a kind of translator who makes sure that the crew understands what the flight controllers are doing and vice versa. Contrary to what many people think, the capsule communicator tells the crew only what the flight director tells him to tell them. The flight controllers make their reports and recommendations to the flight director, who evaluates them, decides on a course of action, and then has the communicator relay instructions to the crew. In making the relay, the CAPCOM makes sure that the instructions are understood by the crew. Sometimes he also needs to interpret the crew's response for the flight controllers. That doesn't happen very often, since the controllers in the room are familiar with crew procedures, having in most cases helped to write them.

Even though the CAPCOM's job doesn't involve a lot of creativity, he does have job security since, under normal circumstances, he is the only one allowed to talk to the crew. There are rare exceptions when the crew requests a private conversation because of a medical problem. When that happens, the flight director, capsule communicator, surgeon, and network controller go down to the communications long-lines console on the first floor of the control center, a console that functions as a switchboard. Working from that position, a communications tech sets up a direct circuit to the ground station that has contact with the spacecraft. To maintain privacy, this circuit is isolated from the system that normally distributes the air-to-ground conversations to a worldwide audience. Private medical conversations are unlikely today since the surgeon's console, immediately to the left of the CAPCOM's position, is vacant. That's not unusual. The doctors participate in only a few simulations before each mission, mostly to maintain their familiarity with communication procedures and data display formats.

Behind the surgeon's console, in the same console row as mine, Larry Keyser, the assistant flight director, or AFD, is holding an animated conversation with Cliff Charlesworth, the Green Team flight director. There are four teams assigned to the mission, each covering a nominal six-hour shift. The teams train to support particular critical mission phases. Charlesworth's Green Team supports launch. Gene Kranz's White Team supports the crew's descent to the lunar surface. Glynn Lunney's Black Team gets the crew back off the Moon to dock with the Command Module. The Maroon Team, led by Milt Windler, a newly selected flight director, covers the fiery return to Earth.

The Green Team leader is a remarkably nondescript man with sandy hair and a medium build progressing toward the paunchy stage. His most distinguishing feature is an upper lip that he keeps twisted into an attitude of casual disdain. It gives fair warning of the type of encounter you're likely to have with the man. Sarcasm and abruptness are his constant companions. One of the flight controllers had remarked that Charlesworth has a personality "like an old sneaker." No one argued the point.

The duty flight director (FLIGHT) is, as a drill sergeant once explained his own role to me, the "head motherfucker who be in complete charge." When time permits, most decisions in the control room are made by ad hoc committees. Their exact membership depends on the nature of the problem at hand. The flight director is always the chairman. If the problem is really major, the committee might include not only the flight controllers directly involved, but also experts from industry and members of the NASA hierarchy like Dr. Robert Gilruth, the director of the Manned Spacecraft Center, and Dr. Christopher Kraft Jr., the director of Flight Operations. The committee's decision-making process seems erratic and disorganized. The central element is a relentless structuring and restructuring of the facts of the case into arguments and counterarguments until the group arrives at a proposed course of action that "makes sense." In time-critical situations, the committee might consist of just the flight director, the flight controller involved, and the CAPCOM. The flight controller makes the best call he can, the flight director agrees, and the decision is voiced up to the crew by the CAPCOM in a matter of seconds.

In the rows of consoles below the flight director's console, flight controllers in various attitudes, sitting or standing, singly or in small groups, drink coffee and talk quietly. Most are ready to go and wait expectantly. As I watch the flight director's back, a look of fading hope appears on the assistant flight director's face, and a slight shrug of Charlesworth's shoulders signals the end of their conversation.

The flight director turns away, picks up his coffee cup from his console, and starts down the console row threading his way through an obstacle course of empty chairs.

"Are you going to get this thing to work today, NETWORK?" he says as he reaches my console.

"Everything is ready to go, FLIGHT. No problems. I did want to ask you…" My words trail off in a verbal wake behind Charlesworth's back as he passes by on his way to the coffeepot.

While I am attempting to talk to the flight director, I hear the simulation coordinator call George and report that the crew is in and ready. They settle on starting the first simulation run with a ten-minute pre-launch count beginning at 12:40 Greenwich Mean Time. George passes the word to the display technician and is about to pass the word to the rest of our crew. As I turn around he asks, "Did you copy that?'

"You bet, one-two-four-zero start," I respond, as I lean forward to punch up the flight director's voice loop on my keyset. Charlesworth is still on his coffee run so I call his partner. "AFD, NETWORK, on three FLIGHT DIRECTOR." I specify three flight director to distinguish this channel from the channel with the same flight director designation that is used in the second-floor control room.

Keyser turns to face me, "Go ahead, NETWORK."

"The crew is in and they want to start the clock at one-two-four-zero with a T minus ten count."

"Roger, NETWORK," he responds, and then continues, "All flight controllers, this is AFD, on three FLIGHT DIRECTOR. Give me a green light if you're ready for a clock start at one-two-four-zero."

The green light he is asking for is one of three status lights—red, amber, and green—that appear on each flight controller's console. By depressing one of the three colored switches, you could make the same color indicator illuminate on the flight director's panel to indicate readiness or the lack thereof.

Suddenly, just as though some unseen director had shouted at his milling troupe of players to take their places, the controllers begin to settle into their chairs and make last-minute arrangements of checklists and displays as Keyser starts his roll call to confirm their readiness.

"BOOSTER, what's your status?"
"AFD, BOOSTER is ready."
"FIDO?"
"All set, babe."
"RETRO?" Silence. "RETRO, AFD, on three FLIGHT DIRECTOR." More silence. The assistant flight director, hovering somewhere between puzzlement and mild annoyance, stands up to peer over his console toward the trench where a deserted retrofire officer's console returns his glare with its cathode ray eyes. "GUIDO, AFD, have you seen any of the RETRO types?"

"That's negative," responds Will Presley, the duty guidance officer.

The ever-helpful flight dynamics officer, Dave Reed, follows with, "No sweat, AFD, we don't need those guys anyway."

As if in agreement, Keyser continues his roll call.

"GUIDO, how about you?"

"We're GO except for some command loads to the spacecraft that we'll send when the computer comes up."

"Roger, GUIDO."

While Keyser continues his roll call, I check over my notes one more time to see if all of the support count sequences have been completed and everything fixable is fixed or in work.

About the time that I start to move my foot toward the mic switch in anticipation of my own status report, the door flies open with an unnecessary clatter of hardware. A loud voice with a Virginia drawl puts an end to the quiet that had descended on the set just moments before. "Hey, AFD, this is your number one RETRO on the open air loop. I hear y'all been lookin' for me."

The retrofire officer has made his usual dramatic entrance. It is hard to imagine him making any other kind. He looks as though someone had stuffed a Cro-Magnon body into blue jeans and cowboy boots, dispensed with the neck, and then topped this neo-primitive creation with a rough, nearly handsome *Homo sapiens* head. John S. Llewellyn (RETRO) is not your run-of-the-mill madman. Flamboyant, eccentric, and always enigmatic, he is a man whose contrasts are as stark as lunar surface lighting.

Physically, John is one of the strongest men I have ever run into. I mean literally run into. We belong to the same judo club. Trying to put a move on him is like throwing yourself at a brick wall. His powerful form signals his style like a neon sign. He's a redneck's redneck, a bar-fighting ex-marine and part-time cow-puncher. The "No Profanity" sign hanging over the bar at the Singing Wheel, a local flight controller hangout, is a direct tribute to his lyrical skills. At one time, I was told, he played center for one of the college football teams in Virginia. His approach hadn't changed—head down and straight ahead.

Some of his exploits are legendary in this community where everyone colors inside the lines. On another day like this one, late for a simulation as usual and unable to find a parking space, John did what—for him—was obvious. He maneuvered his car up onto the sidewalk and parked it between the wings of the Mission Control building.

But the Marlboro Man exterior is only one facet of John's character. Beneath it there is a mental acuity that allows him to excel in a highly technical and demanding skill—a skill he has practiced since the early days of the manned space program. And there's more—occasional glimpses of a broad cultural background and a genuine compassion for others that are sometimes visible through the cloud of flak that marks his passages.

Like any folk hero, Llewellyn has his conspicuous imitators. As is the case with most impersonators, they lack the intelligence and style to duplicate the original. But almost all of us are unconsciously influenced by his distinctive speech inflection and phrasing. The ubiquitous salutation "babe" that you hear on the control room voice circuits testifies to that influence.

Why does that happen? It may be because we all envy the man's absolute disregard of consequences. Most of us ordinary folk modify our impulses, influenced by what might happen or what people might think. John just doesn't seem to give a shit about those trivialities. He is, to all appearances, totally without fear. That uncomplicated state has a universal appeal even though the notion that he acts out of greater fear than any of us sometimes passes through my mind. Envy on my part? Maybe so. But then again we may not be the imitators. Maybe he's the imitator, an amplifier system that takes our feeble attempts at bravado and broadcasts them back to us larger than life. We think we like what we see and hear and project it back again in a kind of macho ping-pong match.

CHAPTER SIX

While the retrofire officer is getting settled in at his console in the trench, the assistant flight director takes my status report and then completes his roll call, getting green lights across the board. By then, the flight director has strolled past my chair and returned to his console. As the assistant flight director finishes briefing him on our status, the time display rolls over 12:40:00 GMT and the countdown clock starts to move.

"OK, troops, we have a clock start."

It's George's voice on three NETWORK sounding hollow and remote through the fog of my own preoccupation with the steadily declining minutes and seconds on the countdown clock.

I sit and swear silently as my involuntary nervous system does exactly what I'm trying to keep it from doing. Thigh muscles tighten, shoulder blades are suddenly a prominent part of my anatomy, and I wonder about control of my hands as I generate a rush of rationalizing, but ultimately useless, thoughts. This is just a practice run. Everyone feels a little bit like this from time to time. Or maybe just say the hell with what people think, you paranoid clown. Forget the fact that you are the only history major in a room full of physics, astronautics, aeronautics, and electrical engineering degrees, and get on with your job.

Best to do something besides worry about my nervous condition, so I take a quick look at the TV monitor in front of me—a complete blank. "George, are we cleared for display requests?"

"Rog, the TV guide is on channel 2."

I check the guide and find the Telemetry Status Table. As I select the proper channel and call up the display, Don Flippin, the second controller on the telemetry console, confirms what I see on the screen. We have two good simulated sources providing data from our simulated launch vehicle and spacecraft—one data stream through the simulated Merritt Island tracking station, and the other by way of the simulated *Apollo* Launch Data System complex located a little farther south near the Kennedy Space Center headquarters building.

"Did you copy a launch azimuth?"

"Negative," responds George shaking his head from side to side.

I call the guidance officer on his communication circuit, "GUIDO, NETWORK, on MOCR DY."

"Go ahead, NETWORK."

"Rog, can we get a launch azimuth?"

"You bet, babe, what would you like to have?"

Silence—no need to respond to that smart-ass comment.

"OK, NETWORK, use zero-seven-two-point-zero-four degrees."

"Our most humble gratitude for your kindness."

I scribble the numbers on one of my plastic checklist covers with a black grease pencil as I reach for a keyset button that will give me access to NET 2. In the real world it connects our console to a global system of tracking stations. This morning no one is out there except some simulation "black hats," but the idea is to go through all of the motions just as if it were the real thing.

"All stations this is NETWORK on NET 2. Launch azimuth zero-seven-two-point-zero-four. I say again..."

With that task out of the way, there isn't a whole hell of a lot left to do except watch the clock. On launch day we will be making last-minute status and radio checks. The voice loops will overflow with traffic coming from eleven directions at the same time. Picking out the key words that might affect your decisions takes concentration that makes your brain all ears. I wish they could simulate that environment. I know it's coming. I'd like to try it on now just to see. But the voice loops are mostly silent. George and I make small talk about his Great Danes and their trials and tribulations until the CAPCOM starts his T minus ten second count to the crew.

"ELEVEN this is HOUSTON. On my mark we'll have minus ten seconds. Mark minus ten—minus nine, eight, seven…"

This one ought to be a piece of cake, I tell myself as I look up at the steadily diminishing clock total. The first run of the day is always nominal, no problems at all.

"FLIGHT, FIDO, we have a liftoff."

"Roger, FIDO."

After all of the waiting, I'm caught by surprise. Flustered, I grab for my grease pencil with my right hand and try to find the right voice loop for copying a liftoff time—the tracking network has to have those numbers. I punch the talk button on the MOCR DYNAMICS communications loop to raise the volume on that circuit above the background chatter, and scramble to copy RETRO's drawled announcement.

"Liftoff, one-three-three-two-zero-zero-decimal-six-three. Y'all copy that, NETWORK?"

"Say again the last two digits, RETRO."

"Hey NETWORK, y'all need to listen up—try six-three."

"Roger, RETRO."

"NETWORK, you may never be a winner, but you'll always be my hoss."

"Whatever that means it sounds great, RETRO."

I punch off the MOCR DYNAMICS loop and get on Net 2 to repeat the message, "All stations, NETWORK on Net 2, liftoff one-three-…"

At this point the checklist calls for me to report the liftoff time to NORAD, the North American Air Defense Command in Colorado Springs, the agency that keeps track of objects in space. The NORAD circuit is not up for this simulation so I skip the checklist item.

Next to me, George is repeating the liftoff time to the teletype communications center so that they can transmit written confirmation of our announcement. The balance of the mission will be run in ground-elapsed time, or time since liftoff, so it is critical that all stations have the same clock start time.

For two minutes after liftoff, the simulated Merritt Island Launch Annex tracking station (MILA) maintains active S-band track on the Command Module, providing position information, telemetry, and voice links to the crew. Until six minutes after liftoff, the Merritt Island station will also be active on the IU, the Saturn V Instrumentation Unit, to provide telemetry status data on the giant booster. In addition to the simulated Merritt Island S-band tracking, pretend C-band radars[2] at Kennedy Air Force Station and Patrick Air Force Base track the Saturn V rocket.

The crew in the Command and Service Module simulator monitor their displays and make the reports required by their checklists.

"HOUSTON, ELEVEN, yaw maneuver complete."
The CAPCOM responds, "Roger, ELEVEN."
"Roll and pitch program initiate, HOUSTON."
"Looks good, ELEVEN."
Fifteen seconds of silence.
"Roll complete."
"Roger, ELEVEN, still looks good."
"ELEVEN, HOUSTON, you're go Mode One Bravo."

Everything looks good so far. This last transmission tells the crew the technique they'll use if something should go wrong and they have to abort the mission in the next minute or so. Mode One aborts are subdivided into Modes One Alpha, One Bravo, and One Charlie. Each is fully automatic and uses the launch

---

2 The microwave portion of the electromagnetic spectrum is divided into ten bands, each of which has a letter designation, e.g., S and C. See the appendices for more information on the tracking frequencies.

escape tower mounted on the top of the Command Module. The tower contains a solid-fueled rocket motor designed to pull the Command Module clear of the malfunctioning booster. Once clear of the booster, the spacecraft deploys parachutes for a safe return to the surface. The three sub-modes employ slightly different abort sequences depending on the altitude of the spacecraft. Mode One Alpha is a launch-area abort that is in effect from T minus thirty minutes until forty-two seconds after liftoff. Mode One Bravo is used from about 15,000 feet at forty-two seconds after launch up to an altitude of 100,000 feet at one minute fifty seconds.

The tracking station on Grand Bahama Island (GBM) is next up on the Command and Service Module. I check the telemetry display in front of me to see if they have acquisition of signal. I don't remember hearing them announce it, but the data is there and solid.

CAPCOM Charlie Duke tells the crew it is GO for "Mode One Charlie." Ten seconds later I hear the simulated Grand Bahama operations supervisor announce, "GBM, go for command CSM." In the "real" world that announcement would signal the hand over of Command and Service Module two-way uplink lock from the Merritt Island station to Grand Bahama.

"HOUSTON, ELEVEN, inboard off."

The inboard engine on the first stage has shut down as planned.

"Roger, ELEVEN."

Twenty seconds of silence—the data looks good. A glance around the room shows heads bent forward in intense concentration.

"HOUSTON, ELEVEN, outboard out, and we have staging. The S-II is lit, babe."

"OK, looks good here."

Another opportunity to look around the room for a few seconds—checklists are up to date—no problems. The flight director has turned to his left to talk to his assistant. At the front of the room, the dynamic plot of spacecraft position is tracking along the nominal path—no sweat—time to take a deep breath and try to relax the muscles in my back and legs.

"Tower jet, FLIGHT."

The internal report comes a full second before the crew reports the same event. The launch escape tower, no longer effective at this altitude, has separated from the spacecraft.

"HOUSTON, ELEVEN, the tower is gone."

"Roger, ELEVEN, you're Mode Two."

The spacecraft is now above the dense lower atmosphere. If an abort is required, the spacecraft commander will manually separate the Command Module from the booster, reorient it, and use the 20,500-pound thrust of the Service Module engine to make the maneuvers needed for a safe reentry.

Guidance is converging. No problems. The whole thing looks good from here. The data from the simulated ground tracking stations is solid. That's the signal that everything is working in the network department. The situation onboard the spacecraft may be somewhere close to catastrophic. The room is full of other people who worry about that. Our job is to make sure the data—be it good news or bad—gets to those people who can do something about it.

The data quality standards are high, especially for the air-to-ground voice communications with the crew. No one can afford to miss a critical report or an essential instruction. Sometimes I wonder that the link works at all. A voice signal from the spacecraft in orbit around the Moon is modulated onto a high-frequency radio wave along with spacecraft telemetry and tracking information. This carrier wave transports the signals across 210,000 miles of space, losing power with every mile that it traverses. A whisper arrives at a ground station in Australia, or California, or maybe in Spain. The signal is amplified and shipped by satellite link or undersea cable across thousands of miles to Greenbelt, Maryland, and on to Houston. When it arrives, it better sound like the crew is sitting next to you in a quiet room. If not, the response is immediate, "NETWORK, FLIGHT, clean up that noise on the downlink."

An organized hunt for the villain takes a lot of cooperative, experienced people who have just the right mind-set. Attitude is critical. That's what makes this whole spaceflight thing work. The basic principles of orbital mechanics have been known since the days of Johannes Kepler. Isaac Newton provided the mathematical basis for Kepler's laws. The only thing missing was the technology—the technology and the peculiar cast of mind that made the technology work.

I had come to Houston four years earlier with a background in liberal arts, a fuzzy sense of "good enough," and a horseshoe pitcher's faith that you could get points for being "close." The technocrat's state of mind was not only peculiar, it could be damn annoying. I just couldn't fathom people who insisted on a detailed, rational explanation for every occurrence no matter how minor. They could really piss you off with their superior insistence that every part of every system work exactly the way it was designed to work. If it didn't, you needed to find out why. You fixed it. Then you tried again until the thing did exactly what it was supposed to do.

Provided that you don't abuse the facts too much, there is plenty of wiggle room to defend your conclusions about the origin and consequences of the Hundred Years' War. There is no empirical method for testing the validity of your views. Much to my initial annoyance, that's not the case around here. Things work or they don't. The results are immediately available. Damned unsporting—sometimes even embarrassing.

But then, ever so slowly as I watched and wondered, the effectiveness, and even the beauty, of the thing revealed itself. I became a born-again empiricist, a convert to relentless logical inquiry. Sure the science needed to be correct, and the technology had to be available to take advantage of the science. But the important term in the equation is a state of mind, a persistent, systematic, and logical process of inquiry that never settles for "close enough." That methodology would take us to the Moon and back—Saturn V rockets were incidental props.

"Four minutes, ELEVEN. Looks like a simulation."

"HOUSTON, ELEVEN, funny you should mention that. The spacecraft systems are all good."

"Roger, ELEVEN."

Another minute or so of silence as the red lines on the plotboards continue to show nominal values—flight path angle, velocity—everything is bloody marvelous.

"ELEVEN, HOUSTON, S-IVB to COI."

The crew acknowledges, understanding that if the S-II stage of the Saturn booster fails they can abort into a contingency orbit using an extended burn of the S-IVB, the booster's upper stage. Once in orbit, although the chance of a lunar mission is gone, the crew would be safe and alternative missions might be practical.

When I think about the size and complexity of the giant Saturn booster, it's not hard for me to imagine an abort situation. I wonder how it is that the crew members talk themselves into sitting on top of more than five million pounds of fuel and oxidizer while someone puts a match to it. I'll be ready to sit up there when they get a spacecraft big enough to carry me and the twelve guys it will take to hold me down.

In thirty-five seconds or so, the Merritt Island tracking station will hand the booster over to the Bermuda tracking station. Thirty seconds later, Grand Bahama will hand the spacecraft over to Bermuda. Today, of course, the handover won't be accepted by a station on a subtropical island, but by a simulation guy less than a mile away. The ground tracking stations are never included in this type of simulation. But they do participate in other types of testing designed to make sure that they are mission ready. Network validation tests are run to check out the computing and tracking systems at each station prior to a mission. The computer programs used at the tracking stations are developed at the Goddard Space Flight Center. Theoretically, after the programs are checked out at Goddard, they are ready to be slipped into the computers of our standardized worldwide tracking stations. But there are always minor differences between station configurations that make it essential to run a series of qualification tests. Sometimes that means that you have to come crawling in, in the middle of the night, to chat with a crew of bloody cheerful Australians and listen to an endless sequence of parameter verifications. That's when the magazines in the console drawer become so much more interesting.

CHAPTER SEVEN

The handovers to Bermuda are made without incident. In five minutes the simulated spacecraft will be inserted into a simulated Earth orbit. This is going to be a sweet, sweet nominal run. How nice!

At eight minutes and forty seconds the Saturn second stage shuts down. A second later it separates and the third-stage S-IVB engine ignites.

At nine minutes and forty-five seconds after launch, the CAPCOM tells the crew that they now have "Mode Four capability," meaning that they can now use the Service Module propulsion system to abort into a safe orbit in the event of a booster failure. The CAPCOM makes his report to the crew using words carefully agreed on in advance to avoid their being misinterpreted in the modulated, but still considerable, excitement of the launch phase. In an earlier simulation a CAPCOM had told the crew "You are GO Mode Four." The crew had acknowledged and immediately initiated an unnecessary abort to orbit. The word "capability" was inserted to make clear the difference between being able to do it and having to do it right now.

In about a minute and a half, the simulated tracking ship *Vanguard* will monitor a nominal insertion into orbit.

"FLIGHT, BOOSTER, the engine has gone hard over. Better tell them to get off."

The nozzle of the S-IVB's single engine is mounted on gimbals. Movement of the nozzle controls the direction of flight. In this case, the nozzle has apparently gone to maximum deflection, putting the spacecraft stack into a continuous turn.

"Rog, BOOSTER. CAPCOM?"

"ELEVEN, HOUSTON, go Mode Four. The booster engine is hard over."

"Roger, HOUSTON, Mode Four."

So much for the nominal case. The crew starts into their abort checklist. EECOM confirms Command and Service Module, S-IVB separation as the crew prepares to use the Service Module engine to boost into a safe orbit. I grab my own checklist while I reach up and punch the transmit button.

"All stations, NETWORK on Net Two, we have an abort—Mode Four. I say again—abort—Mode Four."

As I transmit I can hear George on the internal net, "All stations, NETWORK, Mode Four abort."

"RTC, roger."

"TIC, roger, Mode Four."

"TRACK copies."

"COMM CONTROL, roger."

"COMM TECH copies."

I scan down the checklist looking for my next action. My spine is a tense curve now. Literally sitting on the edge of my chair, I lean forward, right arm extended, hand positioned on the top edge of the console just above the keyset.

I hear Charlie Dumis on the flight director loop: "FLIGHT, EECOM, looks like we lost our spacecraft data."

The instrumentation and communications officer, who is responsible for all spacecraft links until they reach the ground station antenna, jumps in on top of Dumis, "NETWORK, INCO, your loop. What's the problem?"

Charlesworth is next up, "NETWORK, FLIGHT, my loop. Have you got some kind of problem?"

"NETWORK, BERMUDA, Net Two."

In the millisecond I take to decide who's on first, George answers the Bermuda call. With Bermuda covered, the choice is easy. Ignore the two flight controllers and talk to "the Man." I reach for the keyset to punch up the flight director's loop, strain to hear the Bermuda report, and glance at the telemetry status display to confirm what I already know. "FLIGHT, NETWORK, we're checking."

And in the background, "Roger, NETWORK, System One has failed. We'll get System Two configured for CSM data as soon as possible."

This all sounds like bullshit to me. This had to be a system glitch that the simulation people were trying to cover up. They rarely direct problems at us. They focus on the flight crew and the flight control positions that deal with the booster and the spacecraft. Wrong choices there can cost lives. Ground systems are robust and redundant. A failure is not likely to produce catastrophe. We're like the superintendent of an apartment building on Eighth Avenue. When your toilet stops working you call us. We get things moving again so that you can get on with your business.

But simulation glitch or not, you have to play the game. George is on it, "TIC, NETWORK, how does your *Vanguard* data look?"

During the launch phase, the tracking ship *Vanguard* is parked about one thousand miles southeast of Bermuda to bridge the Bermuda–Canary Islands gap. The Command and Service Module maximum elevation angle is about eight and one-half degrees for a nominal launch. In this case it may be lower, but the ship has already had acquisition of signal.

"NETWORK, TIC, we are processing *Vanguard* data."

"FLIGHT, EECOM, we have data."

"Roger, TIC, processing *Vanguard* data."

George acknowledges the telemetry controller's report—then says to me off the net, "Let's hand it over. We have an abort and no S-band track on the Command and Service Module. The Bermuda air-to-ground has to be on the backup VHF link."

I press down on the microphone switch, "FLIGHT, NETWORK, we'd like to hand over to *Vanguard*."

"Any problems?" Charlesworth replies, addressing his question to the room in general. No response. "Go ahead, NETWORK."

George responds before the last syllable arrives, "RTC, NETWORK, hand over to *Vanguard*."

"RTC, roger."

"B-B-BERMUDA, VANGUARD, RTC on Net Two. Stand by for CSM handover, uplink mode six-zero-two-zero-zero."

Seconds later, '"BERMUDA is ready."

"VANGUARD is ready."

"Hand over on my mark: Five-four-three-two-one-mark."

"VANGUARD is Go for command CSM."

In twenty seconds the job is done and the situation seems to be about as normal as it can be in the middle of an abort to orbit. I start to uncoil a little bit, pulling my right hand back from the top of the keyset where I've had it rigidly poised to work the communication circuit selection buttons. About ten degrees from vertical, as I move my body from the lean-forward to the lean-back position (which is, by the way, one of life's more significant rotations), I uncage my head, which has been locked in a straight-ahead mode, and glance left toward the center of the room. In a split second it becomes clear to me that I shouldn't have permitted myself that liberty—Nemesis, the goddess of divine payback, always make a prompt response when hubris shows up on the big display screens in the sky. I see that one of two things is happening, neither one of them desirable. Either the console video displays are holding a fixed position and the entire room is moving steadily downward relative to the fixed displays, or every video display is in rapid vertical motion. The second hypothesis seems more reasonable. But to a man who is beginning to feel like he fell into a bag full of electronic worms, either situation is within the realm of possibility.

I go back into the coiled position, and reach for the keyset just about the time that I can hear the arrival of more help than I really need.

"NETWORK, AFD, what's going on?"

"NETWORK, RETRO, y'all are translating the display too fast even for me to read it."

Ignoring all of the help I'm getting, I punch up the man who can really help, "DISPLAY, NETWORK."

"Rog, NETWORK, we're checking—stand by."

"NETWORK, FLIGHT, is there any chance you can fix the TV for us?"

Concentrating, listening for a follow-up from the display controller, I don't have time to answer. I raise my left hand in a peace sign and turn toward the flight director's console.

"I think NETWORK is trying to tell me to shut up," responds Charlesworth, addressing the world at large.

You bet your ass I am, passes through my head.

"NETWORK, DISPLAY, we have a problem with the sync generator."

I could have told you that!

"What's your estimate, DISPLAY?"

"About fifteen minutes, NETWORK."

"Too much time, babe. Can you patch in a generator from another system?"

"Stand by, NETWORK. I'll check."

Twenty endless seconds of silence pass with data displays in perpetual motion and a dozen pairs of eyes locked on my rigid persona.

"NETWORK, DISPLAY, the patch is in work—about another minute."

"Rog, DISPLAY."

"FLIGHT, NETWORK, about another minute. We're patching in a new sync generator."

"Any time it's convenient for you, NETWORK."

The estimate from the display controller is optimistic, so George and I endure another two minutes trying to look casual and on top of the problem in spite of the glaring, endlessly flickering eyes of our video accusers. Then, suddenly, relief is at hand. The displays stabilize and the display controller makes a totally unnecessary report on his success in correcting the problem.

With the TV problem squared away and spacecraft data flowing smoothly, the world momentarily becomes brighter. It's time to uncoil again, tentatively this time, so as not to provoke the gods. By now the muscular tension has produced a dull ache in the left testicle that will last the day.

The next three or four minutes pass without incident. It's almost time for handover to the Canary Islands tracking station. I might have missed the acquisition of signal call, so I check the display to see whether we have Canary data. No Command and Service Module data from Canary—better double-check the acquisition of signal time. But before I get to that, "NETWORK, TRACK, are you going to reconfigure Canary?"

Oh shit, oh dear—the checklist! We never finished the abort checklist. In the nominal case, Canary tracks the booster. In the event of an abort, they reconfigure to track the Command and Service Module. The direction to reconfigure is supposed to come from yours truly. In this case yours truly has truly screwed up.

The screwup is real enough, and to make it worse, the simulated world amplifies the simulated consequences by not invoking the safeguards built in to the real-world system. In the real world, the Canary operations supervisor, who knows the checklist better than I do, would have reminded me of the need to reconfigure. But in this world, they let you stumble down the path to catastrophe—it amplifies the didactic impact.

""NETWORK, INCO, where's our Canary data?"

I ignore him and go about the business of fixing the Canary situation. "CANARY, NETWORK, reconfigure for CSM support."

"Roger that, NETWORK," responds the simulated ops supervisor, barely concealing his fiendish glee. As I direct the station change, George informs the flight director that we will have data momentarily, blithely ignoring the cause of the problem. We continue to ignore the calls from INCO. We breathe more easily a few minutes later when data is restored and it is clear that the spacecraft has achieved a safe, if simulated, orbit. With the issue resolved, INCO goes away, at least until debriefing time.

The interactions with the other flight controllers are quasi-professional, punctuated with the occasional smart-ass comment. The relationship with INCO, the instrumentation and communications systems officer, on this mission promises to be a whole lot more confrontational for organizational, technical, and personality reasons. INCO is making his debut on the *Apollo 11* mission. On earlier missions, the controller responsible for a spacecraft, Command Module, or Lunar Module worried about all systems on that vehicle including communications. That worked in theory. On *Apollo 9*, when there were two vehicles actually on the air at once, it didn't work very well in practice. The remedy was to create a new position to control communications on both vehicles and during extravehicular activity, when what was essentially a third vehicle entered the picture.

That consolidation created a direct interface between a guy who was responsible for all of the communications leaving the spacecraft and passing through the ether, and the guy responsible for those signals at the exit from the ether, the ground antenna—us and them. When a problem occurs there is always an instinct to point across the interface and say, "Not my problem." There are dozens of those kinds of interfaces. The new guy on the block is more likely to point fingers, but mostly some reasonable accommodation evolves.

Unfortunately in this case there is an added complication—the boss instrumentation and communications systems officer. His name is Ed Fendell. He has been with NASA since the beginning of the Gemini Program, serving as a capsule communicator at tracking stations around the world. Ed is a short man, with a bald head and a prominent nose. You have to see him when he is standing face-to-face with you to appreciate him. His head is thrust forward, his arms are at his side and drawn slightly back, his fists clenched. You get the idea that he is about to punch you in the face.

Ed Fendell is good at what he does. In a macho world—and this is truly one of those—most of us can, at least for some period of time, project the image of a hard-nosed, self-propelled son of a bitch. But the image is just that, a role we play. Eventually we stand revealed as the possessor of a golden heart, or at least as the possessor of the ordinary quotient of empathy for our fellow man that distinguishes civilized society. Ed is different. Beneath his arrogant, aggressive, nasty son-of-a-bitch exterior there is an arrogant, aggressive, nasty son of a bitch. Every encounter with the boss instrumentation controller turns into a pissing contest. Even when he's not on duty his troops try on their own version of their boss's foul disposition. Mostly they aren't very good at it. But the face-offs are tedious. In the quiet times off console you have to have a certain respect for the virtuosity of Fendell's meanness. But out there in the schoolyard the bullying wears thin in a hurry.

The simulations supervisor terminates the run and asks us to tear down and recycle the equipment on our end in preparation for another run. While George tends to the task, I collect comments from our troops on the just completed exercise. The debriefing is conducted by the flight director, who simply goes from position to position on the voice net soliciting comments, criticisms, or lessons learned. The crew participates in the sessions, which often take longer than the actual simulation run. More than once, the simulation guys force fundamental rethinking of mission control rules that the crew and controllers had so carefully developed.

If you have in fact sinned, the best strategy is to "fess up," to say it before someone else does, because they will say it, and they'll be less kind than you might be. You confess your sins, promise to fix the problem, and receive absolution from Father Clifford. The notion is that these rehearsals are the place to find your weaknesses and make your mistakes so as not to repeat them when the curtain goes up. The Bermuda system failure is easily disposed of. The simulations supervisor admits that it was their problem—a wrong identification tag for a data stream. The display problem and the fact that I knew more about the fix than my display tech points up the need for a review of our procedures and some training prior to launch day. The *Vanguard* problem is a different story. I had the checklist in front of me. I lost my concentration. The only explanation is that, to borrow an old East Texas expression, I was "all eat up with the dumb shit." That admission is both stressful and painful. I take only modest comfort in the fact that the stress and pain enhance the learning opportunity—I'm not likely to do that one again.

I hope there aren't too many others lurking out there in the dark. This place is filled with people who came here because they had proven themselves on space programs going back to Project Mercury—the dawn of the manned space era. I came here as the result of a chain of quixotic happenings that had more to do with my complete and utter lack of experience. Now I find myself the lead network controller for the first attempt to land on another celestial body. When I sit down at my console I represent thousands of people who operate S-band tracking stations with thirty- or eighty-five-foot antennas on three continents, two-hundred-foot astronomical radio telescopes, a collection of tracking ships and aircraft, and tens of thousands of miles of communication systems that tie them together. Surely, at some point, I'm going to have to wake up and find out that I really shouldn't be here—and I hope it's not today.

When the debriefing finishes, we move on to the next run, and the one after that, until our launch phase understudy crew arrives to relieve us. Someone has to be trained in the event that you are "not available" when the curtain goes up, so they will work the afternoon segment while George and I go off to talk about display system failure isolation and repair.

PART III
AN UNLIKELY ACTOR

CHAPTER EIGHT

Home, for the three years and more that we have so far spent in Texas, has been in the redneck suburb of Pasadena (that's right—Pasadena, *Texas*). It is bounded on the west by the Houston-Galveston freeway, on the north and east by the Houston Ship Channel with its fringe of smoking, flaring refineries, and on the south by the suburb of Deer Park. Pasadena is a mix of Baptist churches, neon café signs, and shotgun racks in the back of pickup trucks. It has no organized center, no municipal focus. A scattered collection of small strip malls provides a degree of coherence to the city much as the ganglia of some primitive species might serve the function of a developed brain without ever quite making the grade. But center or not, they got good old discipline in the schools, crew-cut cops, and a local prohibition ordinance that forces you a mile down Red Bluff Road to get your bourbon whiskey. The pervasive odor of the Champion Paper Mill is a constant reminder of the real limitations of trying to find decent housing on an air force captain's pay.

Up to the northwest you can find some compensation for the shortcomings of Pasadena—the city of Houston, "Baghdad on Buffalo Bayou." In 1836, the Allen brothers set up shop on six thousand acres near the intersection of Buffalo and White Oak Bayous in the new Republic of Texas. John and Augustus were

New York land speculators who had earlier tried to promote some action on Galveston Island. When that didn't materialize, they moved about fifty miles inland and began to tout a nonexistent city that would, they said, become "beyond all doubt, the interior commercial emporium of Texas." They were right.

In 1842, the city fathers started improvements that made Buffalo Bayou navigable down to the Gulf of Mexico, turning Houston into a major port fifty miles from the sea. In 1901, the fabulous Spindletop oil field came in, and the Allen brothers' commercial emporium was on its way to becoming the petrochemical center of the United States.

Nowadays you can drive the Gulf Freeway from Galveston to Houston. As you head north, the terrain on the right is dominated by the refineries of Texas City and Pasadena. On the left, you see flat coastal plain dotted with scrub oak. Ahead you see nothing but highway and sky—that is until you reach Exit 43 near a major artery called Old Spanish Trail, where the city springs up instantly, fully grown, as though someone had projected a slide onto the blank blue sky.

If you are looking for a pleasant way to pass a sunny weekend afternoon away from the constant nagging thoughts of how ready you might be to do what you will soon need to do, you can go on past the Old Spanish Trail, exit on Calhoun or Pease, and then turn right on Main Street. Six or seven blocks past the big Foley's department store and a couple of blocks past the old Rice Hotel, you turn left on Congress and begin to encounter the crowds headed for Old Market Square.

The Square is just that, with a collection of more or less antique buildings fronting its four sides, looking over a parking lot that some sensitive son of a bitch placed dead center in the middle of the square. The Square is Houston's version of Wisconsin Avenue in Georgetown or any one of the small streets just north of Washington Square in Manhattan. Most of the nineteenth-century buildings are home to cafés, restaurants, boutiques, craft shops, and an occasional pawn shop. On a spring weekend, there is likely to be a sidewalk art exhibit set up in the Square with works by local artists. Bookstores are noticeably absent. On the side streets leading to the Square, you might pass the usual jugglers and mimes, and maybe even a full-bearded hippy type soliciting contributions for KPFT, the local Pacifica radio station. A Pacifica station is an anomaly in this town. The locals respond to their message of peace and love by blowing up their transmitter from time to time.

On the Square, you might find that the parking lot has been cleared for the day, the pickup trucks with their gun racks replaced by food stands serving Tex-Mex or Cajun delicacies. The sun is hot. The people have possession of the Square. An unexpected crash of drum and cymbal echoes from a parking garage on the northwest corner of the Square. A fat, black man in frock coat, top hat, and sash steps out of the shadowy depths of the garage with a funereal gait. Behind him, still in the shadows, are other shuffling black figures, their positions marked by the glint of faint sunshine on polished brass. The first crashing, reverberating sounds settle into the unmistakable rhythms of a New Orleans jazz band's mournful rendition of "St. James Infirmary." Clearing the shadows, led by their solemnly strutting bandmaster, the musicians emerge and begin a circuit of the Square followed by a not-so-solemn crowd of young imitators playing air trombones and make-believe drums. Later, in the evening when the food stalls and jazz bands are gone, you can sip some wine in the courtyard at La Carafe. The court is no more than twenty-five feet square surrounded by multistory brick buildings. The house wine is mediocre. The jukebox offers only one artist— the voice of Edith Piaf and her soulful but endless lamentations drift constantly upward into the blue-black patch of sky above the courtyard.

If Market Square doesn't suit your tastes on a particular weekend, there is always the Houston Zoo at the south end of Hermann Park. You can get there by going down Old Spanish Trail past the Astrodome and then turning right on Main Street. But if you go on a Sunday, late in the morning, the better way is the route straight through the middle of downtown. The city on

Sunday morning is a civilized thing—quiet streets marked with sharp architectural shadows, reflections in department store windows, and leisurely strollers with a copy of the *Houston Post* tucked under their arm. Freed from the need to compete for space or move with the flow of the crowd, you can slow your pace and make compositions in your mind—the sharp light at the end of an alleyway silhouetting rusted fire escapes, a mom-and-pop corner grocery whose faded window posters invoke a sweet, sad nostalgia. The Sunday morning sidewalks belong to the city's ghosts.

Down Fannin Street, the Warwick Hotel, with its red canopies and manicured grounds, marks the transition from city alleyways and grocery stores to city park. Just beyond the hotel, where Main meets Montrose, you emerge into a traffic circle where Sam Houston looks down from his bronze charger. A steep grassy hill on your right, near the Miller Theater, is the home of long-haired hippy types who throw a mean Frisbee. Farther on around the circle, the balloon man's merchandise is a multicolored marker for the entrance to the zoo.

There's no charge for the zoo's colorful kaleidoscope—the silver flash of wet seals, goldfish beside green lily pads, or the dry dusty gold of a coiled copperhead. The children's petting zoo is a study in contrasting behavior. The critters stand patiently, even expectantly, waiting for attention. My two little ones combine eagerness and reluctance in a tentative first touch.

After a dozen trips to this park, watching the children, and even the adults, as they discover the exhibits is more of an attraction then the animals themselves. The only continuing exception is the massive, shaggy Siberian tiger. His endless measured pacing from wall to tiled wall in the near-tropical heat amplifies the sense of solitary captivity. It speaks to me of a crushing confinement without rationale or escape. A rush of sympathy, a sense of uselessness—those are the souvenirs I take away after every visit.

Move along, pilgrim, there's nothing you can do here. You have your own problems. It's mid-July. Market Square, the

Houston Zoo, the entire city of Houston—all are about to become stage settings, scenic backdrops for the drama unfolding a few miles to the south. Against that backdrop, in the middle of all the players milling around back stage, there are some of us struggling to master the bit parts we will play in the upcoming spectacular.

A Russian named Yuri Gagarin had supplied the driving force behind this production when he became the first man to go into space on April 12, 1961. Less than a month later, on May 5, 1961, Alan Shepard took a suborbital ride on a rickety looking Redstone rocket. Whatever its scientific value, and some argued it wasn't much, manned spaceflight had turned into an international pissing contest designed to prove some kind of political and ideological superiority. *Sputnik*, Gagarin, the Bay of Pigs—embarrassment piled on embarrassment. We had to fix all of that! We had to do something dramatic, something very dramatic—we needed a technological high-wire act—preferably one where the wire-walkers work without a net!

CHAPTER NINE

Just twenty days after Shepard's flight, on Thursday, May 25, 1961, the New York Yankees defeated the Boston Red Sox at Yankee Stadium by a score of 6–4. On that same day, President John F. Kennedy made a special address to a joint session of Congress:

I therefore ask the Congress, above and beyond the increases I have earlier requested for space activities, to provide the funds which are needed to meet the following national goals:

First, I believe that this nation should commit itself to achieving the goal, before this decade is out, of landing a man on the moon and returning him safely to the Earth. No single space project in this period will be more impressive to mankind, or more important for the long-range exploration of space; and none will be so difficult or expensive to accomplish. We propose to accelerate the development of the appropriate lunar spacecraft. We propose to develop alternate liquid and solid fuel boosters, much larger than any now being developed, until certain which is superior. We propose additional funds for other engine development and for unmanned explorations—explorations which are particularly important for one purpose which this nation will never overlook: the survival of the man who first makes this daring flight. But in a very real sense, it will not be one man going to the moon—if we make this judgment affirmatively, it will be an entire nation. For all of us must work to put him there.

I spent that day, as usual, at Manhattan College in the Riverdale section of the Bronx. I was thinking about ten final exams that I would have to take in three exhausting days. If I thought about it at all, I would have paid more attention to the Yankees score than to the president's speech. He had set a challenging goal. Coming as it did in the same month as Shepard's fifteen minutes in space, I had to admire his *chutzpah*. He called for all of us to work to put an American on the Moon—typically inclusive, but abstract, political rhetoric. I had no idea that the "all of us" meant me—in person, in a control room, in Houston, Texas.

That thought never occurred to me. If it had, I would have heard my inner voice come online in a near shriek, *You have got to be kidding. You're a liberal arts geek, studying history because the good Brothers at Bishop Loughlin High School told you that you have zero math skills—and you've got the grades to prove it.* The voice would have been dead right and that flight of whimsy would have ended in an abrupt crash of realism.

The international contest that Gagarin had kick-started went on through the end of Project Mercury and into the Gemini Program. The Project Mercury goals were modest—baby steps into space—put a man in orbit, see if he could do his job when he got there, and get him and his spacecraft home safe. Gus Grissom made a suborbital flight in July 1961. They recovered the pilot, but the spacecraft went to the bottom of the Atlantic. The safe part seemed to need a little work.

I spent that summer, as I had a couple of earlier ones, hauling furniture up and down three or four flights of stairs in Greenwich Village, or Brooklyn Heights, or on Staten Island. I had won scholarships to both high school and college. My college scholarship didn't cover boarding at school. I commuted every day from my parents' house in Queens to school in the Bronx. On weekends during the school year, I sold hardware or dished up fast food at Harvey's Burger and Bun to earn money for gas and books. Humping furniture paid better, so in the summer months I paid up my International Brotherhood of Teamsters dues and reported to the Mayflower terminal in Astoria, Queens, not far from the Queensboro Bridge. The boss was Warren John, a tough little guy with a buzz cut and a cigar butt that jutted out from the right side of a perpetual snarl. The word around the lot was that he had left the Patterson, New Jersey, Police Department under questionable circumstances. We shaped up every morning just like they did on the docks. There were maybe twenty-five of us on any given day who stood in a group outside the terminal office. Warren came out with a sheaf of papers and did some pretend calculations to make it look like he hadn't already made his decision. He pointed with his right middle finger, a cigar butt clutched between forefinger and thumb—"You, and you, and you," down through the list until he had the men he needed. "That's it for today. The rest of you can go home."

When the counting was done, we went into the terminal office to collect the shipment paperwork and meet the over-the-road driver we would be working with that day. "This is your lucky day, college boy! I saved you a four-bagger up in the Bronx with a grand piano and no fuckin' elevator. Have a nice day, and be kind to the shipper lady or I'll cut your balls off and ship them to Canada."

"Thank you, sir, may I have another."

Sometimes there really were four flights up and a grand piano. But mostly it was Warren John bullshit. Long-distance drivers new to the big city just shook their heads in disbelief. There were four or five of us college kids, and we worked every day. I found out later that we were Warren's secret weapon. Summertime was his busiest season. It brought more than the normal quota of what Warren described in his more rational moments as "problem shippers." They were people with inbound shipments who had already complained to the originating city about the quality of the service, or people with outbound shipments who were proving to be picky about the packing and handling of their stuff. Warren's "college boys" got all of those jobs. He knew we would be polite, circumspect, and sympathetic about the damage to a cheap Van Gogh print when his regular drivers and helpers might respond with a hearty "Fuck you, lady. That's what you got insurance for."

The regular crew of drivers and helpers were a mixture of guys who had been on the road too long and taken too many pills and others who might have just finished doing two years for armed robbery. Oddly enough they understood that the "college boys" gave them protective cover and bigger tips. They made our day as easy as they could. They treated us well. They looked out for us. More than once, as you sized up a stack of five book cartons, you would hear a gruff voice coming from a figure five feet square with a name like Vinnie or Dominic, "Lemme take that, kid. I don't want you hurtin' yourself." After a day, sometimes a sixteen-hour day, they would drag you off to some local bar and insist that, "You don't wanna end up doin' this forever, kid," and hold themselves up as examples of just how fucked up you could get. Some nights I went home and picked up a textbook. At the end of the summer I found out that my long-time sweetheart, Mary Lou, the girl who had lived around the corner since I was seven years old, was going to have a baby. NASA wasn't the only one that needed to do more work on the safety thing.

On December 27, 1961, Mary Lou and I were married by Father Thomas Ryan at St. Anastasia Church in Little Neck. Both sets of parents disapproved, but they didn't have a better plan. We spent two nights at a motel near the cold but sunny beaches of Montauk Point, celebrating the troubled beginning of our new life. A kind neighbor named Pauline Powers, a widow needing a bit of extra cash and maybe even some company, gave us a temporary place to live. Less than two months later, John Glenn, aboard *Friendship 7*, became the first American to orbit the Earth. The launch vehicle was a modification of the Atlas intercontinental ballistic missile, with nearly five times the thrust of the Redstone missile that had put Shepard and Grissom into space. Both pilot and spacecraft were recovered. I hardly paused to notice. I would graduate from college in June 1962, four months after Glenn's flight. A child was due in the same month.

I had to make some decisions and make them soon about what we were going to do after June. I had done well in the history department. My mentor and tutor raised the possibility of a teaching fellowship at Princeton. I had spent four years in the Air Force Reserve Officer Training Corps program, marching to and fro in Van Cortland Park once a week. In my sophomore year, I had been the drill sergeant for the marching band. On St. Patrick's Day we followed the green line down Fifth Avenue. I can still hear the cadence of "Garryowen" beat out on the snare drums and overlaid with melody by fifes and trumpets. On Opening Day we played the national anthem standing behind second base at Yankee Stadium with the two baseball teams lined up along the first- and third-base lines. Whitey Ford scratched his balls in the middle of "the rockets' red glare."

My cadet time made active duty with the air force a career alternative. Princeton—even the name was magic. But I was fed up with the stress of driving for the "Big 4.0." I had a child to support and I didn't know much about how I could work that out on a teaching fellowship. The air force paid regularly and took care of dependents. And most importantly, the military held out the promise of both service and adventure. I was tired of studying history—time to make some.

I had inclined toward the military since my last year in high school. I wanted a job with a purpose that went beyond paychecks. The thought of thirty years selling light fixtures for General Electric was too grim to contemplate. During my last year in high school, I had applied to and been accepted by the Naval Academy and the Merchant Marine Academy, which also delivered a navy commission. After taking the navy physical, I received a form letter telling me that my eyesight was poor. That was no surprise. I had worn glasses since I was sixteen years old. The spoiler was the last paragraph, which promised ominously that "further deterioration of my vision might result in denial of a commission upon graduation." I discovered later that this was a cover-your-ass form letter, since the real likelihood of degradation great enough to deny a commission was unlikely. But at the time I had no one to turn to, no one who understood the military bureaucracy or was willing to help me find someone who did. I did a kind of expected-misery calculation that balanced four years of demanding cadet life followed by possible denial of a commission against four years in the more relaxed Reserve Officer Training Corps environment followed by the same denial. The only drawback to the Reserve Officer Training Corps option was that it meant a reserve commission as opposed to the prestigious regular commissions awarded to the academy graduates. I was willing to accept that trade-off. I applied a third scholarship that I had won, my New York State Regents Scholarship, to pay my way at Manhattan College, a small, all-male institution that had high standards, a good reputation, and was close enough for a daily commute.

Four years after I started at Manhattan, on May 24, 1962, Scott Carpenter made three orbits of the Earth aboard *Aurora 7*. Carpenter overshot his planned reentry mark and splashed down 250 miles off target. On June 12, I walked across the stage of the college auditorium to collect my diploma and something called the Draddy Medal for academic excellence in history. At the close of the ceremony, a group of us peeled off our academic gowns to reveal the blue dress uniforms underneath, raised our right hands, and became officers and gentlemen. My parents pinned on my gold bars. I was a distinguished graduate so I received a regular commission just like the academy grads. My wife had other more urgent business. She had delivered our daughter, Traci Ann, just three days earlier.

CHAPTER TEN

A set of orders assigning me to the 305th Bomb Wing (Medium) at Bunker Hill Air Force Base in north-central Indiana came along with the shiny new, gold bars. I was to report on August 24 for duty as a flight commander in a security police squadron. And so, in the middle of August, I said good-bye to my mother as I went out the front door of the Little Neck house. My parting words were, "I'll see you in twenty years." Whatever the future held, it had to be better than the pain and loneliness that had come along with that old house. I climbed into my second-hand Renault and started west. Mary Lou and the baby would follow when I had found us a place to live.

Any inventory of the memories that I associated with the house I was finally leaving behind would be a dismal document. Consider:

Item 1: Back Window Blues—We had moved into the little house on Forty-Third Avenue in the Little Neck neighborhood of Queens when I was about six years old. My mother had been like a classified file, and I didn't have the right clearances. Sometimes she would allow a quick glance inside, "I was born on the lower West Side of Manhattan in Hell's Kitchen." She did make it through high school. And then? And then nothing, no hint of childhood experiences, only the intimation that they weren't pleasant. She was made of some mystical material that repelled both emotion and enthusiasm. My father, a grade-school graduate, was absent, physically and emotionally. He worked at two jobs—gone sixteen or eighteen hours a day. When he came home he still wasn't there except when there was some complaint from our mother about our behavior. Then he came, belt in hand, to terrorize my two brothers and me.

The house was one half of a duplex, probably built in the late 1930s—wood frame, flat roof, shingled exterior walls. We shared a driveway with the house next door. There were two garages in the back. There were two floors and a basement. The front bedroom on the second floor, the largest, belonged to my parents. One door down the hall on the right, my older brother Bob lived in a tiny room just big enough for a single bed, a desk for schoolwork, and a small chest of drawers. At the back, next to the single bathroom, my younger brother Kenny and I shared the cramped third bedroom.

After I moved into that room, I began to masturbate early and often. My mother would see the evidence when she did the laundry. I lived in my head except for sporadic, vocal rebellions. My parents worried. They took me to the family doctor, a man with a neatly trimmed and waxed handlebar mustache who looked like he should be selling used cars. To eliminate the possibility that I was somehow retarded, he sent me off for an IQ test, whatever that was. The score, I have since discovered, was high—very high. The doctor said my problems were obviously due to the vast quantities of milk I consumed every day. Reduce that and all will be well. All was not well. My parents still worried and now they were scared of me. They had the idea that my test score required some kind of parental response that neither one understood.

Houses like ours fronted on four streets that made up a city block with Northern Boulevard on the south, 43rd Avenue on the north, 247th Street on the west, and 248th Street on the east side. Inside the hollow rectangle formed by the streets were backyards with garages, sheds, old cars, junk piles, and tall poles that supported clotheslines strung from the back porches of the houses. The room I shared with my brother was at the back of our house. It had a single window that looked down the length of that dismal cityscape—an Edward Hopper painting full of ghosts condemned like me to never communicate with their fellow creatures. Sometimes tears ran down my cheeks. This is my most vivid, crushing memory of that goddamned house that I had lived in.

Item 2: Rabbit Hole Blues—It was a pretty neat arrangement for an eight-year-old. I went to the local Catholic grammar school. One of my schoolmates and my best friend, Bobby, was the son of a prominent local physician. Mostly they lived in a big white colonial on Morgan Street at the other end of town. But in the spring, as the weather improved, they made weekend trips to the family beach compound at Asharoken Beach near North Port, New York.

Sometimes I got to go along. We did all of the things that kids do at the beach. We swam. We played ball. We chased the rabbits that infested the property. We picnicked on the beach or on the family speedboat anchored in some sheltered spot. At night I went to sleep in a second-floor bedroom in the "big house," lulled by the sound of the waves running up on the beach.

Late one Sunday night, Bobby's mom dropped me off at home. Sunburned and tired, I found my mother in her usual chair, eyeglasses perched halfway down the ridge of her nose, crochet hook busy on another one of those white doilies that covered every piece of furniture in the house. My father was at work, my brothers in their rooms.

My mother looked up as I came into the room, "You're late. You have school tomorrow. Get cleaned up and get into bed."

I dutifully made my way up the stairs. Ten minutes later I crept back down the stairs, now in striped pajamas and blue slippers. My mother looked up again as I turned the corner at the bottom of the stairs.

"I thought I told you to go to bed?"

I stammered, "I—they have two houses out there at the beach. Remember I told you some of that?"

"This is not the time to talk about your beach trip."

"Well, but, I have to tell you something we did. Yesterday we chased a little rabbit and it went into a hole under the stable, the littler house. We blocked up the hole with sticks and rocks and stuff."

"That's nice. Now go to bed."

My voice trembled, a tear started down my right cheek. "Last night I worried hard about the rabbit. If he can't get out he might even die."

"Get to bed. It's too late to worry about some rabbit. He'll get out. They always have another exit. Go do what I told you to do."

I rubbed my teary eyes with my fists, turned, and started up the stairs, my open backed slippers slapping gently at my heels as I trudged up into the darkness.

"Good night, and remember I love you," she called after me.

Item 3: Playing the Blues Blues—Our Zenith black-and-white console television stood in front of the two living room windows, windows that looked out on the house across the driveway from ours. On the opposite wall, my parents sat on a flowered couch. My brothers and I sprawled on the floor. I was the skinny eleven-year-old with the jug-handle ears. It was a Tuesday night and for us, like most of America, that meant Milton Berle.

His slapstick comedy routines, ludicrous skits, and crazy costumes worked just fine for my sophisticated eleven-year-old aesthetic sensibilities. But on this night there was a variation from the fast-paced wisecracking. Berle introduced a guest, a musician, a man with a trumpet whose name I have forgotten. But I can remember how the crystal-clear, but still soft notes of a song they said was called "Summertime" touched a longing new to this eleven-year-old.

When the commercial break came, my mother got up and walked into the kitchen. Without understanding what I had in mind I got up and followed. The kitchen was dark except for the light cast from the open refrigerator. My mother glanced up as she heard me approach.

"Can I do that?"

"Do what?"

"Play, learn to play a trumpet like that."

"Why do you want to do that?"

"I—I don't know for sure. I just liked that so much."

She closed the refrigerator, leaving the room dark except for the weak output of a small nightlight and brushed past me on her way back to the living room, "You know I love you, but not everyone can do that. It takes lots of practice and an expensive trumpet. It costs a lot."

Item 4: Back Window Blues Reprise—A radio on the top shelf of the small desk is tuned to the World Series broadcast. The White Sox have just embarrassed the home team 11–0. A copy of Volume II of Burckhardt's *The Civilization of the Renaissance in Italy* is open on the desk in front of me. I am a sophomore now, facing the midterm season stuck on a relentless treadmill of academic achievement. My mother and I have worked out a secret unspoken agreement, and it's killing me. For her part, she pays no attention to what I'm doing except when I bring home a 4.0 report card. Even then she says nothing to me, communicating her pride and approval to neighbors and friends whose kids complain to me that I am ruining their lives. An academic career that might have been satisfactory, interesting, maybe even fun, has become a compulsive struggle for self-worth, a battle I can never win. I understand now that every fact I commit to memory and every concept I come to understand drives me deeper into my own head and widens the emotional and cultural gap between my parents and me. Burckhardt stares up at me: "Freed from the countless bonds which elsewhere in Europe checked progress, having reached a high degree of individual development and been schooled by the teachings of antiquity, the Italian mind now turned to the discovery of the outward universe, and to the representation of it in speech and in form."

My mind turns not to discovery, but to despair, to crushing loneliness. Tears roll down my cheeks. I get up from my desk and look out the window into empty backyards. I think I see my cardboard-cutout mother standing behind me, reflected in the glass of the window.

"Remember, we love you."

CHAPTER ELEVEN

As I walk into the TV lounge on the second floor of the Bunker Hill Air Force Base Bachelor Officers Quarters, Captain Jim Whitehead, a pilot who flies the KC-135 refueling aircraft, sits sprawled in one of the motel modern lounge chairs, his right leg resting on the arm of the chair, his sage green flight suit unzipped halfway down his chest. Egon Schmidt, a General Electric technical representative who advises the air force on the care and feeding of the jet engines used on the B-58 Hustler, sits on a small couch just to Whitehead's left.

Whitehead looks up from the baseball game he has been watching on the black-and-white TV and says, "You look like your dog died."

"I just had a call from my wife."

"Wasn't she supposed to show up today? Aren't you supposed to be on your way to the airport?"

"Her flight was diverted to Chicago because of the weather."

Whitehead just then seemed to notice the rain and lightning outside the windows. "Why don't you go get her? It's only about 150 miles."

"My old Renault is overheating. A guy who knows about that stuff says it has removable cylinder sleeves. Antifreeze is leaking under the bottom of the cylinders into the crankcase. I can't break down with a new baby in the car."

Whitehead reaches into the pocket of the flight jacket that he had hung over the back of his chair. He pulls out a set of car keys and tosses them onto the small table that sits in front of Schmidt.

"It's the gray Buick in the lot. I'm going on alert for three days, so I don't need it."

I look at the keys, but make no move to pick them up.

"You can drive a car with an automatic transmission, right?"

"Yes, sir, yes, sir, I can. But at this time of the month there's about ten dollars in my wallet."

Schmidt, a short, chubby man with wavy blond hair pushes his right shoulder forward and rolls his body so that he can pull his wallet from his hip pocket. He counts bills onto the table next to the key ring.

"Fifty dollars should get you there and back. Pay me when you can."

I pick up the cash and car keys and head for the door. I go out this door feeling like I've found a better home. Five hours later, I knock on Mary Lou's door in a hotel near O'Hare. Holding on to each other, we try to get our new family through a short night in a strange place, a place farther from home than we have ever been.

Early the next morning, we start for our new home in Bunker Hill, Indiana, a town covering about one-half of a square mile with a population of about nine hundred on a good day. Downtown Bunker Hill consists of a single street where you could go to the bank or get yourself a haircut. The barbershop has three or four nail kegs filled with peanuts. The customers eat the peanuts and toss the shells on the floor. They didn't have anything like that back in New York City.

The house on North Elm Street where we would live had originally been a single-family home that the landlord had made into upper and lower apartments. It has no number—it is just "the first house on North Elm." We are upstairs, up one flight to a rickety porch, and then to the door. Inside there is a sort of living room dominated by an oil furnace that stands nearly in the center of the space. The furnace is fed by a fifty-five-gallon tank that sits out on the porch. It provides the only heat for the room where it stands, and for the bedroom, kitchen, and bathroom. If you leave water in the tub on a winter night it freezes solid. The tank on the porch has no gauge and is liable to run out of fuel. I learn how to work copper tubing and install a second tank.

Sergeant O.C. Parr, his wife, Glenda, and their infant daughter live in the downstairs space. They are Texans. They are friendly and kind. O.C. can fix stuff that breaks. Glenda supports my wife as she adjusts to the multiple traumas of a new baby, a husband groping to find his way in a new world, and life in a tiny Midwestern town.

Bunker Hill Air Force Base, my first duty station, is just about two miles west of town, close enough so that the explosive start of a B-58 afterburner lifts you two inches off the bed. The base had opened as Bunker Hill Naval Air Station in 1942 to train navy, marine corps, and coast guard pilots. Shut down after the war, the air force reopened the base in 1954. Five years later, the 305th Bomb Group arrived with its B-47s. In 1961, the 305th became one of two units in the air force to receive the new B-58, a delta-wing multiengine medium bomber that looks like it's supersonic even when it's standing still.

My assignment, in August 1962, is to the 305th Combat Defense Squadron, the unit within the bomb wing responsible for the security of the aircraft and the nuclear weapons they carry. I am to be a flight commander responsible for thirty-five young security policemen. They give me about two days' orientation, a day to qualify at the pistol range, and a couple of weeks of on-the-job training. Then they drop me into the big middle of the worst nuclear confrontation in history.

Just about seven months earlier, in February, the United States had imposed an economic embargo on Cuba. In September, Congress passed a joint resolution authorizing the use of military force in Cuba if American interests are threatened. A tense standoff follows.

On October 3, *Sigma 7* with Wally Schirra on board makes a six-orbit engineering test flight. The mission lasts a little over nine hours. On October 14, a U-2 aircraft photographs missile sites in western Cuba. The missiles—with one-megaton warheads—can reach almost the entire continental United States, including every Strategic Air Command base, like the one at Bunker Hill, Indiana. On October 22, President Kennedy announces a maritime blockade to cut off shipments of missiles and military equipment to Cuba.

That same day, the Pentagon orders US forces to defense readiness condition 3, DEFCON 3, an enhanced state of readiness. On October 23, for the first time in history, they order the Strategic Air Command to DEFCON 2, one step short of weapons release in response to imminent or ongoing attack. The 305th responds by putting any bomber capable of flying on a fifteen-minute alert. They hang a nuclear weapon on anything that looks like it might make it to a target. Our squadron operations officer, Lieutenant Wayne Moore, a friendly Texan with a degree in architecture, warns us to be careful where we park our cars. We might come out to the parking lot and find a weapons pod slung underneath it. They convert the Bachelor Officers Quarters into alert quarters for the additional bomber and tanker crews. We guard the alert aircraft, crews, and weapons storage area around the clock. Our regular force is way too small for the task, so we have help from "security augmentees." They are cooks, bakers, truck drivers, and whatever, who have been released from their squadrons, given basic weapons training, and sent to support the security police. Their parent organizations don't release their very best to us.

With my own troops and this raggedy-ass crew of recruits we muddle through the long nights of the Cuban missile crisis. I am a warm body. I can carry a sidearm that I am marginally qualified to use. I can stay awake all night, sort of. I am the junior lieutenant in the squadron. All of that adds up to twelve-hour night shifts six days a week. I have no idea what I am doing. I am "qualified" to point and fire my weapon, with no idea when that is legally justified. The rules of engagement—when could you kill somebody—nobody had talked about that. I know less about the tactics for repelling an attack on the base than Major General Stanley's "novice in a nunnery."

And if I am more dangerous to friend than foe, my unwilling recruits could be even worse. On a night early in November, Staff Sergeant Billy Johnson, my flight sergeant, and I are checking perimeter sentry posts at the far end of the main runway. Johnson is an Indiana native. He is about medium height, carries just a little too much weight around his middle, has a broad face with a prominent forehead topped by blond, crew-cut hair. He is professional and mostly soft-spoken. We had worked together almost since my arrival on base. He tries to teach me about being an officer. He tries to teach me about squirrel hunting, a favorite local pursuit. The trick, he said, is to sit quietly at the base of a tree and click the safety of your rifle on and off until the sound attracts a squirrel. He never did turn me into a successful squirrel hunter. I am kind of happy about that part.

Mostly our sentry checks mean bringing the troops coffee or a sandwich to keep them from expiring of boredom. Johnson drives our standard air force blue pickup truck. I sit in the right seat with the window rolled down searching for the guard on duty—a new conscript standing his first shift. Johnson flashes the prearranged pattern with the truck lights—no sign of our sentry. He turns off the taxiway onto a narrow road flanked by ditches on both sides that leads out to a navigation beacon. We roll slowly and finally come to a stop just short of the end of the road.

Johnson tries the signal again. In the last flash of the lights I glimpse a black silhouette scrambling up out of the roadside ditch. I hear the bolt of an M-1 carbine go back and then forward as a round goes into the chamber of the weapon. The movement is so quick that I can't focus on the moving figure. When focus returns I am looking into the muzzle of the carbine. It is six inches from my forehead.

"Wagner, what the fuck are you doing?" Johnson demands from behind the wheel.

I decide not to make any sudden movements or noises. I can make out Airman First Class Theodore Wagner looking down the barrel of the weapon with a scary, stupid grin on his face. Wagner is on loan from the roads and grounds section of the Civil Engineering Squadron. They have not sent their very best. Wagner had once upon a time during his fifteen years of service worn two or three more stripes than he wears on this particular night. Various encounters with the military justice system had taken them away.

"What the fuck are you doing?" Johnson repeats.

"I'm guarding my post, Sarge, just like we did it in Korea!"

I think Johnson shakes his head in disbelief. I don't dare turn my head to see.

"You dumb fuck! If you take a look around you'll see that we are not in fucking Korea. Now swing that muzzle away from the lieutenant's face and clear that fucking round."

Sergeant Johnson had selected a limited but apparently effective vocabulary for dealing with the situation. As Wagner swings the muzzle to his right I tentatively reach up and follow its path, trying to convince myself that it is really going away. After Wagner clears his weapon, he comes back up to the window of our truck.

"Give me the fucking magazine, Wagner!"

"But Sarge, I won't have no ammo to hold off the enemy."

"You've got a radio. If you see any bad guys give us a shout. We'll bring back the ammo and a strike team to save your sorry ass. In the meantime read your post orders and find out how to make a proper goddamn Indiana kind of challenge."

Wagner hands me the magazine. I toss it into the back of the truck as Johnson backs out of the side road onto the taxiway. With Wagner neutralized, the rest of the Cuban crisis passes peaceably enough. From time to time some of the local boys spend too much time in some roadhouse and then try out our perimeter security. The sentries stop them just outside the fence every time. The Indiana State Police do the rest.

CHAPTER TWELVE

Finally, on November 15, the Strategic Air Command stands down from DEFCON 2 and things go back to peacetime normal. That means working a rotating shift schedule—three days, three swings, and then three midnights followed by three days off. There is still no formal training. Slots in the Air Police training school are scarce. On-the-job training is still the only alternative. Another Texan, Chief Master Sergeant Bobby Bulls, the senior noncommissioned officer in the squadron, coaches me on how to direct the response to a Broken Arrow or a Bent Spear, accidents involving destruction or damage to a nuclear weapon. The squadron first sergeant, the "first shirt," Technical Sergeant "Iron Pants" Osborne, teaches me something about disciplinary measures that I can use when my troops don't do right. Mostly that means Osborne holding a brief meeting with the alleged perpetrator out behind the barracks. Technical Sergeant Casey Sutton, one of the shift commanders, spends his time pissing and moaning about how come it is that he has to be hanging around on the midnight shift when there are so many fuzzy-faced lieutenants to do that job.

The highest ranking security police officer on base is Major Boyd, the deputy commander for security and law enforcement, who reports to the base commander. Once upon a time I may have known his first name, but I soon forgot. Lieutenants don't have much cause to remember the major's first name. The major is a recalled reservist. In civilian life he is a sergeant in the Texas Rangers. He looks the part—picture Andy Griffith with wavy, gray-streaked black hair and a face furrowed by too much Texas sun and wind. His slow Texas drawl is the perfect medium for his folksy, avuncular messages.

"Dick," he says one day over cups of coffee at the flight-line snack bar, "I been to two hangings, a goat rope, and a buzzard fuck, but I ain't never seen nothin' like this."

He has a way of starting his conversations so as to really get your attention. "I don't understand what a clever college boy like you is doin' here wanderin' around the flight line all night. There ain't no future in it. Take a look at me—top cop on this base with a couple hundert troops—and still a piss-ant major. Did you know that the top cop in the whole goddamn air force is just a colonel? You need to be findin' somethin' else to do, boy!"

"Yes, sir," I nod politely as lieutenants often do when listening to a senior officer.

The major's message stays on the edge of my consciousness as I feel my way along in this still-new environment trying to see if this line of work really does suit me. At this point the possibility of being "just a colonel" doesn't sound bad. But I begin to put my daily experience into two columns: "Stay" or "No-stay."

On the stay side there is an attraction, a vicarious glamour, in serving in one of only two B-58 units in the United States Air Force. Created by Convair, it is the first supersonic bomber built by a Western power. It looks the part. The other bomber aircraft in the air force inventory have a traditional rounded shape. From a distance they might be mistaken for a cargo aircraft. The B-58 crews call them BUFs for short—Big Ugly Fuckers.

There was no way to mistake the purpose of the B-58—function follows form. Its needle-sharp nose, its delta wings, and the single weapons pod slung between its long-legged landing gear make you think of an angry dart meant to deliver something ugly, and deliver it in a hurry. It looks fast—and it is. In March 1962 a B-58 set a transcontinental speed record flying nonstop from Los Angeles to New York and back again in just four hours and forty-one minutes. It flew both the eastbound and westbound legs at an average speed of more than one thousand miles per hour.

A third of our bomber force is on fifteen-minute alert. Fully armed, the bombers sit in shelters next to the runway. There are frequent exercises to test the force response time. On one clear, cold December afternoon, Sergeant Johnson and I park our pickup truck at the far end of the taxiway from the alert area. Central Security Control comes up on the radio and announces an alert force exercise in progress. We can't see what is going on in the alert area, but we can imagine the raucous sound of the klaxon and bomber crews scrambling out of the alert quarters. We hear turbojet engines screaming to life. We pull off to the side of the taxiway and look back in the direction of the alert area. For a minute or two we see nothing. Then Johnson points down the taxiway, "Coco exercise—here they come."

He had explained to me earlier that alert force exercises come in four flavors. For an Alpha exercise the crews would scramble to the alert shelters and board their aircraft. For a Bravo exercise they started their engines. Coco exercises involved the aircraft taxiing to the runway and readying for takeoff. When the exercise terminated, they taxied back to the alert parking pads. There was also a Delta exercise that required the alert force to take off just like they would for the real thing. Delta exercises were usually reserved for use by the headquarters' inspector general during a full-up no-notice inspection.

There was one other case that Johnson thought I needed to understand. "If you see the alert force taxiing out to the runway and no one notifies you of an exercise, you have to act fast."

He is trying hard to be serious—too hard.

"Uh-huh, and do what?"

"You have to get into the defensive position."

"And what, pray tell, is that?"

Johnson looks around with this fake conspiratorial air as though someone might be listening.

"This is top secret stuff."

"Uh-huh?"

"OK, so what you do is to put your head down between your knees as far as you can."

"And then?"

"You kiss your ass good-bye because the Russian missiles are on the way."

From our vantage point alongside the taxiway we watch the B-58s approach. They look like enraged wasps in a raggedy line astern as they swerve slightly from side to side to avoid the exhaust of the aircraft in front. Their ominous weapons pods are framed by main landing gear that look too spindly to keep them from scraping the concrete. The air above and behind them is distorted by the heat of their engines. Johnson shouts to be heard above the engine noise, "This is joinin' up stuff!"

I can only agree—not only "joining up' but "staying on" stuff.

Six weeks later, my sergeant and I are working the midnight shift. We are prowling the alert area on foot in minus-ten-degree cold to check on our sentries. As we work our way along a line of shelters, each one housing an alert force bomber, we are challenged by the point guard assigned to each aircraft.

"Halt, who goes there?"

"Lieutenant Stachurski and Sergeant Johnson."

"Advance and be recognized."

We move forward with our parka hoods off so the sentry can verify who we are. With the formalities concluded, we check status with each man. Are they getting regular relief to warm up? Do they need coffee or a pit stop? When we are satisfied that everything is as OK as it can be on a night that would freeze the balls off the proverbial brass monkey, we move on to the next shelter.

As we approach the last shelter near the south end of the area, we can plainly see the sentry walking his post, weapon slung on his right shoulder, a white plume of breath marking the opening in his parka hood. We expect the standard challenge as we approach. Nothing happens. But we see that each time he passes in front of the needle nose of the bomber he stops for a second and seems to say something. We move closer—still no challenge. Finally we are close enough to overhear him as he turns his head toward the aircraft, mutters "goddamn piece of junk," and moves on. There is no rule about insulting airplanes. There is one that says, "I will guard everything within the limits of my post."

Johnson interrupts the young man's perambulation, "Likosky, what in the hell are you doing?"

Airman Likosky turns and begins to stutter an embarrassed explanation. He sees me and manages a half-assed salute. "Sorry, Sarge, sorry, sir. What with working swings and midnights this is my fifth night out here in this goddamn cold. Sorry, excuse me, sir. It's like I'll be out here for a thousand nights in a row. I guess I was just looking to get warm by getting pissed off at this thing that's keeping me out here. I just didn't see you."

"You didn't see us because you weren't paying attention to your job. You do recall that that piece of junk does include a nuclear bomb?"

"Yes, sir, Sarge."

"The question is what to do now? We could slap a summary court martial on you for this. You know that don't you?"

"Yes, Sarge, I do," comes the mumbled answer.

"On the other side, you've been a pretty good troop up till this point."

Johnson pauses and glances at me to see if I'm ready to go where he is going. I give him a nod.

"So since this is your first offense, we're going to let it slide. At least as far as the legal stuff goes. That doesn't mean I won't find some weapons in the armory that need cleaning during your next break. You understand?"

"Yes, sir, Sarge. Thanks"

"Now get your ass back in gear and walk that post in a military manner."

Twenty minutes later we come by in our truck with coffee and doughnuts for the troops and make a point of handing some to Likosky.

The next morning I think about Likosky as I crawl into bed to get a good day's sleep. After some tossing and turning I fall asleep. Last night's images stay with me. I dream that I'm sitting in the passenger seat of our truck. Johnson is at the wheel. It's dark. We are stopped in the middle of the main runway. An endless column of armed sentries, with their parka hoods up, shuffle past my open window. As each one passes he turns toward me and Andy Griffith's voice mutters, "You need to be findin' somethin' else to do, boy!"

CHAPTER THIRTEEN

My chance to be somewhere else comes early in 1963. The air force is introducing the Minuteman missile into the Strategic Air Command inventory. They are so desperate for launch crew members that they offer a master's degree in business to any officer who signs up. I sign up—a move that takes me ever farther away from Houston and the manned spaceflight program.

I take my family back to New York and then head west to attend Minuteman basic training—the Missile Launch Officer Course at Chanute Air Force Base in Rantoul, Illinois. This is my first exposure to a complex electromechanical system that I will live with and in for the foreseeable future. Most of my classmates are like me. They don't know a diode from a hole in the ground. It turns out that we need to learn a great deal about holes in the ground. Our missiles and our launch control center are buried deep under the prairie. So they teach us to read functional block diagrams—a kind of cartoon designed for the technically illiterate. We learn the basics of how the system operates.

At the end of April I head west from Illinois to my duty station—Ellsworth Air Force Base near Rapid City, South Dakota. I stay only long enough to get connected with Captain Dean Beach, the quirky little man who will likely be my commander for the next four years. Technically he is the missile combat crew commander and I am his deputy missile combat crew commander—grand titles considering that there are only two of us. We head out together to attend the Minuteman Operational Readiness Training at Vandenberg Air Force Base near Santa Maria, California. On the day we report to school, NASA launches Gordon Cooper aboard *Faith 7* for a thirty-four-hour flight. The only missile I see during my three-week tour is an Atlas. It lifts off from the Vandenberg launch complex, climbs to maybe twenty thousand feet, and blows up. My crew commander and I learn how to run our checklists for normal operations and to respond to emergencies. We learn how to react to Emergency War Order messages—messages that may direct the "release" of our weapons on targets halfway around the world.

My family joins me when I return to Rapid City. We set up housekeeping, as we had in Indiana, in an apartment on the upper floor of a big white house. This one is at 1027 Omaha Drive. Once again a young airman and his family are on the first floor. There's no garage. In January and February you run a long extension cord from the house to a head-bolt heater on your engine block. Minuteman has made Rapid City a boom town. If a Boeing missile worker, a Sioux Indian, a young GI, and a guy in a hardhat walk into a bar on West St. Joseph Street, that's not the beginning of a joke—it's Rapid City in 1963.

My crew is assigned to the 68th Strategic Missile Squadron of the 44th Strategic Missile Wing. There are three Minuteman intercontinental ballistic missile squadrons at Ellsworth Air Force Base. Each one operates five Launch Control Facilities and fifty Launch Facilities, each one housing a single missile. The control centers and missiles are located in the vicinity of the communities of Wall, Union Center, and Belle Fourche. We pull twenty-four-hour alert tours in a Launch Control Center buried thirty feet under the prairie. Certified crews are in short supply in the beginning, so we sometimes pull three tours a week—something like ninety hours on duty.

The work is demanding. At any instant we can be called on to be Dr. Death, dealing out our product in megaton doses on targets we will never see. Crew training and testing standards are understandably stringent. We take a monthly exam on weapons launch procedures. We call it the "you bet your ass" test. The passing grade is 100 percent. Anything less earns you an audience with the wing commander. Strategic Air Command pencils don't come with erasers. Our behavior is scrutinized as part of a "human reliability" program—can't have any crazies down there with the launch keys. We are also subject to periodic "check rides." Launch crews from the Standardization and Evaluation Branch run you through a simulated scenario complete with overlapping emergencies and urgent Emergency War Order execution messages. A "major error," a procedural mistake that endangers your own crew or results in an unauthorized weapons release or a nuclear accident, earns you an immediate relief from duty and that unpleasant audience with the wing commander.

The rewards that come with this regimen are elusive. When you come up out of the ground a day after you went under, you can entertain the notion that you kept the world safe for democracy for another twenty-four hours. That notion doesn't produce much in the way of creative satisfaction. Yeah, you sat there with your finger on the trigger, but all you get for that is a tired trigger finger and the question of whether or not you would ever pull that trigger.

My relations with my crew commander are strained. We are allowed to sleep in shifts during our twenty-four-hour tours. He tells me that it would be a good idea if I polished his boots while he is sleeping, the way he did for his commander when he was a junior officer on an air crew. I demur. He suggests that he might give a direct order. I suggest that I have been trained to recognize an illegal order when I hear one. The tension is amplified by the forced togetherness of twenty-four hours in a concrete and steel cocoon isolated from the world above ground. One morning, without explanation, he shows up for our pre-departure briefing totally bald—every hair is shaved from his head. Our squadron commander doesn't see that as particularly "reliable." Captain Beach is investigated and finally found to be stable enough for duty. He ends up with a written warning about "bizarre hair styles" that violate regulations on appearance and dress. I end up on another crew. I move my family into a house on base. In June 1964, the new Manned Spacecraft Center in Houston opens for business. My son Dale is born in the Ellsworth Air Force Base hospital in October.

My second crew commander is Captain Ray Hamel, a New Hampshire native who piloted a B-52 before coming to Minuteman in search of a graduate degree. He is motivated and knowledgeable. We quickly achieve Instructor Crew status. That leaves us a notch above the ordinary "crew dogs" and a notch below the evaluation crews. Hamel has this in-your-face relationship with the evaluation crews. They come after us. We end up the only crew in the wing to ever complete an evaluation without even a single minor error—none, *nada, niente.* Hamel's drive to get it right is communicated through example rather than exhortation. There is little strain involved in following his lead. Whatever minor strain there might be is balanced by a relaxed sense of humor that is frequently coarse and sometimes outrageous. On duty, we both wear side arms. The weapons are there to presumably protect the launch code documents and launch keys we have around our necks. The notion that we are going to shoot at each other in some imagined Dr. Strangelovian scenario is beyond bizarre. The first thing you do when you go on duty with Hamel and the eight-ton blast door closes to seal you in is to hang your weapon on one of the equipment racks. When it comes his turn to get his four hours of sleep, he takes the launch code documents from around his neck and hangs them on the rack next to his weapon. He turns in with the comment, "If you need these help yourself. Don't wake me up. I don't want to know."

Most of our excursions into the underworld are marked by a dull, repetitive sameness. Occasionally we get an ugly surprise. December 5, 1964, is one of those ugly surprise days. We are scheduled to start a twenty-four-hour alert tour at Launch Control Facility Lima. Our pre-alert briefing that morning sounds just like a hundred others we have heard. The briefing officer gives no hint that there might be trouble waiting for us at Lima flight—big trouble.

Lugging our packs of winter survival gear, we file out of the briefing room and walk the short distance out to the flight line where H-1 helicopters wait with their engines running and their rotors swinging menacingly through the air. Ducking under the blades, Hamel and I, with two other crews, scramble aboard the chopper. Today is my day to ride in the copilot's seat just to the right of the pilot. The others settle into their seats in the cargo compartment behind the pilot and strap themselves in. Airborne at 500 feet and 110 miles per hour we start our morning commute. The dark shapes of the Black Hills loom up to the west. To the north, the solitary summit called Mato Paha by the Lakota and Bear Butte by the Europeans dominates the sweep of prairie just to the east of the Black Hills. Farther to the east, the prairie stretches toward Chicago with its winter brown surface randomly broken by the glint of sunlight off the white surface of frozen stock ponds.

Less than thirty minutes later the pilot adjusts the chopper's throttle and the pitch of the rotor blades to hover over the landing pad outside the chain-link and barbed-wire security fence that surrounds the Lima Launch Control Facility support building. Except for the fence with its sliding electric security gate and a forty-foot-tall high-frequency radio antenna, the building could pass for one of the single-story ranch houses that dot the prairie. It houses sleeping quarters, a kitchen, and a recreation room that support a security strike team and transient maintenance people. Supporting those troops is an important but secondary function. The primary reason for the existence of the Lima support building is invisible: the Minuteman Launch Control Center buried thirty feet under the building.

As soon as the chopper touches down, we repeat our crouching dash under the threatening blades. Security troops verify that we're good guys and open the gate. Inside the building,

Technical Sergeant Jackson, the noncommissioned officer who runs things topside, stands by to brief us before we go below.

"Morning, sirs. Everything is running fine. The cooks and I are the only ones here at this point. The security strike team is deployed to Lima Two. They've been gone since last night. We're getting ready for a big uptick in transient maintenance teams. We'll be ready to support."

Hamel gives him a quizzical look. "Support what, Sergeant? What's going on?"

Jackson shifts his weight to his left foot, and looks down to carefully examine the toe of his right boot.

"Sir, I think that maybe Major King is the best one to answer that question."

My boss decides not to pursue it. Jackson is a conscientious dependable NCO. Something serious is going on—best to get below and talk to the guys on duty.

We pick up our gear and make our way to the head of the reinforced concrete elevator shaft that leads down to the control center. As we enter the elevator we step across a yellow line that marks the beginning of the high-security "no lone zone." Anyone who passes that line has to be accompanied by or at least watched by a second person capable of detecting "erratic or unauthorized behavior." Deadly force is authorized to protect the launch control systems. This is serious shit.

Jackson had notified the crew that we were on our way down. As we reach the bottom of the shaft, Major Ray King, commander of the crew on duty, swings the eight-ton blast door open. That's strange. Eight-ton doors are mostly the junior officer's job. King is a tall distinguished-looking man who looks like he ought to be the senator from somewhere. His deputy, Lieutenant Bob Lopez, is about my age with dark hair and a perpetual five-o'clock shadow. Both men look as if they had "been rode hard and put up wet." Neither offers a greeting.

We go through the doorway, crouching down to make our way through the low, narrow tunnel that penetrates the outer structure of the control center, and then cross a short steel plate that brings us into the inner structure, the Launch Control Center proper. The outer structure is like a giant Tylenol capsule—a cylinder with hemispherical ends—twenty-nine feet in diameter, fifty feet long—made of steel-reinforced concrete three or four feet thick. The inner structure is basically a rectangular room, maybe twelve feet wide, ten feet high, and twenty-eight feet long, made of steel plates. It is suspended inside the outer structure using a set of four pneumatic shock isolators—huge pistons meant to damp out the shock waves from a nearby nuclear detonation. How nearby? I try not to think about that. The whole idea that you are going to survive a nuclear exchange borders on insanity—I mean, why would you want to?

Anyway, the control room has two desk-like consoles. The commander's console is at the far end. It has an illuminated panel that shows the status of each of the ten missiles and launchers in Lima Flight. Each of the missile launchers is about ten miles from the control center, connected by underground cables. The deputy commander's console, my duty station, is halfway down the right side of the enclosure. Alongside of each console there is a small panel with a spring-loaded, key-operated launch switch. Both crew members have to insert their keys and then rotate them at the same time to launch the missiles. It's simple—you turn the key and then you assume Sergeant Johnson's defensive posture.

Except for a small bunk and a latrine, the space between the consoles is crammed with equipment racks. Everything is painted institutional green. Under the floor there's a motor generator that runs day and night. The whine of the generator and the sound of cooling air being forced through the equipment racks drive the background noise level up close to the threshold of pain. Any fluctuation in the sound of the generator adds panic to the pain.

Before Hamel can even drop his gear on the bunk, King takes him by the arm and pulls him in the direction of the commander's console. One glance makes it clear what it is that King wants my boss to see. A single red light shines near the top of the Lima

Two status display. I know what it says even before I come close enough to read its ominous message: "Warhead Alarm." Below the red light other indicators show that both the inner and outer security perimeters of the launch facility have been violated.

My boss lets his survival pack fall to the floor. King points at the light. "We had a maintenance team on-site at Lima Two last night. They were supposed to work on the inner security circuitry. About half an hour after we cleared them in, the Warhead Alarm came on. Right about then the maintenance guys called in. They said that they had been working in the launch tube equipment room when they heard a roaring sound. They felt a strange vibration and maybe even saw some smoke. They weren't sure. They were scared shitless. We told them to pull back to the access gate and maintain security until the cops got there. Then we ran our checklist and put everybody on notice about what we had—maintenance control back at the base, our own command post, and the SAC headquarters command post."

He pauses to catch his breath and then continues. "A maintenance team, with some troops from munitions maintenance is on site now. DROPKICK," he says using the communications call sign for the SAC headquarters command post, "seems to be really nervous about this one. I don't know what they know that we don't, but they're being super cautious. They told us to maintain radio silence. They don't want anyone overhearing what's going on. So we rigged up a special landline voice circuit connecting Lima Two to DROPKICK, our own command post, and maintenance control back on base. Right now the maintenance crew is getting ready to roll back the silo blast door so they can see what's going on. If I were a betting man, I'd say that we're leaving you guys with a Broken Arrow."

"A what?" I blurt out without thinking.

Hamel gives one of those "shut your face, Lieutenant" looks and turns back to King. "Do you think it's that bad? Do you think the thing may have burned or be damaged enough to release radiation?"

"I don't know for sure," King admits. "But you guys are going to find out."

We finish the crew change checklist, and Hamel reports the changeover to our local command post. While I open and then close the blast door to let the other crew out, Hamel punches up the communication circuit to Lima Two. "LIMA TWO, LIMA CONTROL, comm check. How do you read?"

"You're loud and clear, CONTROL. How me?"

"You're also five-by-five."

"CONTROL, TWO, would you pass on to DROPKICK that we have the tool in place and we're about to start opening the blast door."

The duty controller at the SAC command post responds, "DROPKICK is online and copies LIMA TWO—standing by for silo opening."

We wait and wait some more. It takes time to move a thirty-ton hunk of concrete and steel.

"DROPKICK, LIMA TWO, we have the door open enough to see the missile. It's gone!"

Hamel and I looked at each other.

"LIMA TWO, DROPKICK, say again. What's gone?"

"The reentry vehicle, the warhead, it's not there. All we can see is the top of the third stage. It shows some damage and signs of burning, but the warhead is gone. The only explanation we can up with is that there was some kind of explosion at the top of the third stage that separated the reentry vehicle and dropped it down into the silo. We think that maybe one of the retrorockets on the top of the third stage fired. Stand by five and we'll give you a recommendation on where to go from here."

"DROPKICK is standing by."

"DROPKICK, LIMA TWO. We're proposing that we rig up the bosun's chair and lower one of our munitions maintenance guys down into the silo to see what kind of problem we're up against. We've got a volunteer. He'll carry a safing tool and safe the ignition circuitry in each stage as he goes down."

"Stand by, LIMA TWO. I'll get you an approval."

Ten minutes later, "LIMA TWO, you're cleared to proceed. Our accident advisory board wants you to make sure that your volunteer has a Geiger counter and wears a radiation dosimeter. Have him make readings as he goes down and be ready to extract him if the dose rate exceeds the standards."

"Roger all of that, DROPKICK. We're proceeding."

We listen, hardly breathing, as the maintenance team lowers the warhead specialist into the silo. He reports as he safes each missile stage. And then, "OK, I'm about twenty feet above the silo floor. With my light I can see the reentry vehicle on the bottom of the silo. It looks like it hit one of the missile support columns on the way down. There are pieces scattered all over the place. The high-explosive initiator may have broken up. Could be high explosive scattered around in that debris. I'm picking up some alpha radiation. Can you all get me out of here?'

They get him out of there. For the next couple of hours the local and headquarters accident teams work on options and come up with their plan. They all agree that it would be a very bad idea to try to retrieve the warhead with the missile still in place. The detonation or burning of the warhead high explosive might just set off the thousands of pounds of solid rocket propellant sitting just above the silo floor.

Our local maintenance control had anticipated the need and positioned a transporter erector vehicle at Lima Two. It is basically a tractor-trailer. You back it up to the edge of the silo and then raise the trailer box straight up so that it is directly over the mouth of the silo. A majorly powerful winch lifts the missile out of the ground. Once the missile is secure they lower the trailer back to the horizontal position and haul it away. That whole process takes hours. But finally they lower a munitions team into the silo to start recovering the warhead.

What happens then? Well, the damn thing goes off. There is a blinding flash and most of western South Dakota disappears. It vaporizes all of us! OK, OK, not funny—sorry about that—but it is hard for me to avoid the specter of annihilation. Ray Hamel is totally calm through the whole exercise, maintaining that the warhead has so many safety circuits that it won't ever go off—even when you want it to. I can't decide whether that's good news or bad news.

The munitions maintenance troops report that the impact with the missile base ring tore the arming and fusing system loose from the warhead. The arming and fusing system contains the warhead batteries so there is no power available to initiate an arming sequence. There is some high explosive scattered around, but no radiation leakage—at least none that anyone will admit to. They pick up the pieces. It is careful, dangerous work. And I guess everyone keeps their mouths shut because none of the media, local or national, ever pick up the story.

The graduate study program doesn't ease the stress or make the assignment any more rewarding. The work is not so much hard as it is boring. When I signed up for a business degree there were a lot of things that weren't clear to me. One of those was the requirement to take courses like business law. Cost accounting—yeah, that could be interesting and even challenging. But business law! After I complete all of the undergraduate prerequisites, I look forward to the graduate courses and see more business law and other stuff that looks equally tedious—a master's degree in ennui. Virgil Grissom and John Young complete the first manned *Gemini* flight onboard *Molly Brown* (*Gemini 3*) on March 23, 1965. Overwhelmed by the tedium of business anything, I quit the MBA program in April. Two months later, Astronaut Ed White makes the first American "space walk." In August, Gordon Cooper and Pete Conrad make the first use of fuel cells for power and test space rendezvous systems aboard *Gemini V*. I am looking at the bleak prospect of a couple of more years buried alive deep under South Dakota dirt.

Then one day the Fates, Clotho, and her sisters, wonder if they might twist my predicament into an amusing diversion. My wife and I meet one of my squadron mates at the base service station. He wants to know if I have seen "the list." No, what list? The one posted on the bulletin board at the personnel office. He saw it today when he was there for a records check. Uh-huh—so?

Your name is on the list. Uh-huh—so? It's a list of people they want to go to Houston to interview for jobs at NASA. Don't fuck with me. No, no—call them, check it out. I do.

Within the week I'm putting on my best civilian suit in a motel room on NASA Road One across the street from the Manned Spacecraft Center. The interview is a blur. The NASA types are kind. I suspect they are wondering, "What is this guy doing here?" I have the same question. I don't ask it. Six weeks later I get orders for Houston. The Fates rub their hands in anticipation—this is going to be funny as hell.

CHAPTER FOURTEEN

We start south from Rapid City in December across the empty sand hills of Nebraska. We are two kids and two adults in a green VW bug. The emptiness around us magnifies the feeling of being adrift without a home—even if the condition is only temporary. My squadron mates, unhappy perhaps that they would stay and I would go, ask me only half jokingly if I know the way to Texas. I tell them I don't, but I do have a plan. I'll tie a snow shovel to the front bumper of my car and drive south until someone asks, "What's that?"

We follow the figurative snow shovel to a single-story, three-bedroom house at 3802 Crawford Drive in a working-class neighborhood of Pasadena. I install my family in their new quarters and go to work. Mary Lou is left alone again, this time with two small children. She is submerged in an alien culture. The people speak our language, but they speak it so slowly that you can't remember the beginning of the sentence when they finally reach the end of it. The winter is mild. The summer when it comes will make you feel like you're in Sri Lanka. After June 1, the children will refuse to go outside. That may be just as well. The place is populated by every venomous critter known to mankind—water moccasins, coral snakes, and some other really nasty species. I keep a long-handled shovel on the carport to ward off the evil spirits. There are days when I need it.

Most of our neighbors on Crawford Drive are refugees from the Cajun country of Louisiana come to work in the oil refineries and steel mills. There are a couple of exceptions. Chet Brantley and his wife live right next door. He is a Philco-Ford employee who works at the space center as a communications technician. Our paths will cross in a way I never imagined. Across the street there is a family originally from Pecos in far-west Texas, Orville Maddux, his wife, Barbara, two pre-teen boys, a younger daughter, and their incongruous pet, Fifi the poodle.

Orville Maddux served a tour in Korea with the Texas National Guard. After the war he migrated to Houston. He drives a tractor-trailer for Alamo Trucking. One trip is enough to convince me how hard he works. He runs only at night. We leave Houston as the sun sets, drive south west two hundred miles to Alice, Texas, swap trailers, and head back to Houston. Maddux is a careful professional. He keeps a feather duster under his seat and a .45-caliber handgun under the mattress in the truck's sleeper cab. When he stops for a traffic light he is apt to pull out the duster and give his dashboard instruments a once over. The weapon, he explains, is for any of "them sons-a-bitches" that take advantage of tired drivers who pull over to catch a nap. He doesn't show me the pistol. I take his word that it is there. Maddux drives these night runs hoping to accumulate enough money to move back to Pecos and open a service station. He is a first-class mechanic who doesn't mind spending some time helping a dumb-ass college kid change out a generator or a fuel tank on his beat-up VW.

Maddux is a quiet, soft-spoken man who seldom raises his voice. His wife is none of the above. Barbara Maddux sounds a lot like Minnie Pearl, the country comedienne of Grand Ole Opry fame. She is loud, boisterous, and fun. "Kiss my ass!" is her favorite response to any input that doesn't completely satisfy her expectations. Underneath all of that bluster is a kind and giving person. She and my wife become good friends. I am happy that Barbara is there when my working hours inevitably begin to get way too long.

I start work in the middle of the *Gemini 7–Gemini 6* space rendezvous mission. I expect that they will put me someplace where

I can do minimum harm. I call that one right. My new job is in the Flight Operations Scheduling Office in the Flight Support Division. The Scheduling Office prepares, distributes, and monitors the calendar for all Manned Spacecraft Center internal and external testing—some two hundred to three hundred tests a week. Monitoring and updating the schedule is a three-shift operation with a scheduler always on duty.

My particular assignment is to handle all of the testing that involves Houston and the worldwide tracking network. My boss is Ray Mackey, a NASA transplant from the White Sands missile range. He favors turquoise-ornamented bolo ties and tries to teach me some words of Navajo. Mackey's boss, head man of the scheduling operation, is Russ Nickerson, a short man with an expensive haircut and a lot of gold jewelry. My workmates include representatives of the three major control center contractors: IBM, Philco-Ford, and UNIVAC.

NASA is about halfway through the Gemini flight program and is flying unmanned *Apollo* tests. Six manned flights during Project Mercury established the feasibility of manned orbital flight. Kennedy's challenge upped the ante. After a lot of soul-searching and some infighting, NASA decides that lunar orbit rendezvous gives them the best odds for getting a crew safely to the Moon and back. To make that technique work they have to extend their knowledge beyond the basic information provided by Mercury. They need to know how to locate, approach, rendezvous, and dock with another vehicle. They need to know how to work outside a spacecraft. They also need to understand more about the physiological effects of extended spaceflight.

In the fall of 1961, NASA invented the *Gemini*, a two-man spacecraft launched on the Air Force's Titan II rocket, to collect the information they needed. Another air force rocket, the Agena upper stage, is fitted with a docking collar to serve as a docking target. The first operational mission takes place in March 1965.

In parallel with these proof-of-concept flights, NASA sets about developing the spacecraft they need to execute the mission.

Work on the *Apollo* spacecraft started in November 1961. Design and development of the Lunar module started a year later.

NASA and their contractors have to design, develop, and test new hardware and software for both spacecraft. The pace of testing is near frantic. The control center has to do more on any given day than the designers had ever planned on. When I stop to think about my assignment in the big middle of all of that, I have the notion that I am staring up from the bottom of a deep dark hole of ignorance. I respond by going where I have always gone—in search of a book, the book, whatever book—the one that will supply knowledge and comfort. After a short but panicky search I find two that I hope will keep me from embarrassing myself. The *Mission Control Center Houston Familiarization Manual* prepared for NASA by Philco-Ford is just a month old. The book provides written descriptions of the systems that make the control center work—Communications, Command and Telemetry, Display/Control, and Real-Time Computer Complex. But there's more, much more—page after page of functional block diagrams of the systems and subsystems. The format is familiar. I have a place to start.

I still need to deal with my total ignorance of the tracking stations that connect the control center to the spacecraft. This time I am saved by the *Proceedings of the Apollo Unified S-Band Technical Conference* held at Goddard Space Flight Center in July 1965. This is brand-new technology. The thirty or so papers in the report "constitute a first handbook pertaining to the *Apollo* Manned Space Flight Network." The words are there and so are the blessed block diagrams. The "goes in to" and "goes out of" lines have strange labels—pseudo-random noise code and pulse code modulated telemetry. The function blocks have mysterious descriptors—Phase Detector, Bandpass Filter, Voltage Controlled Oscillator. That's all OK. The Manned Spacecraft Center has a technical library where I can learn the vocabulary. Some basic "pidgin" technical talk lets me begin to communicate with the people who operate and maintain the control center equipment. Some of them think my questions are stupid. Some think they're annoying. Some think they're both of the above. Most are mystified by my frank admission of ignorance—ignorance is not a manly virtue in the world of steely-eyed missile workers. But they are flattered by my appreciation of their expertise and they help me. A Bendix contract employee named Lee Haislip working in the scheduling office at Goddard helps me work my way through the tracking station flow diagrams.

I work shifts just like all of the other scheduling types. I learn some stuff. During a swing shift on March 16, 1966, I get a dramatic look at how the Mission Operations Control Room works. *Gemini 8* is launched from the Cape at 10:41 a.m. (CST) with Neil Armstrong and Dave Scott onboard. The objective of the mission is to rendezvous and dock with an Agena rocket already in orbit and perform a series of maneuvers in the docked mode. My job isn't related to the ongoing mission. The network controller commands all of the mission resources. With everyone's attention focused on the *Gemini* operation, it is deadly dull in my little back room. So at about five o'clock I set out in search of adventure.

I have a good idea of where I can find some. Just around the corner and down the hall from my duty station are the doors of the VIP viewing room. Normally, with a mission in progress, the doors are guarded and a special pass is required to get past the guard. Tonight the doors are unattended—it is a routine night in what appears to be a routine mission. I decide to go in and watch the show for a bit—it beats sitting alone in the back room looking at a schedule on the wall.

I go up the stairs into the darkened room and find a seat about halfway down toward the large glass windows that separate audience from actors. About two rows down from me sit three or four astronauts. There are maybe a dozen other people scattered around the room. As I sit down, one of the astronauts, Jim McDivitt I think, looks up from the sandwich he has been working on to remark with mock solemnity, "They really got themselves into it this time."

His mates give laughing agreement. I don't know what he is talking about. But it doesn't take long to figure out that some part of this mission is going wrong. The astronauts and the other spectators in the room are intently watching a knot of people gathered around the flight director and CAPCOM consoles. At this point in a mission, that grouping can't mean good news. As I watch the urgent gestures and worried expressions of the duty flight controllers, I become aware of their voices being broadcast by the viewing room speaker system. There is something wrong there too—crisp and clean has been replaced by a hint of panic. Conversations on the voice loops are fragmented and urgent. *Gemini 8* must be in deep trouble.

Both John Hodge, the duty flight director, and Gene Kranz, his relief, are at the flight director's console. Qualified people are in short supply. The two have decided to work two twelve-hour shifts to cover this mission. Hodge is a British engineer who came to the Space Task Group at Langley via Canada. He looks like somebody you might share a pint with at your local pub. He has a distinguished, kind face and an accent that seems appropriate to his appearance and at the same time out of place on the flight director's voice net. Eugene F. "Gene" Kranz is an ex–air force captain who joined the Space Task Group after a year of aircraft flight test engineering with McDonnell Aircraft.

The contrast between the two men is striking. Kranz looks like the archetypal leader of men—blond crew cut, square jaw, a ready but controlled laugh, and a hearty hi-ho, Silver. In any ordinary setting he seems slightly out of place. Like an actor trained to scale up his voice and gestures to the magnitude required by a broad stage, Kranz is a little larger than life until you put him down at center stage behind the flight director's console. In that setting, he is a cross between Superman and your high school football coach. He practices an active style of leadership that demands he constantly chatter to his teammates—to get them organized, to motivate them, to make them feel secure as an integral part of the team—yay, team! I wonder if his chatter makes the flight controllers feel manipulated. I think I would feel embarrassed and maybe even annoyed. Maybe he's just not my style. Or maybe it's the cold eyes that don't smile with the rest of his face. They seem to signal a kind of functional fixedness—you match his prototype of the good follower or not—if not, there is no recovery. You must be a Boy Scout. He is determined to provide adult leadership. Maybe I'm supersensitive. Quiet but firm leadership looks like the better alternative—gung ho doesn't sit well with me. But a lot of these guys are fresh out of college and short on experience. Maybe they need adult leadership. I wonder what John Llewellyn thinks. Whatever his leadership style, Kranz on stage can put on an awesome display of calm and collected. I would see that tonight.

Listening to the sporadic air-to-ground traffic, the nervous questions on the internal voice net, and the conversations with the flight controllers stationed at the remote tracking sites, I begin to get a picture of the events that created the alarm I see on the faces in the control room and the viewing room. The *Gemini 8* crew accomplished the first-ever docking in space connecting with the Agena over the tracking ship *Rose Knot Victor* at 06:33 ground elapsed time. About seven minutes later, at *Rose Knot Victor* loss of signal, the combined spacecraft disappeared over the radio horizon in apparent good order. At 07:17 Jim Fucci aboard the tracking ship *Coastal Sentry Quebec* established contact.

"GEMINI EIGHT, CSQ CAPCOM. Comm check. How do you read?"

"We have serious problems here...we're tumbling end over end up here. We're disengaged from the Agena."

"OK. We got your SPACECRAFT FREE indication here... What seems to be the problem?"

"We're rolling up and we can't turn anything off. Continuously increasing in a left roll."

"Roger. GEMINI EIGHT. CSQ."

"We have a violent left roll here at the present time and we can't turn the RCSs off, and we can't fire it, and we certainly have a roll...stuck hand control."

Soon after the docking, the combined vehicles started a series of wild gyrations. Thinking the Agena was the villain, the crew undocked. The spacecraft, instead of stabilizing, went into an uncontrolled rolling motion. Post-flight analysis would show that the failure was caused by an electrical short in the attitude control system. A thruster continued to fire, putting the vehicle into a roll at rates up to one revolution per second. Increasingly disoriented by the continuous motion, Neil Armstrong managed to regain control using the thrusters of the reentry control system. By the time the vehicle stabilized, the control system needed for a safe return to Earth had been compromised. Mission rules required that the flight end as soon as possible.

Now, as I watch, Hodge gives up his seat and directs his controllers to hand over their positions to Kranz's team. I wonder about changing crews at this point, but the logic becomes apparent. The flight directors have decided that they need to return the crew to Earth as soon as they can. The reentry system has already been compromised. Kranz and his White Team have trained for reentry. Hodge tells his team to turn over their stations to the fresh team and stay close to provide whatever information they can on the emergency.

Coming up on the flight director's loop, Kranz directs his flight controllers to shut up and listen up. Heads rotate in the direction of the flight director's console. There are looks of surprise and even relief. Absolute silence reigns in 1.2 milliseconds. Kranz gets on with the business of relieving *Gemini 8*. He instructs his controllers to get off the voice loops for a few minutes, get with their support troops, and make up a prioritized list of the things they need to know about the condition of the spacecraft. By the time the spacecraft comes up for its next pass—this time over Hawaii—Kranz intends to have a consolidated, prioritized list of things to ask about and things to look for in the telemetry downlink. Methodically, he puts together the story of what might have happened and what can be done about it. He makes sure that every loose end is collected and firmly held by someone in the room. Through it all he continues to exhort his troops in a tone calculated to encourage the fainthearted.

At 07:38 ground elapsed time over Hawaii, the capsule communicator advises the crew, "Roger. Copy, GEMINI, and be advised they're planning to come into a -3 area. They're looking into 6 or 7-3 at this time. They would like you to enter Module 4 and the ATM computer. Over."

"OK. We'll go ahead and do that."

"And also get into retro attitude as soon as possible. Over."

The -3 recovery area is in the western Pacific off the coast of China. After collecting status data and assessing what more needs to be done before reentry, the flight control team decides that the reentry will be made on orbit seven.

At 09:13, Hawaii tells the crew that the destroyer USS *Mason* and a rescue aircraft, Naha Search One, are on route to the splashdown point. Less than an hour and a half later, the *Gemini 8* spacecraft hangs below its main parachute on its way to a safe landing. Kranz and his White Team have done their jobs.

Two months later, NASA delays the launch of *Gemini 9* when its Agena target vehicle falls into the Atlantic Ocean seven and a half minutes after launch. To keep something flying, the Gemini Program cobbles together the Augmented Docking Adapter, an unpowered *Gemini* docking collar. They launch it in June on an Atlas booster. The shroud that protects the adapter during launch fails to separate, eliminating the possibility of docking. The *Gemini* crew practices rendezvous techniques and comes home. In mid-July *Gemini 10* docks with an Agena target and then uses the Agena's propulsion system to rendezvous with the *Gemini 8* target vehicle. *Gemini 11* flies two months later, docks with an Agena target, and then sets a *Gemini* altitude record of nearly 740 miles. Between February and August, there are also three test flights of the new Saturn IB booster. The pace is frenetic. Sometimes on the midnight shift I think I can hear the control center creak and groan under the electromechanical load.

Not everything that I learn during that first year has to do with flight control operations. I learn, for example, how it is that the Fates caused me to be where I am. The scheduling office where I work is part of the Flight Support Division, a large organization responsible for operating the Mission Control Center and its interfaces with launch facilities and tracking stations. Our division chief, the agent of the gods, is one Henry "Pete" Clements, an air force lieutenant colonel. He had connected with Chris Kraft during the *Mercury* days at the Cape. Kraft was impressed. He asked the air force to lend Clements to NASA for the duration. The air force agreed. He became Kraft's assistant for *Gemini* and followed him to Houston where he became one of Kraft's division chiefs. Along the way, Clements had suggested in a letter to Air Force Chief of Staff General Curtis LeMay that the air force send officers to NASA to train for an eventual air force-manned space program. LeMay agreed. Clements headed up the team that selected the air force candidates.

One night at a party, I ask him how it is that I ended up on his list. It was an experiment, he responds. He thought it might be interesting to see how someone with my background—a "liberal arts puke," I think he called me—would do in the NASA environment. I ask him if it was kind of like "hire the handicapped—they're fun to watch."

"I wouldn't quite characterize it that way," he responds with a wan grin, "but yeah, something like that." Clements is more than a little bit eccentric—he frequently refers to himself in the third person as "Prince Henry." His story rings true.

One year after my arrival, Ray Mackey decides to go back to New Mexico. I become head of the Scheduling Group in his place. I have eight contractor types working for me and one NASA employee, a Jewish kid from New York City who races a Lotus sports car on his days off. I like his style. *Gemini 12* launches on November 11 to complete the *Gemini* flight test program.

We have another party on Friday January 27, 1967. This one is an air force Dining Out—all of the officers are in their formal mess dress uniforms. Prince Henry is called away to answer a phone call. He disappears. When I reach home, my neighbor Chet Brantley, one of the air-to-ground communications techs, calls and asks, "Have you turned on your TV?"

"No—why?"

"They're dead. There was a fire on the pad—all of the crew members are dead."

Apollo-Saturn 204, scheduled to be the first manned *Apollo* spaceflight, is sitting on the launch pad at Kennedy Space Center. Astronauts Gus Grissom, Edward White, and Roger B. Chaffee had been in the spacecraft practicing launch procedures. In the early evening hours, a fire broke out in the crew compartment. The pure oxygen atmosphere in the cabin intensified the fire. It consumed the interior of the spacecraft and asphyxiated the crew members. These men are the first casualties of the United States space program.

My wife and I watch the gruesome television reports late into the night. The mood of the people I talk to the next morning at work is a jumble of disbelief and deep sadness, interrupted at intervals by the hope that the accident is not the result of some choice they made, no matter how small, that added to the accumulation of details that produce most accidents. We all of us suffer from a certain amount of tunnel vision. I don't know much about the spacecraft and the design decisions that make it what it is. But I have, out of necessity, been watching the progress of the testing needed to validate the tracking station software. The program is ambitious. It is not going well. The likelihood of meeting the launch schedule is diminishing. I think that the rush to put the first manned *Apollo* into orbit may turn out to be the real culprit responsible for this sad, sad loss. A friend of mine, another air force officer who works in the communications section, is custodian of the Houston copies of the crew voice tapes relating to the accident. He plays them over and over again for the accident investigators. He wakes up in the middle of the night, his sleep shattered by anguished screams. We both hope that if this accident doesn't destroy the program things will go on at a more deliberate pace.

Floyd L. Thompson, director of NASA's Langley Research Center, takes charge of the accident inquiry board. Eventually the board recommends a series of changes in design, engineering, manufacturing, and quality control. The overarching message is that NASA's rush to the Moon had relegated crew safety to a minor consideration with predictable results. Safety is a command responsibility. Constant emphasis and example are needed to make it work. NASA management had neglected that responsibility.

While the investigation is going on, NASA and its contractors use the time to catch up on their work on the Lunar Module, the Saturn rocket, and the Manned Space Flight Network. My personal situation changes too during that summer and early fall. Prince Henry is transferred back to Patrick Air Force Base in Florida. He takes over as chief of the Network Division, in the office of the Department of Defense (DOD) manager for manned space flight. The DOD manager's office coordinates air force support for NASA's manned flight program. That support includes the use of facilities at Cape Kennedy, the use of air force tracking stations, and selected air force people, people with tracking station experience who are assigned to work for NASA in Houston. Four of those people are assigned to the Operations Section, Operations Support Branch here in the division where I work. "Operations" is the key word in these titles. They along with their NASA counterparts are network controllers—the guys who sit at the console two positions to the right of the flight director in the Mission Operations Control Room and operate the *Apollo* ground tracking and communications system.

Shortly after the Prince's departure, I find out that I am being transferred to the Operations Section. I will get to sit in the front room. I don't know why this is happening. I don't ask. I have to believe that the Prince has struck again. Sam Sanborn, the NASA branch chief, seems glad to have me—manpower is in short supply. I am going to work in *Apollo* Mission Control. I'm just arrogant enough to think that the stuff I learned in the scheduling office will get me by. I started out on a search for adventure. So far the emphasis has been on search. Now adventure seems to have found me. This fuzzy-headed young captain is going straight from summer stock to Broadway.

CHAPTER FIFTEEN

The transition to the new organization is mostly cordial. The majority of the people working as network controllers are air force. They are used to people coming and going. Their reception is matter of fact—just one more "new guy" to get up to speed. There are three NASA types. Two of them, Dave Young and Joe Vice, are welcoming and generous with their knowledge and their friendship. The other one, Ernie Randall, is a slender man with sandy hair and a crooked, boyish smile. If there is such a thing as a senior network controller, Ernie meets the requirements. He is a small-town boy from Ada, Oklahoma—an electrical engineer. He joined NASA in 1963, the same year that I transferred in. But he comes with extensive experience in mission control center operations, accumulated working on a major air defense program for the air force. In Houston, he works the network position on the first *Gemini* missions. He worries some about his place in history and his career. His reaction to me is more guarded. The Philco-Ford contractors who work as assistant network controllers are patient and helpful.

There is no formal training program. The equipment is too new, and qualified people who might put together a program are in short supply. The training we do get is a grab-ass mix of on-the-job learning and orientation visits to network tracking stations. I go to the tracking stations at Corpus Christi, Texas, and Merritt Island, Florida, for weeklong tours.

The Merritt Island station is adjacent to the Kennedy Space Center and provides launch and orbital support. I make that trip with two fellow "students," Earl Carr and Bob Chapman. Earl is a Philco-Ford troop. I don't know exactly what it is that he does. He's tall and slender—a native Texan and damn proud of it. He looks like he should be playing bass behind Bob Wills. Bob is an air force captain like me—training to work as a command controller.

Our trip coincides with the launch of the *Apollo-Saturn 501* mission on November 9, 1967. This first flight of the Saturn V, the largest rocket ever launched, is either (a) an inspired act of faith that will make it possible to meet the Kennedy schedule for landing a man on the Moon, or (b) a desperate gamble made in hopes of salvaging that same schedule, or (c) all of the above. The normal procedure is to test new rocket stages one at a time before combining them for an "all-up" test. Pressed by Dr. George Mueller, the associate administrator for Manned Space Flight, NASA management decides to make this first flight an all-up test. The first and second stages of the vehicle sitting out there on the pad at Launch Complex 39-A have never flown before. This will be the first-ever launch from Pad 39-A. The unmanned *Apollo* spacecraft at the top of the stack will test the vehicle's heat shield at lunar reentry velocity for the first time.

In spite of big-league hangovers, we manage to collect ourselves at five in the morning and head out toward the Cape. Bob and I take some minor comfort in placing the blame for our sorry state on Earl Carr's shoulders. The previous evening he had declared that our initiation into the rocket launch culture would be woefully incomplete without a tour of the bars and strip joints on Highway A1A in Cocoa Beach. Motivated by anthropological curiosity about the manners and mores of the native tribes, we tagged along. Now we are paying the initiation fee as we station ourselves just in front of the Air Force Range Operations Control Center. From there we can see the launch pad and listen to the range countdown on loudspeakers. Even from where we are standing, a couple of miles southeast of Launch Complex 39, Von Braun's machine looks massive in the chill, early morning light. Its three stages tower 363 feet above its mobile launch platform. Fully fueled it weighs more than six million pounds. Yeah, it's big and it's heavy, but when it moves it will move fast, really fast. After liftoff the first stage will burn for just two and one-half minutes, developing seven and one-half million pounds of thrust as it consumes over five million pounds of fuel and oxidizer and pushes its *Apollo* payload upward more than thirty-eight miles. That's more than two hundred thousand feet in less than three minutes. Stage two will operate for just about six minutes. It pushes the vehicle up to 115 miles, more or less. Operating for less than three minutes, the third stage will increase the spacecraft's speed to the required orbital velocity of 17,500 miles per hour.

When the engines ignite, at one second after 7:00 a.m. (EST), I have the incongruous impression that the rocket's towering column of flame is pushing the Earth down instead of pushing the vehicle up. The nozzles of the five first-stage engines rise clear of the launch umbilical tower in complete and utter silence. About the time I begin to think how strange it is to see all of that fire and not hear a thing, the first of a rapid-fire sequence of explosions punches me in the chest. I stagger half a step backward. The control center shudders and shakes as if it is about to come apart. The ground rolls and jerks under our feet. We steady ourselves and watch the giant machine climb up its column of flame, propelled by this continuing series of explosions. We watch until there is nothing left to see but a trail of white smoke in the sky. It's hard to believe that I see what I am seeing. It's even harder to believe that I am here to see it.

We collect ourselves and head back to Texas. The Saturn boosts its S-IVB third stage and the *Apollo* test vehicle into a 115-mile circular orbit. After two orbits, the third stage reignites, boosting the spacecraft into an elliptical orbit with a high point of more than 10,500 miles. The Command and Service Module separates from the S-IVB and fires its Service Propulsion System engine to send it out to 11,000 miles. Another Service Propulsion System burn increases reentry speed to 25,000 miles per hour, simulating a return from the Moon. The test vehicle survives reentry. It lands ten miles from the target landing site.

Training back at the Mission Control Center consists mostly of spending time on the command, telemetry, tracking, and communications consoles to get a first-hand feel for the jobs of the team members you are supposed to supervise. The troops are interested in having you understand what they are doing so the experience is productive, even if it has its share of not totally accidental "gotchas."

Apollo 5, the first test of an unmanned Lunar Module in Earth orbit, flies in January 1968. A little over two months later, on April 4, *Apollo 6*, the second Saturn V flight-test vehicle, launches from Kennedy. Severe longitudinal oscillations, the so-called pogo effect, shake the vehicle for thirty seconds, two engines of the second stage cut off early, and the S-IVB upper-stage engine fails to reignite for a simulated translunar injection burn. The public doesn't pay much attention to the cascade of failures—on that same day Martin Luther King Jr. is shot and killed in Memphis, Tennessee.

Redesign of the *Apollo* spacecraft and the Saturn V goes on through the summer. In September, the air force personnel system serves notice that I have been selected to attend Squadron Officers School in residence at Maxwell Air Force Base in Montgomery, Alabama. The school is the first in a series of professional development courses that the air force requires. It is a good system, a system that provides a common base of expertise as you advance in rank. Most officers take the courses by correspondence. In-residence assignments are rare and coveted. I am reluctant to go, coveted or not. I feel like I still have too much to learn about what it is that I'm supposed to be doing. I want a seat in the control room for one of those upcoming missions. Prince Henry thinks otherwise. I wonder if the Fates are screwing with me.

I spend fourteen weeks in Alabama. The academic and physical workload hovers right around the overwhelming point for the full duration. Because of the war, the school is short of instructors. I have judo training so I am drafted to teach self-defense classes. The competition is fierce. Some of my classmates just back from tours in Vietnam have strange ideas about what constitutes fun. I stop one of them from doing me real harm by laying a forearm across his face with enough force to blacken both of his eyes. I win the award for the best academic performance in my unit.

Along with the rest of the planet, I watch *Apollo 7*, the first manned *Apollo* flight, and *Apollo 8*, the dramatic Christmas flight around the Moon, on TV. The two missions demonstrate that we can put a crew into orbit around the Moon and return them safely to Earth. Success depends on a complex navigation and control system that reaches from the Real-Time Computer Complex in Houston, through the tracking network, to the guidance and control systems on board the spacecraft.

Apollo 9, my first chance to sit in "the big room," is meant to demonstrate the remaining capabilities needed for the landing mission. It is the first test of the Saturn V in full-up lunar configuration. It carries the largest payload ever put into orbit—the Command Module *Gumdrop*, the Lunar Module *Spider*, and their three-man crew. They will check out the Lunar Module systems on orbit and demonstrate the maneuver and rendezvous techniques essential to the lunar landing.

Figure 3: The *Apollo 9* Orange Team. Pete Frank, our flight director, is seated on his console at the center of the picture. On the far left in the striped shirt is CAPCOM Stu Roosa. I am at the center rear, in my air force uniform. My console partner, Bob Gonzales, is standing in front of me slightly to my left. (NASA photo)

Except for crew rest periods, the mission time line is crammed with critical test activity. Pete Frank, rookie flight director of the Orange Team, works the rest periods. I am his rookie network controller. The new guys always get the third shift—*Apollo 9* is no exception. The mission lifts off from Launch Complex 39-A at 10:00 a.m. (CST) on March 3. The Command Module splashes down in the Atlantic on March 13 with every major mission objective met. During ten days in orbit, the crew docks with the Lunar Module and extracts it from its shroud on the S-IVB. They open the hatches on both spacecraft to demonstrate extravehicular crew transfer. They undock and then demonstrate rendezvous and reconnection after a separation of six hours and 113 miles. They fire the Service Module engine seven times to adjust the spacecraft orbit. After the eighth firing, a retrograde reentry burn, they splashdown within 2.7 miles of their target point. None of this happens on my watch.

The *Apollo 10* stack—Saturn V, Command and Service Module, and Lunar Module—moves from the Vehicle Assembly Building to Launch Complex 39, Pad B while *Apollo 9* is still in orbit. A few weeks later, NASA confirms that *Apollo 10* will be a lunar mission—a full-up dress rehearsal for the *Apollo 11* landing. It will be the fourth manned *Apollo* mission in seven months.

I scarcely notice *Apollo 10*. Because the intervals between launches are so short, the training and testing cycle for the next mission overlaps the operations cycle for the current mission. Flight and ground control teams work alternate missions. I worked *Apollo 9* and now I am part of the team preparing for *Apollo 11*. Is that happenstance or calculated intervention by the Fates? I have no idea.

But wait, there's more. I am astonished to learn that I am assigned as network controller for both the launch from the Earth and the launch from the Moon. Just goddamn amazing! And the gods still aren't finished. In April, Sam Sanborn, my branch chief, tells me that I am to be the lead network controller for the *Apollo 11* mission, responsible for the readiness of the entire ground operations team. Mostly that means keeping things coordinated and making sure all of the contingencies are covered.

How can that be happening? Prince Henry is too long gone to have pulled that string. This must be a default thing. The veteran controllers want to work other mission phases they consider more demanding than the two launches—the lunar descent and landing, and the first Moon walk. I am left with the launch from Earth and the primary network controller title that goes with that assignment. I'll settle for that—it's pretty heady, even terrifying, stuff for a guy who knows more about Pliny the Elder than he does about Hohmann transfer orbits. I keep looking over my shoulder to see if the gods have dispatched Nemesis to punish me for my disproportionate good fortune by bringing this teetering cantilevered construction crashing down onto the hard rock of reality.

While I wonder why all of this is happening for me, the preparations for the landing mission go on. The *Apollo 11* hardware, the boosters and the spacecraft, are delivered to the Kennedy Space Center before the end of February. Assembly of the stages begins immediately after the delivery of the first Saturn stage and continues during early March while *Apollo 9* is in orbit. On April 14, the Command and Service Module is put on top of the stack. By the time *Apollo 10* launches on May 18, the *11* team is beginning a series of integrated training exercises that simulate each of the critical phases of the mission—launch, translunar injection, lunar orbit insertion, descent orbit initiate and landing, ascent and rendezvous, and reentry.

On top of all of that, I am trying to solve the language problem that has plagued me since my first day on-site. I try like hell to understand how things work. But just as I think that I am on the verge of real understanding, someone drops an indecipherable differential equation that shuts off my advance. In the end, I find that the path to real understanding is open only to the initiated, to the people who can speak in algebra, trigonometry, calculus, and differential equations. I am back at school, working nights at the Deer Park Community College to learn the language. My workmates find that amusing. I take all kinds of crap when I sit at my console during a late-night telemetry test working on a linear algebra book. My boss, Sam Sanborn, encourages me. A NASA network controller named Dave Young goes out of his way to help. I have a long way to go before I can claim even minimal fluency. But there is, even at this early stage, a promise of access to a powerful juju.

CHAPTER SIXTEEN

On May 20, the *Apollo 11* stack moves from the Vehicle Assembly Building to the launch pad. To support a July 16 launch date, ground crews need a go-ahead to load hypergolic fuel and oxidizer on board the spacecraft by June 12. So on the twelfth, Sam Phillips, the *Apollo* program director, and his staff gather in a slab-sided building near the Smithsonian Museum in Washington for a conference call to discuss the July 16 date. On the line with Phillips are George Low, Gene Kranz, and Dr. Charles Berry in Houston, Lee James in Huntsville, and Deke Slayton and Rocco Petrone at the Cape.

The discussions go on for an hour and a half. The results of the *Apollo 10* mission, which was completed just about six weeks earlier, are a primary topic. Phillips and his team also have to consider the status of the training program for the whole *Apollo 11* team. The flight crew is on the downhill side of a two-year training program that involves two thousand hours of formal training and individual preparation for each man. That load has forced ten-to-twelve-hour workdays, six days a week for the last month. The stress level prompts the *Apollo* decision makers to take a careful look at the crew's health. And of course, the health of the mechanical mission components sitting on the pad at the Cape has to be carefully considered. When the discussion is done—when the status reports and concerns of all the participants have been pushed, pulled, and twisted into a rational structure that everyone can live with, Phillips makes his decision—the *Apollo 11* spectacular will open on July 16.

With the decision made, mission rehearsals become more intense for both the crew and the Houston flight controllers. Everyone pokes and probes his own knowledge and procedures looking for potentially fatal flaws. While we struggle with our preparations and Houston's distorted image shimmers in heat waves generated by record temperatures, the crews at Cape Kennedy continue their launch preparations at Launch Complex 39. Fifteen days after the launch decision, on Friday, June 27, they start their last major exercise—the Countdown Demonstration Test, or CDDT. During the test, the launch-complex ground crews, the flight crew, and the Houston flight controllers will count down the *Apollo-Saturn* stack just as they will on launch day, stopping just short of the automatic ignition point.

On Monday morning, June 30, the newspapers report that everything is going as planned and the crew is going through launch simulations while the pad rehearsal countdown continues. The next day the crew runs more launch simulations and takes a physical exam. Launch complex crews run fuel cell checks. In Houston it is ninety-eight degrees and people are beginning to talk about water rationing. The heat is oppressive. The waiting doesn't help. On Wednesday, Mayor Louie Welch tells the citizens of Houston that they can't water their lawns. Twelve hundred miles to the east, launch pad crews pump millions of pounds of liquid oxygen and liquid hydrogen into the creaking, groaning tanks of the Saturn V. At twelve fifty-one in the afternoon the fueling exercise is complete. During the last hours of the Countdown Demonstration Test, the crew does not go on board their spacecraft as they would on launch day. There's no point in sitting on top of millions of pounds of explosive fuel and oxidizer any more often than you really have to. Their turn will come on Thursday. After the propellants are off-loaded, the crew enters the Command Module and runs through their launch procedures.

With their procedural checks done, the crew starts back to Houston to spend the Fourth of July holiday with their families. On Friday, July 4, the newspaper says that 241 Americans had died in Vietnam in the last month despite a twelve-day lull in the fighting. I feel guilty that I am here and people I know are over there getting killed. I console myself with the thought that I have put a Southeast Asia volunteer statement in my personnel records. If the air force in its infinite wisdom wants me here instead of there, then so be it. In Saigon, the high temperature is ninety-three degrees. It is ninety-nine degrees in Houston. Everyone sort of rests.

On Saturday, the crew holds a one-hour news conference at the Manned Spacecraft Center. Neil Armstrong announces that the Command and Service Module and the Lunar Module will have call signs COLUMBIA and EAGLE. Doctor Berry, the flight surgeon, worried about possible contamination of his charges, continues his campaign to dissuade President Nixon from dining with the astronauts the night before launch.

On Monday July 7, the *Apollo 11* tracking network is placed on "mission status." The network director at Goddard Space Flight Center has turned over the worldwide tracking system, which normally watches over unmanned probes headed to the Moon or to a nearby planet, to the Manned Spacecraft Center to support preparations for *Apollo 11*. This is a major milestone for those of us in the ground support business. The Houston network controller now has operational control of resources reaching around the world in a belt that extends thirty degrees north and south of the equator. A couple of years ago, I had never heard of the tracking station at Honeysuckle Creek, Australia. Now it's mine for the duration.

Until the mission is over, the network controller's console in the Mission Operations Control Room will be manned around the clock. We are the first on stage. For three or four nights we will be the only ones in the control room. We are working regular shifts now. The regularity makes it clear that what has been about to happen for so long is really going to happen. A historian ought to appreciate the significance of the moment. *This* historian doesn't dare think about the historical significance of the moment. More significance equals more pressure. I am feeling enough of that, thank you very much. Let the pundits worry about history. History comes with a dustbin. I don't want to end up there. Keep your head down and go over your procedures for the ten thousandth time.

During the days just before we take up the shift schedule, I spend most of my time working with Rod Reining, one of the tracking controllers on my team. We work on procedures for managing the network tracking stations during the lunar ascent phase of the mission. For weeks, Sam Sanborn, along with George Ojalehto, the network controller who will work the lunar landing, and Rod's boss, Tom Sheehan, have been working on elaborate procedures for the descent phase. I haven't paid too much attention. They have a full, competent crew working that problem. But one afternoon at about two o'clock, as I sit at my desk working on the network launch countdown procedure, Rod plops down on the government-issue gray chair alongside my desk. He puts his right forearm on my desk like he means to stay until he says what he needs to say. The expression behind his GI spectacles is as serious as I have ever seen. There's a set of I-mean-business furrows in his broad flat brow.

Rod has watched his boss work on the lunar descent emergency procedures. The experience convinces him that we need to apply the same logic to the lunar ascent. I am skeptical. I argue that the two situations are different. Once the spacecraft is in lunar orbit, the Lunar Module will separate from the Command and Service Module. At about 101 hours after liftoff, when the vehicle is behind the Moon and out of view of ground stations, the Lunar Module will fire its engine, making a retrograde burn to lower its orbit and start the approach to the lunar surface. About an hour later, the lunar spacecraft will emerge from behind the Moon. The Houston flight controllers will then have about nine minutes to look at telemetry and tracking data and make a GO/NO-GO decision for powered descent initiate, the sequence of engine firings that will put the vehicle on the surface of the Moon. This will be the critical moment for crew and flight controllers. The mission rules make it clear that without voice and telemetry you are NO-GO for powered descent initiate. After a quarter of a million miles, billions in taxpayers' money, and three deaths, the crew will have to give up and boost back up to rendezvous with the Command and Service Module. For the want of two-way lock between the spacecraft and a ground station in California or Madrid, voice and telemetry will be lost—for want of voice and telemetry the landing will be aborted and a national dream will go unfulfilled. You have to do whatever you can to reach out and make the electronic linkup work. The consequences of failure make anything less flat-out unacceptable.

Launch from the lunar surface after a successful landing is in a different category. You have to try it at some point or face a cold lonely death on an alien surface. Once you decide to do it, there are no intermediate GO/NO-GO points where the flight controllers need to make an input. Glynn Lunney, the Black Team flight director, had caught the spirit of the thing exactly at the beginning of our first team meeting on the lunar ascent phase. He had dropped a copy of the flight plan on the conference room table and remarked that the ascent operation was "like the Israelis going to war." Once it started there wasn't much you could do about it. There would be no abort for lack of voice contact or loss of telemetry once the ascent engine was fired. There would be no turning back. Armstrong and Aldrin would have to continue the maneuver with or without support from Houston.

Reining makes a persuasive counterargument. Loss of data is not cause for an abort. But the presence of data might allow the flight controllers to see and correct an impending malfunction that isn't apparent to the crew. Think about how many measurements we see on the ground. The crew displays are limited. The crew might see a tenth of the available measurements.

We also have to deal with the anytime liftoff case. The *Apollo* missions are being flown during a solar maximum period. A solar flare is a real possibility. A flare would likely be followed by a solar particle event, a dangerous flux of deadly super energetic protons capable of penetrating the thin skin of the Lunar Module and the crew's spacesuits. The particles might reach the Moon in as little as four to six hours. The crew would have to get off the Moon as soon as possible and seek shelter in the Command and Service Module. There would be little time to make Lunar Module configuration checks. It would pay to have a plan to cover this "bug out" scenario.

I am convinced. We set about the task of putting together a contingency plan similar to the one being put together by the descent crew. Why hadn't we thought about this sooner than two weeks before launch? Good question. When I was a cadet we were allowed only three responses to serious questions such as that: "Yes, sir. No, sir. No excuse, sir." The last one applies.

On the same day that the NASA tracking network comes under the operational control of Houston, Monday, July 7, the press reports that the crew's pre-departure dinner with President Nixon has been canceled. The crew runs lunar ascent/rendezvous simulations at the Cape. On Tuesday, July 8, they run launch-abort simulations. On Wednesday, the simulators at the Cape are hooked up to Houston for the last integrated launch-abort simulations.

In parallel, Rod and I coordinate our contingency procedures with our Instrumentation Support Team and the Black Team flight controllers. When we finish, we hope that we have done what we can to get Armstrong and Aldrin safely off the Moon and into lunar orbit.

PART IV
BEGINNER'S CALL

CHAPTER SEVENTEEN

At 7:00 a.m. (CDT) on Thursday morning, July 10, the temperature in Houston is already in the eighties and on its way to another of the ninety-degree highs that are becoming routine. To the east in Cocoa Beach, a one-hundred-degree day is about to happen. The motels along highway A1A are already accumulating a jumble of luggage, screaming kids, and impatient parents. Nearly a million tourists are gathering on the coast. A thousand police and volunteers are on standby to deal with them.

Later that same day, as the hands of the clocks in Cocoa Beach show 8:00 p.m., another clock a few miles to the north begins to count down from ninety-three hours. For the next six days, it will measure the progress of the final preparations for the spectacle the tourists have come to see. The clock is on the wall of a gigantic firing room at the Kennedy Space Center where launch controllers will oversee preparations for the liftoff of *Apollo 11* from Launch Complex 39. The firing room is one of four situated on the third floor of the four-story reinforced concrete Launch Control Center. The control center sits on the southeastern side of the Vehicle Assembly Building, just three miles away from the Saturn V booster that looms over Launch Complex 39-A. At peak, contractor, NASA, and air force controllers will man nearly 450 consoles that allow them to monitor the status of their respective spacecraft, launch vehicle stages, and support equipment.

Technicians begin to supply electrical power to the Saturn V, energizing the nervous system of the giant robot that will enable the July 16 production. Step by carefully documented step, ninety-three hours of work will be done during the one hundred and thirty-three hours and thirty-two minutes between 8:00 p.m. on July 10 and 9:32 a.m. July 16 (EDT). The forty hours and thirty-two minutes not dedicated to pre-planned work are broken down into a series of "built-in holds." At the designated hold times, the countdown clock will be stopped for the duration of the hold to allow work crews to rest and clear problems that have arisen during the count. The clocks in the Mission Control Center begin to count in sync with the Firing Room clock even though Houston's first active participation in the launch pad operations is still some thirty hours away.

The stage manager of this vast preparation effort, the man who will make sure that the required actors and their props are on stage when the lights go up for act one, is the NASA space vehicle test supervisor, call sign CVTS. Like any stage manager he has a prompt book that he will use to "call" the show. His is an eighty-two-page time-sequenced document, the *Apollo/*Saturn V Countdown, Test and Checkout Procedure Number V-40300, dated July 3, 1969. It describes who will be where, when they will be there, and what they will do when they get there in order to make the rocket and its crew ready for their debut.

Safety drives the overall timing of the work sequences. Dangerous tasks that require the pad to be cleared of all nonessential personnel and radio silence to be in effect are done early so as not to interfere with the final phases of the countdown. During the so-called pre-count, the period between T minus ninety-three hours and T minus twenty-eight hours, technicians install Command and Service Module explosive ordnance, install the spacecraft cover that will protect the crew during launch, turn on spacecraft power, and load the spacecraft's liquid oxygen and liquid hydrogen tanks. Booster service crews install F-1 engine ordnance and hypergolic cartridges on the first stage, hook up vehicle destruct system initiator detonators, and make a closed loop check of the launch vehicle Digital Range Safety Command System components.

The supervisor of range operations reports that the Air Force Eastern Test Range is ready to support the "official" countdown beginning at T minus twenty-eight hours. The Merritt Island Launch Annex tracking station begins its Site Readiness Test in preparation for its first interface with the spacecraft at T minus twenty-four hours. The station is adjacent to the Saturn launch complex at the Kennedy Space Center but is owned and operated by the Goddard Space Flight Center. During the countdown it will serve as surrogate for the entire tracking network in confirming the compatibility of the *Apollo* stack and the ground systems.

Once the official countdown begins, crews spend the next twenty hours preparing the launch vehicle for the start of fuel and oxidizer loading at T minus eight hours. They complete the four-hour process of installing launch vehicle flight batteries. Other crews begin Lunar Module stowage and cabin closeout. HOUSTON FLIGHT notifies CVTS that the Mission Control Center is ready to support the countdown. The Merritt Island station completes its system testing. Technicians in Houston, at the Merritt Island station, and on the launch pad conduct end-to-end command and air-to-ground validation tests.

At T minus eleven hours and thirty minutes, the Houston control center begins to come online. Building 48 fires up its generators and begins critical power support for the control center. Technicians in the control center run diagnostics on the IBM 360/75 mission computers and on the UNIVAC 494 communications-switching computers. Other crews run validation tests on individual pieces of equipment, voice recorders, high-speed printers, and status display modules, and then string them together, testing at each step to be sure the end-to-end system will be ready when the lights go up for act one.

The countdown clock stops when it reaches minus nine hours. It remains stopped for the next eleven hours while pad crews fix problems or rest up for the final push. In Houston, crews continue their methodical process of test, connect, and test again until the wideband recorder is connected to the communications processor, and the communications processor is connected to the mission operations computer, and the mission operations computer is connected to the group display system, and recorded wideband tracking data produces the correct plot on the group display at the front of the control room. Toe bone connected to the foot bone, foot bone connected to the ankle bone—now hear the word of the Lord.

While the duty network controller and his team put the building together, I crawl into bed without any real hope that sleep will come. It is just 8:00 p.m. Houston time. I have to be on station at 6:00 a.m. the next morning. If I could put my internal turmoil on hold I just might be able to come on stage bright eyed and bushy tailed. No chance of that. The phone rings even before I can shuffle and scrunch my pillows into the sleep configuration. I try to ignore it. My wife picks up and seconds later opens the bedroom door.

"It's for you. Somebody from communications, they said."

"Hello."

"Hey, Dick, this is Chuck Ritchie. Sorry to bother you."

Ritchie is one of the NASA communications controllers.

"What's the problem?"

"Ernie Randall called us a few minutes ago. He wants us to change the air-to-ground configuration at MILA."

Ernie is one of the NASA network controllers assigned to the mission.

"He wants to do what?"

"Change the air-to-ground setup—that's what he said."

"Change from the configuration we tested during the Countdown Demonstration Test we just ran?"

"That's what he said."

"The answer is not 'no,' it's 'hell no.' I don't even want to know what he thinks he's up to. We fly with what we tested."

"You bet. We all felt that way, but we needed someone who outranked him. See you in the morning."

"Yeah, early in the morning."

I hang up the phone and get my head on the pillow. As I try to settle in, the odor from the ashtray on my wife's night table reaches across the room and puts a headlock on my awareness.

Nice move, dumb shit—quitting smoking three weeks before launch day! No more of those carcinogens for you. You'll be cancer-free and lead a long, happy life—if you don't have a nervous breakdown between now and reentry.

I haul myself out of bed and pad down the hall with the ashtray in hand. Two minutes later I'm back in bed. Just as soon as my head touches the pillow and my eyes close, swarms of relentless, toxic, sleep-killing doubts race through my consciousness.

Have I done all I can? What did I miss? Can I do the right thing when the stress level goes up to mission maximum? There's no way to say, is there? You just might screw up and kill somebody! There's no way to say for sure is there?

Yeah, yeah, OK, but the guys who designed this thing built in safeguards and redundant systems to protect against a screwup by guys like me. Besides, I'm a bit player. I'm not like the real flight controllers who have to make the life or death calls. I just keep the pipes open. Yeah, and if one closes at the wrong time? So what? That's just a small thing, right? A small thing? You know damn well that accidents happen when the small things pile up and send the best designs crashing to the ground.

Yeah, well, whatever—those guys who are going to ride that thing had their eyes open when they signed up—I can only do my best—leave me alone!

I run this trap line of doubts, doubts that attack my confidence like piranhas on a drowning pig, trying to counter them with logical, comforting constructs. At the end of my run I am back where I started—the clock in my head keeps counting, the flight director glares at me in disbelief, rockets explode in giant fireballs.

An hour and a half before the end of the eleven-hour hold, with launch just ten hours away, players from around the world begin to crowd two-by-two onto the margins of the stage. The Canary Islands tracking station and the tracking ship *Vanguard* report that they are ready to play their parts—their Site Readiness Tests are complete. The communications controllers at Goddard and in Houston run end-to-end circuit checks to connect the two stations to the network. Tests of the stations' telemetry, command, air-to-ground, and tracking systems follow in turn. The stations at Honeysuckle Creek in Australia and on the island of Guam are the next in this process of getting beginners to the stage. They are followed by Bermuda and Hawaii. Texas and Carnarvon, Australia, are next, followed by Ascension Island and Madrid. Goldstone in California completes the call.

Minutes before the hold ends, the space vehicle test supervisor, CVTS, comes up on communications channel 111 and asks for a go-ahead to resume the count. The supervisor of range operations, the Merritt Island operations supervisor, the Houston flight director, the Command and Service Module test conductor, the Lunar Module test conductor, the Launch Vehicle test conductor, the test support controller, and systems safety all answer in the affirmative.

The clock begins to count down from T minus nine hours. An hour later, the pad crews get down to serious business. They finish pressurization checks on the S-IVB third stage and load the vehicle's tanks with liquid oxygen. In sequence they load the tanks of the second and third stages—more than four million pounds for the three stages. Loading liquid hydrogen, the fuel that will combine with the oxygen to drive the second and third stages, is the next step in the booster countdown sequence. Crews load more than two hundred thousand pounds into the two stages. Earlier in the launch preparation cycle, they had loaded almost 1,500,000 pounds of RP-1, a kerosene-like fuel much less volatile than the super cold liquid oxygen and hydrogen, into the first stage. By the time the clock counts down to T minus three hours, the launch vehicle stands fueled and ready, looking like a living, breathing thing with great clouds of white vapor escaping from vents in the three stages as super cold gases boil off into the hot, humid Florida air.

As the launch vehicle loading proceeds, the flight crew members awaken, undergo a medical examination, eat breakfast, and don their spacesuits. When the launch vehicle loading is complete, the crew leaves the Manned Spacecraft Operations Building for Launch Complex 39. At T minus two hours and forty minutes, they board a high-speed elevator that will take them up 320 feet to their spacecraft. I give up on my mostly unsuccessful attempt at sleep. My wife mumbles something that sounds like "good luck." I grab a quick breakfast and point the Volkswagen down Red Bluff Road in the direction of the Manned Spacecraft Center.

PART V
CURTAIN TIME

CHAPTER EIGHTEEN

I reach the space center at 5:30 a.m. Extra security guards man the gates to deal with the increased traffic. The Mission Control Center parking lot is already crowded. This day is different from all of those other days when I walked past the security desk into the Mission Operations Wing. The hallways and the elevators are full of important people on critical missions. Dutch and his crew of cable thieves are nowhere to be seen. Their work is done—at least I hope it is.

I open the door to the control room and start down the aisle toward the network controller's console. My anticipation turns to hard-edged, nervous reality. At the right front of the room I see, projected on a ten-by-ten-foot television display, the image of the Saturn V, 363 feet of metallic balloon inflated with millions of pounds of super cold, volatile fuel and oxidizer. The cold liquids boil over, releasing white plumes of gas. The machine looks as though it is straining to be released from the hold-down clamps that keep it Earthbound. For a fraction of a second I am aware that I am not the only one waiting for the great machine to become airborne. There are tens, maybe hundreds of millions of people watching that same machine and the people like me who are supposed to make it work.

Dave Young and his partner, Captain Ron De Cosmo, the duty network controllers, brief my partner, George, and me on the status of the Mission Control Center and tracking network. There are no major problems—so far, so good. By T minus two hours, the handover is complete. They wish us luck and head off to the Network Support room where they can plug in and monitor the launch. Even after a midnight shift, no one thinks about going home to bed.

We have a third person at our console today. Major John Monkvic will keep the console event log so that George and I can focus on what is about to happen. He is the senior officer in our small group. Like me, he is wearing his air force uniform. That's the rule. Day-to-day you wear what the NASA guys wear—white shirt, skinny tie, and trousers in some subdued tone. When mission time comes, you put on your military suit to highlight the role that the air force plays in this production—nothing unusual about that. But in this case, you have to ask yourself why the major has chosen to wear a pair of darkly tinted aviator's sunglasses in an already dimly lit room. Good question. He wears them any time he comes into the control room. He doesn't say why. The silence fuels speculation.

Figure 4: The author, Major John Monkvic with his signature sunglasses, and George Egan, who is partially visible nearest the camera. (Screen shot from a NASA documentary film)

The most plausible of the speculations goes something like this: John is also the only one of us who holds an aeronautical rating. He is a qualified "airplane driver." The rest of us have non-flying ratings. In air force speak we are "ground pounders." The distinction is important. Only officers with aeronautical ratings, rated officers, can command flying units. That makes sense. But it means that those of us who are ground pounders are barred from commanding most of the major units in this air force and holding the rank that goes with those command positions. Given that he is an airplane driver, John may be dealing with an embarrassing problem. It just might be that his eyesight has deteriorated. It is not bad enough to take him off flight status. But he cannot read the displays at the front of the room. When you're keeping the log, that much visual acuity is essential. Sure, he could just put on a pair of eyeglasses. But self-images are hard to escape. John keeps his intact by showing up in the control room wearing a pair of macho, but nevertheless prescription, aviator sunglasses. He takes a lot of shit from the other controllers for that one. It doesn't change his mind.

I glance down at the log book in front of John and then up at the countdown clock that subtracts second after second from the time remaining before this drama begins in a cloud of fire and smoke. I ran away from academic history to try to make some real history. The realization that I am now doing that leads to a strange duality. Sitting here watching myself do what I am doing, I wonder with a mix of historical detachment and real-time fear how well I will do it. The historian looks over John Monkvic's shoulder to make sure that that he is keeping an accurate record of the event. Other historians will need that record someday.

Today there's little time or space for the historian. I need to get down to the business at hand. As I try to focus, lines from *Macbeth* come to mind. I think about the poor, unlikely actor who is about to "strut and fret his hour upon the stage." I hope with all my being that my part in this drama does not turn out to be "a tale told by an idiot, full of sound and fury, signifying nothing."[3]

I am aware of the bizarre incongruity of Shakespeare in mission control. But the lines linger in my head. As they persist, I notice, with more than a little astonishment, that my poor player is himself dividing like some primitive protozoan. Now the historian is joined by two newly morphed personalities—a steely-eyed missile worker, he of calm, collected demeanor and voice—and a panicky liberal arts puke hanging on by his fingernails while his butt cheeks clench the cushion of the chair. There are three of us now, crammed into that chair with its mistreated cushion.

I take a three-ring binder from my briefcase and flip through the launch and translunar injection checklists. The neatly printed pages are reassuring—they suggest that I know what I am doing. I hope to God that's true—we're about to find out.

There's not much time to look at the book. Five minutes after we change crews, we focus on a sequence of command system checks between the Command Module and Houston via the Merritt Island tracking station. A check of the Abort Advisory System is next. In turn, the flight director, flight dynamics officer, booster systems engineer, and guidance officer transmit a command through the Merritt Island station that illuminates a light on the left side of the spacecraft's main display panel. The light is marked ABORT—it means get off—save your ass—this mission is broken—no one is going to the Moon today! I'm happy we don't have one of those ABORT command modules on our console. Keeping the plumbing working is challenge enough for some of us.

We lean forward in our chairs as though being close to the communications panel might help us sort out the conversations on a dozen communication loops. This is quasi–Tower of Babel time. Everyone speaks the same language—sort of. But the conversations are uncoordinated, layered one on top of another, as

---

3   *Macbeth*, Act 5, scene 5, 25–28.

controllers go about their individual business. You have to listen hard to the circuits where you do your primary business— Net Two, the communications loop that connects the Houston network controller to the worldwide tracking network, and Three Network, the internal loop that is reserved for our in-house support team. You listen hard for the boss on Three Flight Director. In the background there are six or eight other loops. You try to sort them out so you can follow the progress of the countdown. The simulations don't come close to duplicating the "confusion of tongues" that comes with the real thing.

The command checks are successful. The flight director gives CVTS a GO for the release of the last high-altitude weather balloon. At ground level, the crowds of excited rocket watchers enjoy a near perfect day—eighty-four degrees with a six-knot southerly breeze and a scattering of light cumulus clouds. The SRO, the supervisor of range operations, reports that the Eastern Test Range launch danger area is clear. BEACH BOSS, the launch site recovery forces commander, reports that the launch area recovery force helicopters are on station, manned and ready. The *Apollo* spacecraft Launch Escape System is armed. The RSO, the range safety officer, makes his final launch-vehicle command-destruct checks. At T minus thirty minutes CVTS asks HOUSTON FLIGHT for a GO to begin the launch-vehicle terminal count sequences at T minus twenty minutes. Without a millisecond of hesitation, Charlesworth affirms that Houston and the worldwide network are ready.

I hope he's right. Last night's conversation about changing the air-to-ground configuration keeps jabbing at my comfort level. At T minus fifteen minutes, the spacecraft will go to full internal power. An end-to-end check of the crew communications circuits follows the power transfer. The checks validate two voice communications systems—very high frequency radio, and a Unified S-band voice link. The very high frequency transmitter-receiver equipment operates pretty much like your AM radio at home except that you can talk back when it talks to you. It is used for voice communications with the ground stations during launch, and near-Earth phases of the mission. The Unified S-band voice link is combined with spacecraft commands and tracking data and uplinked on a single radio beam. It is used during deep-space phases of the mission when the spacecraft is not within very high frequency range of a ground station. At shift change the team we relieved had assured us that no changes had been made to the voice communication configuration we tested during our last launch pad exercise.

Yeah, yeah, easy for them to say. But you won't really know until they make the T minus fifteen minute check, will you?

The communications check is still five minutes away. I have to be patient.

Patience my ass—I'm going to kill something. I know I am early, but I press the transmit pedal, "COMM TECH, NETWORK."

"Go ahead, NETWORK."

"Have you verified MILA's status yet?"

"Negative, I was going to wait until nineteen then I'm going at him."

Forty seconds later, "MILA, Houston COMM TECH Net Two."

"Go ahead, HOUSTON."

"Roger, verify that you are configured for Houston's simplex voice check."

"Negative, HOUSTON, we are waiting for a little later in the spacecraft sequences to configure. I will inform you when we are."

"OK."

I am locked on to the air-to-ground voice checks. George has been trying without success to call up video displays that show the predicted tracking station coverage for Earth-orbit number one, "DISPLAY, NETWORK."

"DISPLAY."

"It must have happened now for five or six times. When I select on a channel, any channel, I get an overlay of channel seventy-six."

"OK, you know which channels you were calling when you got these overlays?"

"It varies. One time it was channel seventy-four—another time seventy-five."

"Which monitor are you using?"

"Right monitor, console eighteen."

"OK, we'll see if we can find anything wrong back there."

As soon as George gets off our comm loop, I'm back on the case.

"COMM TECH, NETWORK."

"Go, NETWORK."

"OK, have they come back and verified their configuration yet?"

He doesn't have to ask whose configuration, "Negative, they have not. I asked them and they said negative. They are waiting on MSTC (Spacecraft Test Conductor) to give them the word."

I stretch my patience and wait another thirty seconds.

"COMM TECH, NETWORK."

"Go, NETWORK."

"Query them again."

"Roger."

"MILA, HOUSTON COMM TECH, Net Two."

"Go ahead, Houston COMM TECH."

"Roger, verify that you're configured for Houston's voice simplex checks."

"Negative, we're still waiting for the spacecraft sequence."

"Ah, Roger."

After another twenty- or thirty-second pause, the MILA operations supervisor reads my mind and decides to put a stop to the neurotic nonsense. "HOUSTON COMM TECH, MILA, Net Two."

"Go ahead."

"Roger, we will give you a reconfiguration at the TCP sequence number one eight dash five four nine."

"Roger, that."

Freely translated, that means, "Get off my back, Houston."

You knew he had to wait until they reached the right sequence in the Test and Checkout Plan. You've been looking like a jerk!

Suitably chastened, I turn my attention back to the progress of the overall countdown. At T minus fifteen minutes, MSTC reports, "Spacecraft going to full internal power."

Simultaneously, George begins our final check of control center readiness.

"All stations, NETWORK. Stand by for status check."

"TIC?"

"GO."

"TRACK?"

"GO."

George steps down through the rest of his list. He gets a simple, crisp "GO" for each of the building systems until he reaches the last entry, the emergency power generator system housed in the building next to mission control. Backup power is not called up for simulations—they only support the real thing. This is the real thing.

"BUILDING FORTY-EIGHT?"

"We're on mission status, maximum support—we're GO."

This last message is delivered in a deep but nervous voice by a man not used to being up on the communication net. Nervous or not, there is a distinct note of pride in his voice.

With the status check done, George turns his attention back to his TV display. The words "Dumb shits!" muttered under his breath indicate that he can now see what it was that he was trying to see, and that he doesn't much like it.

"TRACK, NETWORK."

"NETWORK, TRACK."

"I don't want to interfere with the launch preparations, but when you get a chance, check the masking on Goldstone for that TV pass we're expecting."

The response is immediate. The tracking guys have been looking at the same data. "It will be very severe."

"Roger."

I don't know what problem George is chasing. I would like to ask. But I don't have any attention to spare. I am locked on to Net Two listening for the Merritt Island ground station to confirm their air-to-ground configuration. Finally, at T minus twelve minutes,

"HOUSTON COMM TECH, MILA, NET 2. MILA is configured for your simplex check."

The word "simplex" means that this first check will test the very high frequency and S-band voice circuits one after the other. Now we're ready to get this thing done.

"FLIGHT, NETWORK. MILA is configured for the simplex check."

"Roger."

"HOUSTON, this is TANANARIVE. Has HOUSTON announced a correct launch azimuth yet?"

Get off my circuit Tananarive—I'm trying to hear these voice checks.

George responds, "Negative."

The question from a guy on an island off the southeast coast of Africa reminds us that we are running late on the guidance officer's announcement of the launch azimuth.

That step in our checklist will have to wait just a few more minutes. CVTS comes up on the circuit, "FLIGHT, perform your comm check and verify completion."

The CAPCOM, the capsule communicator, Bruce McCandless, is on the job, "APOLLO ELEVEN, HOUSTON, on VHF. How do you read?"

"Roger, Bruce, read you loud and clear."

"APOLLO LMP, this is HOUSTON on S-band. How do you read?"

"HOUSTON, you're loud and clear."

"Roger, you're the same out."

One more check to make.

"MILA, HOUSTON COMM TECH, Net Two."

"HOUSTON COMM TECH, MILA."

"Roger, verify you're configured for CAPCOM simo check."

"It's in work."

This time the CAPCOM will transmit on the very high frequency and S-band links at the same time.

Come on, you guys—come on. The whole goddamn world is waiting.

"HOUSTON COMM TECH, MILA. MILA is configured."

I punch the push button for the flight director loop and press the transmit switch, "We're configured, FLIGHT."

"Roger."

McCandless copies my report to the flight director and makes his call, "APOLLO ELEVEN, CAPCOM, how do you read?"

"HOUSTON, APOLLO ELEVEN CDR, loud and clear."

Everything checks OK. I can breathe easy—maybe not easy—but easier. At this point, we have verified that the Merritt Island station can communicate with the spacecraft. Now we have to confirm that we can talk to the downrange ground stations that will relay our communications to the spacecraft during the boost to orbit. We also need to check the stations' overall readiness to support the launch. We accomplish both objectives by making the status checks on Net One, the circuit that will carry spacecraft air-to-ground voice after liftoff. During a mission, only the CAPCOM and the crew use Net One. Everyone else on the planet listens to it. This is my first time up on Net One during an actual launch operation. I swallow hard and start my poll of the downrange stations, "All stations, NETWORK, Net One, final status for launch."

"MILA?"

"GO."

"GBM?"

"GBM is GO."

"BERMUDA?"

"BERMUDA is GO."

"VANGUARD?"

"VANGUARD is GO."

"CANARY?"

"CANARY, NETWORK, Net One."

"CANARY, NETWORK, Net One."

No answer. The station on Grand Canary Island, ninety miles off the northwest coast of Africa, will have the spacecraft in view just after nominal orbit insertion. If the boost phase is something less than nominal, contact with the crew could be critical. George tries a different circuit, "CANARY, NETWORK, Net Two."

"Go ahead, NETWORK."

"Answer up on Net One for a status check."

A defensive voice responds, "I answered up three times. You didn't hear it."

"Try it again. We didn't hear you."

Another voice comes up on Net Two, "CANARY, GODDARD VOICE, you're extremely weak on Net One."

"NETWORK, GODDARD VOICE, CANARY is extremely weak on Net One."

"CANARY, GODDARD VOICE, go to Net Two for your status check."

After what seems like three months, "GODDARD VOICE, CANARY, Net Two, how do you read?"

The communications controller at Goddard has reconfigured Canary's circuits switching Net One from a faulty satellite link to the underwater cable that had been carrying Net Two voice.

"Loud and clear."

"NETWORK, GODDARD VOICE."

"GODDARD VOICE, NETWORK."

"Do you want to get status from CANARY now? We have his Net Two on GOSS CONFERENCE."

GOSS CONFERENCE is an alternate designation for Net One.

"CANARY, NETWORK, Net One."

"NETWORK, CANARY, how do you read?"

"You're loud and clear, CANARY. Thank you!"

Just as I am about to breathe again I look at my checklist and see that I still haven't heard the guidance officer's launch azimuth announcement. Wake up, wake up—this one is for real!

"GUIDO, NETWORK, my loop."
"Go."
"Launch azimuth?"
"Plus zero-seven-two-point-zero-six."

Just as I depress the Net Two talk button on my communications panel, "MILA, COMM MANAGER, Net Two. I still don't see your modem idle pattern on Net Five."

Get off my damn net. You've got your own circuit. Use it!

"Break, break, COMM MANGER, break, break, launch azimuth zero-seven-two decimal zero six degrees, zero-seven-two decimal zero six degrees."

At T minus eight minutes and thirty seconds, CVTS comes up on his voice circuit, "HOUSTON FLIGHT, CVTS, 111. Verify GO/NO-GO for start of automatic launch sequence."

He is looking for confirmation that Houston is ready for the terminal countdown sequencer, a computer located in the mobile launcher, to take automatic control of the vehicle countdown at T minus three minutes and seven seconds. This is a major decision point. A GO for automatic sequence is equivalent to a GO for launch.

Our internal procedures call for the flight director to make a roll call of the Houston flight control team at T minus ten minutes in anticipation of the query from CVTS. Charlesworth chooses not to make the status check. He responds without hesitation, "Verify GO."

At T minus eight minutes, "HOUSTON TV, TRACK."
"Go ahead, TRACK."
"My data shows that Goldstone will be out of masking from one hour, thirty minutes, forty seconds until one hour, thirty-one minutes, fifteen seconds."

We can't believe those guys on the Track console are still working that problem.

George interrupts, "OK, let's drop that one then—too close to launch."

I glance over at George. "Do you think they've been watching the stuff they should be watching?"

"We can find out."

He depresses his transmit pedal, "TRACK, NETWORK, how do you look on high-speed data?"

"One more minute before I get high-speed USB. IP data is coming in and looking good."

The range safety officer uses Impact Prediction data generated by air force tracking radars to monitor the flight of the booster. That air force tracking data provides an additional input to the Houston tracking programs.

"TRACK, NETWORK, have you got both IP computers up green?"

"Stand by, we'll double-check."

"NETWORK, TRACK, both IP computers are up."

They seem to be where they should be on their pre-launch checklist as the countdown clock keeps moving us ever closer to liftoff.

A launch pad technician comes up on the space vehicle test supervisor's circuit, "Swing arm nine will be retracted to the fully retracted position on my mark, 10-9-8-7-6-5-4-3-2-1-mark."

The bridge that connects the spacecraft to the Launch Umbilical Tower and provides a line of retreat in an emergency is gone. The crew is alone with their machine, connected by the tenuous electronic thread that will have to sustain them for the next two hundred hours.

"NETWORK, COMM CONTROL. We have a good Net One to Canary."

I glance over at George with an expression that asks, "What the hell does that mean?" Have the communication wizards at Goddard changed the Net One air-to-ground configuration that we just put together and checked out not three minutes ago?

Oh shit, oh dear! Should I go up on the net for a voice check and interrupt the count seconds before the start of automatic sequence? I don't even know for sure if they changed anything.

George reads my mind. "Mission rules: Canary air-to-ground's not mandatory for launch. We're still GO even if they hosed the connection."

George is right. The mission rules wizards have classified Canary spacecraft voice as "Highly Desirable."

Easy for them to say. Suppose they have to abort to orbit? I think they're going to need that link to make sure everyone understands what's going on.

"We need to find out what the hell the comm guys mean by a "good Net One to Canary."

As I finish the sentence I glance down at my checklist—I'm behind again. "COMM TECH, NETWORK."

"COMM TECH."

"Stand by to verify ASTRO COMM patched to air-to-ground one long-line."

The ASTRO COMM Launch Circuit is a cable connection that allows the Mission Control Center and the Launch Control center to speak to the crew through the Saturn's umbilical connection while it sits on the launch pad.

"ASTRO COMM is patched to air-to-ground one long-line—it is."

"It is already?"

"Not to air-to-ground one. It's patched to air-to-ground long-line which is air-to-ground PBI in-house."

"Roger, that's air-to-ground one long-line."

You guys sound like Abbott and Costello doing their "Who's on First?" routine. What the hell is all of the confusion about? Just do it the way you did it during the Countdown Demonstration Test. This has nothing to do with the in-house configuration. You need MILA to patch that landline to their Net One so that the CAPCOM can monitor the traffic on that loop and use it if he needs to. That's all—it's that simple!

The flight director comes up on his loop, "OK, all flight controllers were coming up on automatic sequence. BOOSTER, how are you?"

"We're GO, FLIGHT."

"EECOM?"

"GO."

"G&C?"

"GO."

"TELCOM?"

"GO."

"NETWORK, you got it all—everything up?"

We weren't expecting a status check at this point. I give George a panicked look. He shrugs his shoulders. We still don't know what our Canary air-to-ground status is. It's not mandatory—it's not mandatory!

"That's affirmative, FLIGHT."

I listen to my own voice as I give the final go-ahead—lots of steely-eyed missile guy steadiness—pretty convincing considering that the status of the Canary circuit plummeted to "unknown" seconds before my report.

"APOLLO ELEVEN, this is the Launch Operations Manager. The launch crew wishes you good luck and Godspeed."

"Thank you very much—know it will be a good one."

"CDR, STC, how do you read me?"

"Loud and clear."

"OK, Neil, have a good one."

"Minus three thirty."

The pad countdown procedure calls for time announcements every ten seconds between T minus three minutes and thirty seconds and T minus forty seconds. From T minus forty until T minus fifteen seconds they will be made every five seconds. From T minus eleven seconds until liftoff the call-outs will come every second. The historian wants to stop and appreciate the moment—to inventory the feelings generated by immersion in this very first attempt to land on the Earth's bright satellite. But the announcements feed a feeling that the list of things to do and the list of things to worry about are expanding in an inverse relationship to the time remaining. There's no time for personal assessment—posterity will have to take care of itself.

Where the hell is Brantley? Why hasn't he checked the ASTRO COMM status?

"MILA, NETWORK, Net Two."

"NETWORK, MILA, Net Two."

"Rog. Do we have the ASTRO-COMM circuit patched to the air-to-ground one long-line?"

"They should be. Stand by."

"Minus three ten."

"Firing command initiated."

"NETWORK, MILA. They are hooked up."

"Roger. Thank you."

"Auto sequence minus three."

"Start sequence initiated."

BOOSTER comes up on the flight director's loop, "Auto sequence, FLIGHT."

"ROGER."

"OK all flight controllers, we're in auto sequence. Stand by."

"Minus two fifty."

"Minus two forty."

"ECS on internal cooling."

The spacecraft has switched from pad-supplied cooling to its own onboard system.

"Minus two ten."

"Minus two minutes."

"Minus one fifty."

There's an eerie silence now, punctuated by the ten-second time announcements. It looks like we are really going to do this thing.

"Minus one forty."

"Minus one thirty."

"Minus one twenty."

George comes up on our internal loop, "COMM CONTROL, NETWORK."

"Go, NETWORK."

"What's the configuration for comm at Canary?"

"Comm at Canary?"

The communications controller sounds like George just asked him about the current temperature on the far side of the Moon. "Comm at Canary—is he all normal?"

"He's all normal. That's affirmative."

"He's on satellite?"

"Roger."

Suspicions confirmed. The Goddard communications manager has switched out a tested circuit and replaced it with a circuit that failed its initial test. Of course they would have checked the circuit before they used it to connect Goddard to the Canary Islands. In theory it should work just fine when they make the Houston-Canary connection. But sometimes theoretical stuff gets complicated when you try to put it into practice. There is nothing to do now but wait and worry for the twenty minutes between now and Canary acquisition of signal.

"S-II pre-press complete, FLIGHT."

"Roger."

"Minus fifty seconds."

"Power transfer complete."

The Saturn is on internal power—ready for engine start.

"Minus forty seconds."

The systems that the mission rules call out as "Mandatory for Launch" are now "Highly Desirable." Only an impending catastrophe will stop the count. I hope we're ready for this!

"S-I pre-press complete, FLIGHT."

The giant first stage is ready for engine start.

"Minus thirty."

"MCC recorders to flight speed."

"GRR."

"Roger, GRR."

The Saturn guidance and navigation system has been holding a fixed vertical and north-south orientation. It just stays put, guarding against any drift that might jeopardize the system's knowledge of its starting point on the launch pad. At Guidance Reference Release, the system is free to begin its navigation calculations based on that starting point.

Finally we hear what has become the ritual chant of the space age overlaid with a series of terse announcements that signal the final sequences in the countdown.

"Ready for ignition."

"Ten-nine—"

"Ignition sequence started."

The Saturn computer staggers the ignition times of the five engines to prevent a massive shock caused by simultaneous start of all of the engines. The center engine starts first, followed at quarter-second intervals by diagonally opposed pairs of the other four.

"—eight-seven-six-five-four-three-two—"

"All engines running."

"Commit."

The engines come up to full thrust, generating 180 million horsepower. The hold-down clamps that have held the Saturn in place until full thrust is achieved release the giant rocket.

"—one-zero."

"Liftoff, we do have a liftoff."

Five access arms on the launch umbilical tower support lines that provide electric, propellant, and pneumatic service to the Saturn stack until the very moment of launch. As the vehicle rises off the launch pad, the umbilical connections drop from the booster and the access arms swing away. The umbilical disconnect triggers a liftoff signal. The signal starts the first of seven time-phased programs that the onboard computer will use to control the Saturn.

"Clock start, FLIGHT."

I steal a glance at the projection TV—the launch vehicle exhaust envelops the umbilical tower in an angry cloud of fire, smoke, and steam. An avalanche of ice formed by the super cold propellants separates from the skin of the rocket and crashes down into the firestorm as the great machine inches upward.

At plus ten seconds the launch operations manager reports, "Tower clear." I think I hear a touch of relief in his voice. The Saturn is clear of the launch umbilical tower. The launch team's work is done. They have guided the space vehicle through the first four hundred feet of its mission. The next five hundred thousand miles are up to us.

CHAPTER NINETEEN

From his vantage point at the top of a towering column of fire, Armstrong reports, "Roger. We got a roll program."

McCandless acknowledges, "Roger. Roll."

Sitting on the pad, the Saturn guidance system is aligned to a nominal launch azimuth of ninety degrees—due east. Airborne now, it climbs straight up and rolls counterclockwise to align with the launch azimuth of seventy-two degrees—just north of due east. The adjustment simplifies upcoming maneuvers designed to point the vehicle's nose downrange and allow it to pick up the horizontal velocity it needs to achieve orbit.

"DYNAMICS, this is RETRO. Liftoff one three plus three two plus zero zero point seven eight."

This is the number we are waiting for. I scribble it down on the bottom of my launch checklist page. John Monkvic copies it into the log and circles it with a red pencil.

I go up on Net Two to pass the numbers to the network stations.

"All stations, NETWORK. Liftoff one three—"

"Break, break, GBM has AOS."

"FLIGHT, range safety is nominal."

"Roger, RSO."

Just as I am about to try my announcement a second time, Armstrong updates the vehicle status, "Roll's complete and the pitch is programmed."

The Saturn has reached the launch azimuth and is about to pitch over to point its nose downrange.

"MILA, TRACK."

"Go ahead, TRACK."

"Do you still have bad angles?"

"Roger."

Receivers on the S-band antenna are supposed to sense the edges of an incoming radio beam and point the antenna directly at the source of the signal. There's too much signal now—there are no edges to detect. The antenna angles are unreliable. But there are other sources of tracking data. We can live with this one. I try again.

"Liftoff one three plus three two plus zero zero point seven eight. GET clock start one three plus three two plus—disregard."

I have lost it. I'm supposed to round the time to the nearest second. My head won't work! Oh, shit, oh dear! The entire mission plan from liftoff to splashdown is written in terms of time from liftoff—GET or ground elapsed time. A mistake means massive confusion.

I warned you about getting into this. You are an arithmetic illiterate! What are you going to do now? OK, OK, be quiet, I got it!

"One three plus three two plus zero one."

I imagine that the whole world has seen my confusion. Head down in embarrassment, I glance at the television display on my console. As I look at the status of the incoming data, I realize that I heard Grand Bahama announce acquisition of signal. But I haven't heard the follow-on announcement that they have two-way lock and can accept commands for the spacecraft. It's taking too long. But my command guys don't seem alarmed. I decide to trust that Glenn Spears will do the right thing.

McCandless advises the crew, "Stand by for One Bravo. Mark, One Bravo."

I like the sound of that. Over the months of launch training, the abort mode call-outs have changed character from prelude to possible disaster to measure of mission success. Every call you hear puts the spacecraft closer to a safe orbit.

At forty-four seconds Armstrong confirms, "One Bravo."

"FLIGHT, range safety is in the water."

"Roger, RSO."

If range safety has to terminate the flight, the spacecraft will come down in the ocean. That's a good thing.

"Roger, how are you, BOOSTER?"

"We're GO, FLIGHT."

"Good at one minute, CAPCOM."

"APOLLO ELEVEN, HOUSTON. You're good at one minute."

"Roger."

The Saturn rocket is four miles high and a mile downrange. It has already exceeded the speed of sound. I still need to pass the launch time to NORAD. They keep track of objects in Earth orbit so as to distinguish them from incoming Soviet ICBMs. We need to help them do that.

"NORAD, NETWORK."

At plus one minute fifty-eight seconds McCandless signals, "Stand by for Mode One Charlie," and then confirms, "Mode One Charlie."

I try again, "NORAD, NETWORK."

The Grand Bahama operations supervisor comes up on the loop, "GBM is GO for command CSM."

The NORAD duty controller responds to my second call, "Go ahead, NETWORK."

Is this guy super calm or what? He sounds like I woke him up—your, my air force is always alert—sort of.

"Launch azimuth zero seven two point zero six. Liftoff time one three plus three two plus zero one."

"Would you say again on that?"

I repeat the transmission.

"Uh, rog, got it. Thank you, HOUSTON."

Sorry to have bothered you, brother—back to sleep!
Charlesworth comes up on the flight director loop.
"Staging GO?"
"BOOSTER?"
"GO."
"FIDO?"
"GO."
"GUIDANCE?"
"GO."
"Good for staging, CAPCOM."
"APOLLO ELEVEN, this is HOUSTON. You are GO for staging."

This is classic Greek drama with Charlesworth as protagonist. His flight controllers fill out the chorus. They make an electronic inspection of the innards of the booster and spacecraft. They evaluate the omens using the mission rules and the laws of physics. They make their predictions and pass recommendations to the flight director. The flight director consults his inner oracle and instructs the CAPCOM to transmit his decisions to the crew—this is how it is supposed to work.

Neil Armstrong reports, "Inboard cutoff."

The center engine of the Saturn first stage has shut down. The CAPCOM acknowledges the report. BOOSTER sees the same event in the telemetry. "We confirm inboard cutoff."

At two minutes and fifteen seconds after launch, the Saturn is twenty-four miles high and twenty-five miles downrange, traveling at more than a mile a second. The first stage has consumed four and one-half million pounds of fuel and oxidizer in those two-plus minutes since launch.

The crew commander continues his terse narrative of mission events.

"Staging."

The four outboard engines shut down. The first stage separates. Retro-rockets push it clear of the upper stage and accelerate its death plunge into the Atlantic.

"And ignition."

The Houston flight controllers monitor the staging sequence using S-band telemetry and tracking data provided by the Grand Bahama and Merritt Island tracking stations. Air force C-band tracking radars at Cape Canaveral, Patrick Air Force Base, and on the island of Grand Turk track a beacon on the Saturn and confirm trajectory status. The Grand Bahama and Merritt Island files take an indirect route to the flight controllers' consoles—going first to Goddard and then on to Houston. The C-band radar tracking files come direct via the *Apollo* Launch Data System—a pair of wideband communications circuits that connect Houston and the Cape.

BOOSTER confirms, "Thrust is GO all engines."

"ELEVEN, HOUSTON. Thrust is GO, all engines. You're looking good."

"Roger. You're loud and clear, HOUSTON."

The historian pulls at the corners of my consciousness and urges me to look up and look around to record the scene at this critical juncture. There's no time for that. I keep my head down and my attention on the voice and data communications quality. If I did look up I would see a bunch of guys just like me—heads down, eyes locked on their console displays.

"We've got skirt SEP."

"Roger. We confirm. Skirt SEP."

The interstage that connected the two stages is gone.

GUIDANCE sees a change in the Instrumentation Unit telemetry. "Guidance initiate, FLIGHT."

The Saturn's onboard computer has changed modes. Until this point, the computer has initiated guidance commands based solely on the time from liftoff. Now it switches to an iterative guidance mode, which calculates the flight path that meets mission requirements with minimum fuel expenditure.

A small solid-fuel motor jettisons the Launch Escape System, pulling the boost protective cover away from the Command Module windows. Armstrong reacts to the sudden, brilliant expanse of sky and sea. "HOUSTON, be advised the visual is GO today."

"Let me know when it converges, GUIDANCE."

"Yes. They finally gave me a window to look out."

"Looks good, FLIGHT—converged."

The Saturn guidance system has found an optimum trajectory.

"CAPCOM."

"ELEVEN, HOUSTON. Your guidance has converged; you're looking good."

EECOM is satisfied with the crew life-support systems. "Cabin stable at five nine, FLIGHT."

"Roger, cabin."

"How are you, BOOSTER?"

"We're GO, FLIGHT."

"GNC?"

"We're GO, FLIGHT."

"SURGEON?"

"GO, FLIGHT."

"We're good at four minutes, CAPCOM."

"ELEVEN, HOUSTON. You are GO at four minutes."

"Roger."

"FLIGHT, FIDO, all trajectory sources agree. We're GO."

Forty seconds later, Charlesworth runs his trap line again, asking each flight controller for status. The CAPCOM relays the result, "ELEVEN, HOUSTON. You are GO at five minutes."

"Roger. It'll—APOLLO ELEVEN. GO."

In a few seconds the booster will have reached the point where the S-IVB third stage can put the spacecraft into a safe orbit if the second stage should fail, a maneuver called contingency orbit insertion. FIDO comes up on the flight director's communications circuit, "Stand by for S-IVB to COI capability."

McCandless relays the status to the crew, "Stand by for the S-IVB to COI capability."

"OK."

FIDO confirms the capability, "Mark."

The CAPCOM again relays the status to the crew, "Mark. S-IVB to COI capability."

"Roger."

Armstrong acknowledges and adds, "You sure sound clear down there, Bruce. Sounds like you're sitting in your living room."

This is a report that warms a network controller's heart. I give Monkvic a half-assed grin and hope that he writes that one down in the log.

Charlesworth starts his six-minute check, "BOOSTER, FLIGHT, how are you?"

"We're GO, FLIGHT."

The other controllers all give the same response.

"Roger, ELEVEN. You're GO from the ground at six minutes."

On Net Two, we hear Bermuda report right on time. "BERMUDA has AOS IU."

George responds, "Roger, BERMUDA."

The expected report on two-way lock follows. "BERMUDA is GO for command IU."

The second stage is nearing the end of its short life.

"FLIGHT, BOOSTER, times eight plus one seven, nine plus one one."

"Copy eight one seven, nine one one."

"BERMUDA, TRACK, we show you're not two-way."

"APOLLO ELEVEN, this is HOUSTON. Level sense arm at eight plus seventeen; outboard cutoff at nine plus eleven."

"This is BERMUDA. We confirm two-way on the IU."

"BERMUDA is GO for command CSM."

"Roger, BERMUDA."

"HOUSTON COMM TECH, BERMUDA COMM TECH, downlink is VHF."

The flight director runs his seven-minute check. "Good at seven minutes, CAPCOM."

"BERMUDA, TRACK, still have you intermittent on CSM."

"ELEVEN, this is HOUSTON. Roger. You're GO from the ground at seven minutes. Level sense arm at eight plus seventeen; outboard cutoff at nine plus eleven." Armstrong acknowledges the transmission and then adds, "Inboard cutoff."

BOOSTER sees the same event, "Confirming inboard cutoff."

The flight director acknowledges. The CAPCOM closes the loop. "Roger. We confirmed."

At seven minutes and forty-two seconds after launch, the spacecraft is six hundred nautical miles downrange at an altitude of almost one hundred miles traveling at three miles per second. The plot-boards at the front of the control room record its steady progress toward Earth orbit—the plots for velocity, altitude, range, and flight-path angle trace along the nominal paths.

RETRO reports, "FLIGHT, we're right on the ground track."

"FLIGHT, FIDO, good agreement all sources. We're GO."

"APOLLO ELEVEN, HOUSTON. You are GO at eight minutes."

Without warning, noise overlays the transmissions on Net One. "BERMUDA COMM TECH, HOUSTON COMM TECH, what's the problem on USB?"

"Based on experience USB normally drops out on launch."

"COMM TECH, NETWORK."

"Go ahead."

"You got a problem?" I sound like I'm straight out of the south Bronx.

"He indicates no problem, but says based on experience USB will drop out on launch."

"OK, how's the voice been sounding?"

"Sounds good."

Monkvic and I exchange quizzical glances. The circuit goes quiet just in time for another critical event.

"OK, BOOSTER, how are you for staging?"

"We're GO for staging."

"GUIDANCE, how are you?"

"GO."

"GO for staging, CAPCOM."

"ELEVEN, this is HOUSTON. You are GO for staging. Over."

"Understand, GO for staging. And—"

"Staging—"

"—and ignition."

"Ignition confirmed; thrust is GO, ELEVEN."

The S-band and C-band systems on the islands of Bermuda and Grand Turk track the third-stage burn. The S-IVB and spacecraft are more than 101 miles above the Earth, and almost 900 miles downrange, traveling at 7.5 miles per second.

"EECOM, FLIGHT, how are you?"

"We're GO, FLIGHT."

"GNC?"

"We're GO, FLIGHT."

"SURGEON?"

The guidance officer interrupts the roll call, "Guidance converged, FLIGHT."

The surgeon responds with an emphatic "GO."

"BOOSTER, how are you?"

"We're GO, FLIGHT."

"We're good at ten minutes, CAPCOM."

"APOLLO ELEVEN, this is HOUSTON. At ten minutes, you are GO."

"Roger. ELEVEN's GO."

The INCO picks the middle of the launch phase to worry some more about his first television session. Goldstone is scheduled to receive the signal after the spacecraft reaches orbit. "NETWORK, INCO, do you have the TV times?"

George responds, "Give it to you when I get it."

"Roger."

"Gotta be in orbit first."

Good answer, George!

"FLIGHT, FIDO, all sources agree—we're GO."

"Roger, GUIDANCE, got a predicted cutoff time?"

"Roger, FLIGHT, it's settled down at eleven plus forty-two."

"Are you satisfied with that one?"

"Go with eleven plus four two."

"OK."

"NETWORK, ARIA."

ARIA CONTROL located at Patrick Air Force Base, Florida, operates the fleet of Apollo Range Instrumented Aircraft that fill the gaps between tracking stations and ships.

"ARIA, NETWORK."
"ARIA Three airborne at one three three two."
"Roger."
"APOLLO ELEVEN, this is HOUSTON. Predicted cutoff at eleven plus forty-two. Over."
"Eleven forty-two. Roger."
"BOOSTER, FLIGHT, how are you?"
"We're GO, FLIGHT."
"GNC?"
"We're GO, FLIGHT."
"EECOM?"
"GO, FLIGHT."
"GUIDANCE, how are you?"
"GO, FLIGHT."
"SURGEON?"
"We're GO."
"GO at eleven, CAPCOM."
"APOLLO ELEVEN, this is HOUSTON. You are GO at eleven."
"Good deal."
"FIDO, FLIGHT, how are you?"
"Lookin' good—a little noise on the raw—all sources agree—we're GO."
"OK, we'll be standing by for your confirm."
"Roger that, FLIGHT."
RETRO gives a position update. "FLIGHT, we've cleared the east coast of Africa."
We should have heard from the tracking ship *Vanguard* by now. Their tracking data will confirm orbit insertion. "RTC, NETWORK."
"RTC."
Roger, have we got anything from *Vanguard?*"
"Negative."
"VANGUARD is GO for command CSM."
"Roger, VANGUARD."
Just in time!

Mike Collins confirms S-IVB engine cutoff, "SECO. We are showing 101.4 by 103.6."

The three Saturn rocket stages have burned for just under twelve minutes, boosting the third stage and the spacecraft into a near-circular Earth orbit.

"VANGUARD is GO for command IU."

"Roger, VANGUARD."

"HOUSTON COMM TECH, VANGUARD COMM TECH, you have USB voice."

"Roger."

I take a quick look to my left and see Charlesworth with his head raised as he follows the trajectory plot on the center display at the front of the room.

"Standing by for you, FIDO."

"FLIGHT, FIDO we are GO. Confirm GO."

"APOLLO ELEVEN, this is Houston. You are confirmed GO for orbit."

"Roger."

"FLIGHT, GUIDANCE, G&N is GO."

"Roger."

"Standing by for you, BOOSTER."

"Roger, we have the range safety receiver safe."

"Range safety receiver safe, CAPCOM."

"APOLLO ELEVEN, this is HOUSTON. The booster is safe."

I am still focused on the quality of the Net One air-to-ground voice link, listening for any hiss or squeal that might indicate a problem. The link is useable but nowhere near perfect. I hear *Vanguard* make a report to the telemetry instrumentation controller on Net Two but can't focus on the content. "TIC, NETWORK."

"Go ahead, NETWORK."

"What was his report?"

"He has good signal strength on CSM. It's increasing, it's good.

"OK, it's looking solid now?"

"Roger."

I look at George. If the signal strength is "increasing' there must have been some problem when they acquired the signal. They haven't said. We don't know. It seems to be working now. We'll save that one for the post-mission operations analysis.

"NETWORK, COMM CONTROL, your loop."

George responds to the call. "Roger, I copy."

I have no idea what George has copied. He will tell me if I need to know.

"FLIGHT, BOOSTER, IVB is configured for coast."

"OK, CAPCOM, booster configured for coast. Both spacecraft look good."

"Roger."

"BERMUDA has LOS all systems."

"FIDO from FLIGHT."

"FLIGHT, FIDO, based on the IU vector now—99.7 by 102.5. We'll have some radar data shortly."

"Ninety-nine what?"

"Seven."

"By 102.5."

"All right. And that's based on what again?"

"That's from the booster."

The current estimate of the orbit is based on the data from the Saturn onboard computer. The crew can make their own estimate by looking out the window at the deep black sky above the Earth's curving horizon or watching the line between daylight and darkness move across the face of the planet.

"I'll stand by for your radar data."

George comes up on our internal voice circuit again. "TIC, NETWORK."

"NETWORK, TIC."

"Yeah, how's that Canary Net Six doing?'

"It's holding in now."

"Let us know if you want it restored."

"OK."

Now I know what I missed earlier. There have been problems with the circuit carrying crew biomedical telemetry from the Canary Islands station.

"COMM CONTROL, NETWORK."

"Go, NETWORK."

"OK, are you aware of the problem on Canary Net Six?"

"Affirmative the COMM MANAGER is checking it now."

"OK, if it should go bad, we'll go ahead and restore it."

"Roger."

"APOLLO ELEVEN, this is HOUSTON. Vanguard LOS at fifteen thirty-five; AOS Canaries at sixteen thirty. Over."

"OK. Thank you."

Glynn Lunney, the Black Team flight director, and three of the other flight directors, have been sitting just behind Charlesworth during the launch sequence. Now I hear him calling the launch operations supervisor at Kennedy. "CVTS, FLIGHT."

"Go, FLIGHT."

"We're in a nominal orbit near as we can tell. Everything is working just fine. Cliff sends his regards and three other guys do too. Thank you very much. We appreciate your good support."

"Ah, it's our pleasure."

"NETWORK, ARIA, Net Two."

George takes the call. "ARIA, go ahead."

"Roger, ARIA Four airborne one three three eight."

"NETWORK, TRACK."

"TRACK, NETWORK."

"Channel twenty-three is valid now."

"Twenty-three is fine, thank you."

Channel twenty-three displays a table of predicted times for network station acquisition and loss of spacecraft signals. The table is one of our primary planning tools. The nominal times have been updated based on the actual orbital parameters.

"NETWORK, COMM CONTROL."

"Go ahead."

"Net Six has been restored. He said it looks like Net Five to Canary needs—"

"VANGUARD has LOS."

George follows up on the comment about Net Five, the high-speed trajectory data circuit. "TRACK, NETWORK."

"TRACK."

"You don't need Net Five from Canaries, do you?"

Voices overlap voices. I lose the tracking controller's response in the babble. I hope George deals with whatever is going on.

The CAPCOM comes up on the flight director loop. "Hey, FLIGHT, you know this business of the delta azimuth update?" Only McCandless could get away with that kind of salutation.

"Yeah."

"If we get it why don't we go ahead and pass it up over Canaries since we have been having all of these comm problems at Tananarive?

"OK, we'll get it up at your LOS call."

That's just one more piece of business to be transacted through the Canary station.

"TIC, CANARY do you have AOS?"

"Roger that."

"Then why didn't you follow the goddamned procedure and report it?" I mutter to no one in particular without depressing the transmit switch.

"CANARIES is GO for command IU."

"Roger, CANARY."

"CANARY, HOUSTON COMM TECH, Net Two."

"Go ahead."

The idiot is responding on Net One!

"…HOUSTON COMM TECH. CANARY COMM TECH."

"Roger, are you remoting VHF to Net One?"

"That is affirmative."

Coincident with Canaries' reassuring response, this time on Net Two, a cloud of background noise settles on Net One.

"APOLLO ELEVEN, this is HOUSTON through CANARY. Over."

"NETWORK, FOD TV."

Out of instinct I respond to the call. "Go ahead."

Excuse me! Why are we dealing with these TV people? Doesn't Net One have overwhelming priority?

"Can we turn down the video lines coming to us from the Cape?"

Before I can respond, the crew makes a status report.

"Roger. Reading you loud and clear. Our insertion checklist is complete, and we have no abnormalities."

I can't believe they said "loud and clear." That is the crappiest signal we've had!

"Stand by."

"PROCEDURES, NETWORK."

"PROCEDURES, NETWORK, my loop."

"Go ahead."

"Can we turn down the TV line from the Cape? Do you have any further requirement?"

"Negative."

"OK."

McCandless continues his dialogue in spite of the noise. "Roger. And I'd like to pass up your delta azimuth correction at this time if you're ready to copy."

How the hell can he not hear that? It sounds like somebody poured a can of noise on the circuit.

"Stand by."

"FOD TV, NETWORK."

"Go ahead."

"Take 'em down."

"Roger, will do."

The crew somehow doesn't seem to hear the noise either. You have to wonder how long they can ignore it. "Roger. Go ahead. Ready to copy."

"OK. Delta azimuth correction is plus 0.22, that is plus 0.22, and we do recommend the P52 alignment. Over."

"OK. We'll go ahead with the P52, and detecting angle plus 0.22."

"Roger. And your LOS time at Canary is twenty three thirty seven. Over."

"Twenty three thirty seven."

"HOUSTON. Roger. Out."

I have only the vaguest idea of what that 0.22 number means. Not that I wouldn't like to know—if I had the time. But I don't. I have to stick to my job of making sure those numbers are readable when they reach the crew. At this point I'm not doing all that well. I wonder how they can understand anything in the middle of the noise barrage on the net.

George comes up on the circuit. "HOUSTON TV, NETWORK."

"Go ahead, NETWORK."

"You took down the line from the Cape. The one to the Cape stays up for a while?"

"Roger, also we checked with TRACK. It looks like we have about thirty-five seconds at Goldstone and I think we ought to reevaluate doing that since it takes about twenty seconds to lock up on him."

"OK."

Enough with the TV schedules.

"COMM CONTROL, NETWORK."

"Go, NETWORK."

"You got any words from VOICE on why that circuit is so noisy from Canary?"

"We'll check it."

"It's useable, but it's the noisiest one we've seen yet."

"Right."

And now the inevitable call comes. "NETWORK, FLIGHT."

"FLIGHT, NETWORK."

"Do we have any kind of problem at Canary?"

"We're checking on it, FLIGHT. We had a problem on the circuit before liftoff and restored it on the sub cable. We're looking at it again."

Why are you telling him all of that? He doesn't need to hear your sad story. He needs you to clean up that noise. "COMM CONTROL, NETWORK."

"Go."

"What's the status on Canary? Can we do anything?"
"We're checking."
"Roger."

The hissing, crackling noise on Net One seems to get louder. It begins to roar! Every controller in the room seems to stop what they're doing and glare in the general direction of the network controller's console.

"NETWORK, TRACK."
"TRACK, NETWORK."
"Yeah, I think we may have given TV the wrong impression there. We have masking for most of the pass at Goldstone at one hour twenty minutes, however, uh—"

Not again! I look past Monkvic and give George my best "What the fuck?" look.

"NETWORK, RETRO."
"RETRO, NETWORK."
"OK, call channel twenty-two please."

Per procedure, Llewellyn wants our coordination on a teletype message he is about to send that will synchronize the timing of the tracking station computers.

"Roger, RETRO."

I look carefully at the liftoff time in the message. It looks good. But I don't want to trust to memory—not a good day to make an error. Monkvic is in the same mode. He flips back to the liftoff time in his log book, checks it against the TV screen, and gives me thumbs-up.

"RETRO, NETWORK, my loop."
"OK, call channel twenty-two."
"I've called it up and it looks good."
"OK, that's the one I'm sending out at Canary LOS."
"Roger."
"Thank you a lot."

The thank you, delivered in a soft Virginia drawl in the middle of a cascade of terse flight control communication, is typical Llewellyn.

The communications guys have still not answered my earlier call. I try again. "COMM CONTROL, NETWORK."

George leans forward in his chair and talks to me on the open air loop.

"We're about a minute and a half from Canary loss of signal. I think we should hold what we got. Even if it's noisy it sort of works. If we take the circuit down to check and restore it, the pass will be over before we get it done."

"Disregard, COMM CONTROL."

"FIDO from FLIGHT."

"Go ahead."

"Did you ever get an orbit from radar?"

"We have confirmation from Canary. The residuals are real low. We're going to take it from Canaries and give it to you then."

George wants to confirm his suspicions on the configuration of the Canary air-to-ground circuit. "COMM CONTROL, NETWORK."

"Is Net One on the satellite or the cable? From Canaries."

"Satellite."

"Roger."

"OK."

"NETWORK, TIC."

George answers, "Go ahead."

"We had a momentary line drop on Net Four. It came back up."

"OK."

This whole pass is turning to shit! There's noise on every circuit!

"How is Net Six doing?"

"It's been holding."

"APOLLO ELEVEN, this is HOUSTON. One minute to LOS Canary; AOS at Tananarive thirty seven zero four in VHF Simplex Alfa. Over."

"APOLLO ELEVEN, this is HOUSTON. Coming up on LOS Canary; AOS Tananarive at thirty seven zero four, Simplex Alfa. HOUSTON. Out."

"CANARY COMM TECH, HOUSTON COMM TECH."
"Go ahead."
"Did you have any downlink from the spacecraft?"
"APOLLO. Roger."
"Just then we had a downlink."
"Roger."
"COMM TECH, NETWORK."
"Go ahead, NETWORK."
"What were you trying to establish there?"
"Well at the time I called them the CAPCOM had went for the second time and I was gonna verify that he had a downlink. And just as I was calling him they did get a downlink."
"OK."
"It was only a short 'Roger.' They were kind of busy."
"TRACK, NETWORK."
"Go, NETWORK."
"OK, what's the status on the Goldstone TV pass? How much good data can we expect?"
"OK. They'll be low on the horizon and masked.[4] And the signal strength will be around minus ninety to minus one hundred dBm."
"How much good TV can we expect?"
"I can't say, George, except that they'll be masked for all but twenty seconds.

A transmission from the Canary operations supervisor overlays the tracking controller's report. "CANARY has LOS all links."

The noise disappears—thank you, Jesus!

"And I guess you were trying to give me an indication of the masking there but I didn't really come up with it."

"OK, they are masked from one twenty-nine to one thirty forty."

"NETWORK, ARIA."

---

4   Local terrain features such as hills can interrupt or "mask" the signals from a spacecraft that is just above the tracking station's radio horizon.

"ARIA, NETWORK, on Coord."

"Roger, we request release of ARIA ONE and TWO from the mission."

"ARIA TWO?"

"ONE and TWO? OK, I believe our understanding was to release them after TLI, all aircraft."

"OK, I guess so, ah, with this launch azimuth they will not be utilized and…"

"OK, that was not the agreement."

"OK, we'll just keep them there then."

"What's their next mission?"

"Say again."

"What's their next mission—their next support?"

"Those two are the aircraft that are at Mauritius and Cocos Islands and they will not be utilized in this and we're using these aircraft—one in a ROC return–and so they've got quite a bit of time."

I have no idea what a ROC return is. This is beginning to sound like an old vaudeville comedy routine.

"OK, is he the one on the schedule for data transfer?"

"Ah, no, SIX and EIGHT are. These are the ones that aren't utilized at all. I agree with you on the rest of the aircraft."

"OK, give them a release.'

"Thank you, sir."

"TRACK, NETWORK."

"Go, NETWORK."

George is still working the goddamned TV problem! "Yeah, say on this Goldstone TV rev, do you know what omni we're going to be on?"

"It will be delta."

"OK, we need to be on delta to get anything out of it."

"Yeah and that's what they should be on."

"OK."

I need to follow up on my last agreement with ARIA Control. "STATUS, NETWORK, on Call."

"STATUS."

"Release ARIA ONE and TWO, please."
"Roger, we'll do that."
"FLIGHT, RTC."
"Go ahead."
"Will you disable aborts?"
"Yes sir, thank you."
"NETWORK, COMM CONTROL, your loop."
"Go ahead, COMM CONTROL."
"We gonna get some times for a Carnarvon-Mercury comsat hand over?"

Communications satellites are new and scarce. We make specific channel sharing arrangements for both the Atlantic and Pacific satellites. "Wilco, stand by."

George flips his checklist open to the translunar injection pages. "I'll get him some times. We're close enough to the nominal mission time line to use the pre-planned numbers."

"FLIGHT, FIDO."
"GO ahead."
"Canary radar—103 circular."
"Beautiful."
"Decimal zero."
"COMM CONTROL, NETWORK."
"Go ahead, NETWORK."
"Carnarvon to Mercury fifty-nine minutes elapsed, five niner minutes."
"Roger."
"Mercury back to Carnarvon."
"OK."
"One hour forty minutes, one hour four zero."
"One hour four zero, roger. Thank you, George."
"NETWORK, COMM TECH."
"Go ahead."
"Do I have your permission to make a voice check with Tananarive before he gets acquisition? Just to check the circuit out."
"Rog."

"OK, I'll get CAPCOM's permission also."

The voice check is loud and clear.

With the crew safely in orbit and preparations made for the upcoming station passes, there's one more bit of business to deal with: the great Canary Islands air-to-ground screw-up. Just as I depress the foot pedal to activate my mic:

"NETWORK, COMM CONTROL."

The very guy I was about to call.

"Canary is all five-by at this time. It's on the satellite. He'll have an RFO for that outage shortly."

"OK, were we on the satellite during the pass?"

"That's affirmative."

"OK, why did we go back off the sub cable which was loud and clear when I finally got to him on the check?"

"Well he just went normal."

He is sounding defensive now!

"That's his normal route, his, his satellite and he went back on it."

"Yeah, but it was screwed up before liftoff and we got him good on the sub cable. And I feel like we should have left him there. But we'll rehash that some other day."

I take a second to look up at the ground elapsed time clock high up on the wall at the front of the room. Just twenty-five minutes have passed since the Saturn lifted off. Most of our stuff worked, even if some of it like the Canary voice was marginal. A quick check of my adrenaline tank shows that the level is already way below what it ought to be at this point in the mission.

CHAPTER TWENTY

The interval between Canary Island loss of signal and Tananarive acquisition allows George and me to stretch, head out for a quick pit stop, and refill our coffee cups. John Monkvic covers the comm loops for us. We get back in position just in time.

"APOLLO ELEVEN, this is HOUSTON through Tananarive. Over."

"HOUSTON, APOLLO ELEVEN. Read you on VHF A Simplex. How do you read? Over."

"Roger, ELEVEN. This is HOUSTON. We're reading you loud and fairly clearly. For your information, Canary radar shows you in a 103.0 by 103.0 orbit. Over."

"Beautiful."

That parking orbit is safe in the short term. But the Eleven crew has a long, long way to go. Think about the Earth in cross-section. Its radius is a little more than 3,400 nautical miles. At 103 miles, the spacecraft is like a tiny bug skating across the surface of the atmosphere. It still has more than two hundred thousand miles to go to reach the planned landing site. To make that journey with minimum fuel expenditure, the spacecraft has to be fired into an extended orbit that will take it to a point in space at the same time that the Moon arrives at that point. That requires that the translunar injection burn take place on the side of the Earth opposite the eventual rendezvous point—over the southwest Pacific between Australia and Hawaii.

In addition to happening in the right place, the burn has to happen at the "Goldilocks" moment—not too early, not too late. The no-earlier-than constraint of one and one-half hours is driven by the time required to perform system checks, both onboard and on the ground, and the need to realign the spacecraft's guidance platform. The lifetime of the S-IVB batteries and the amount of attitude control propellant onboard set the outer limit at four and one-half hours. Taken together, these time and place constraints dictate that the burn has to happen on the second or third orbit.

George and I are getting ourselves organized for that first-opportunity burn on the second orbit. Except for the much discussed television transmission to the Goldstone tracking station during the first orbit, most of the station contact time will be focused on preps for the injection burn.

Ten minutes after Tananarive loss of signal, the spacecraft makes its first contact with the station at Carnarvon, Australia. "APOLLO ELEVEN, this is HOUSTON through Carnarvon. Over."

"HOUSTON, APOLLO ELEVEN. Loud and clear. Over."

"Roger, ELEVEN. We're reading you the same. Both the booster and the spacecraft are looking good to us. Over."

"HOUSTON, APOLLO ELEVEN. Would you like to copy the alignment results?"

"That's affirmative."

"OK. NOUN seventy-one: we used thirty and thirty-seven, four balls one; NOUN ninety-three: plus zero zero zero one six, plus zero zero zero three three, plus zero zero one five two; GET zero zero, four eight, fifteen; check star three four. Over."

The spacecraft guidance and navigation system is aligned on the pad prior to liftoff. Inevitably errors creep in during flight requiring a realignment before the translunar injection burn. The ground controllers recommend that the realignment be done during the first night pass. Using the spacecraft sextant and a computer program called P52, the Command Module pilot aligns the inertial measuring unit platform using two stars, numbers thirty and thirty-seven in the star catalog they carry onboard, one in the constellation Sagittarius and the other in Centaurus. That process is now complete. The required corrections are minimal positive values. The crew is one step closer to the Moon.

"APOLLO ELEVEN, this is HOUSTON. One minute to LOS Carnarvon; AOS at Honeysuckle fifty-nine, thirty-three. Over."

"APOLLO ELEVEN. Roger."

"Roger. And we request you turn up S-band volume for the Honeysuckle pass."

Up to this point the spacecraft's short-range very high frequency radio has been the primary voice communications link. At lunar distances, the S-band communications system has to be used. The station at Honeysuckle Creek is one of the three eighty-five-foot antenna sites that will maintain S-band communications with Apollo. This pass will provide the first in-flight check on a critical air-to-ground link.

"APOLLO ELEVEN, APOLLO ELEVEN, this is HOUSTON on S-band. Radio check. Over."

"Roger, HOUSTON. APOLLO ELEVEN reads you loud and clear."

"This is HOUSTON. Roger. Reading you the same. Out."

"APOLLO ELEVEN, this is HOUSTON. A little over one minute to LOS at Honeysuckle. You'll be AOS at Goldstone at one, twenty-nine, zero two; LOS at Goldstone one, thirty-three, fifty-five. Over."

"Roger, Bruce. Thank you. We expect TV. We've got it all hooked up. We have not yet turned it on. We're ready to do that now."

"Roger. We copy. We'll be configured and waiting for whatever you want to send down."

I glance to my right. George's eyes show the tense frustration you might expect from a man who has already decided that, in spite of his best efforts, the thing we are about to do is not going to work.

"GUAYMAS has AOS IU."

"GYM is GO for command IU."

Beginning at Guaymas acquisition-of-signal, we will have thirty minutes of continuous contact as the spacecraft races through the sky over Mexico, the southern United States, and the Atlantic Ocean. The first test of the spacecraft television system will consume the initial five minutes of the pass. The test conditions are nowhere near ideal. It kind of makes you wonder why they chose to do it now. As the spacecraft approaches the west coast of North America, the stations at Guaymas, Mexico, and Goldstone, California, have overlapping coverage. The spacecraft ground track passes to the south of Guaymas, giving that station the longer viewing period of the two. Guaymas does not have television-processing equipment. It is tracking the Saturn instrumentation unit with its S-band antenna and maintaining very high frequency voice communications with the crew. Goldstone, the station that can process the television, will be looking far to the south into Mexico from the Mojave Desert of California. The spacecraft will be low on the horizon. Its signals will be liable to interruption by elevated terrain. In these marginal conditions, Goldstone has to lock on to the frequency modulated S-band television downlink from the command module.

"APOLLO ELEVEN, this is HOUSTON through Guaymas. Over."

"Roger, HOUSTON. Reading you loud and clear."

"Roger. Reading you the same. Coming up on AOS Goldstone."

"Roger."

"Cecil B. deAldrin is standing by for instructions."

"APOLLO ELEVEN, this is HOUSTON. We are not receiving your FM downlink yet. We are standing by."

"HOUSTON TV, GOLDSTONE. We have the FM carrier—no TV modulation."

"FLIGHT, NETWORK, Goldstone has the FM carrier but doesn't see a TV signal."

"APOLLO ELEVEN, this is HOUSTON. We are receiving your FM downlink now. We are standing by for TV modulations on the signal."

"APOLLO ELEVEN, APOLLO ELEVEN, this is HOUSTON. Radio check. Over."

"HOUSTON COMM TECH, GODDARD VOICE. You are receiving Goldstone air-to-ground."

The crew commander responds to McCandless's communication check and confirms that they are transmitting a television signal on the frequency modulated downlink. "Roger. Loud and clear. We think we are transmitting to you."

"OK. We are not receiving it yet, ELEVEN, although we have confirmed presence of your FM downlink carrier."

"Which switches do you want us to confirm?"

"Stand by."

"TEXAS has AOS CSM."

"TEXAS is GO for command, CSM."

"GOLDSTONE has LOS both carriers."

Cecil B. deAldrin's television directing debut is going to have to wait for a future pass. The crew and the flight control team will devote the remaining twenty-five minutes of this pass to critical translunar injection preparations. The agenda is crowded. The flight controllers prepare and McCandless reads up to the crew the data needed for three maneuvers. One of these is the nominal translunar injection burn. The other two are emergency maneuvers to be executed in the event that the mission has to be aborted after the translunar burn. When the nominal burn is completed, the Command and Service Module will separate from the Saturn S-IVB, turn around, dock with the Lunar Module, and extract it from the Spacecraft Launch Adapter. In preparation for this sequence of operations, the crew extends the Command Module docking probe. They also run a hot-fire check of the small rocket motors mounted on the Service Module that will control the Command and Service Module during this "transposition and docking maneuver."

By the time the spacecraft passes over the horizon at the Canary Island station, these tasks are done and the crew puts their helmets and gloves back on in anticipation of a final GO for the lunar adventure. The Canary pass is a long one—close to eight minutes. Prior to acquisition, the communications controller reports that the wizards at Goddard and the COMSAT Corporation have fixed our problem by increasing the power on the signal between Canary and the satellite. We are skeptical. We are still painfully aware of the troubles we had on the first Canary pass. The communications guys are right—all circuits perform as advertised.

In the background, the investigation of the television test goes on. Ill-advised or not, the test had failed. We have to understand the reason. Although it is a major public relations tool, television is in no way essential to the landing mission. The inquest is conducted on a noninterference basis. The crew reports that the switches onboard are in the correct positions for television transmission. The Merritt Island tracking station reports receiving about a minute of usable television signal near the end of the stateside pass. INCO, the controller responsible for the spacecraft side of the process, immediately, and with some enthusiasm, points out that "you Network guys have some kind of problem at Goldstone." That turns out to be the case. The problem is a faulty cable. The idea that the shortness of the station contact precluded attempts to find and fix the problem is a feeble defense. It's the only one we have.

Our next contact is through Tananarive. The air-to-ground connection is raggedy ass. But the crew is able to confirm that they have armed the pyrotechnic devices that will have to operate during the upcoming mission sequences. In the quiet between Tananarive and the next contact at Carnarvon, the flight director asks for a GO/NO-GO for the upcoming burn. Everyone is ready.

"APOLLO ELEVEN, this is HOUSTON through Carnarvon. Radio check. Over."

"Roger, HOUSTON through Carnarvon. APOLLO ELEVEN. Loud and clear."

"Roger. You're coming in very loud and very clear, here. Out."

"APOLLO ELEVEN, this is HOUSTON. You are GO for TLI. Over."

"APOLLO ELEVEN. Thank you."

"Roger. We'll be coming within range of the ARIA aircraft coverage, here, in about one minute. They're going to try un-linking both on S-band and on VHF this time. So if you turn your—make sure your S-band volume is turned up, we'd appreciate it. And we believe that we'll have continuous coverage from now on through the TLI burn. Over."

To provide coverage of the translunar injection maneuver, NASA deploys aircraft and ships into the vast empty space between Australia and Hawaii. Two Apollo Range Instrumentation Aircraft, ARIA FOUR and ARIA THREE, fill coverage gaps between Australia and the tracking ships during the translunar injection. They provide real-time voice communication between the crew and the Mission Control Center at Houston, and record telemetry data from the spacecraft for later playback.

"APOLLO ELEVEN, APOLLO ELEVEN, this is HOUSTON through ARIA FOUR. Radio check. Over."

"HOUSTON, we read you strength four and a little scratchy."

"Roger. We're reading you strength five, readability about three. Should be quite adequate."

"APOLLO ELEVEN, APOLLO ELEVEN, this is HOUSTON. We're reading you readability about three, strength five. Sounds pretty good. Over."

"Roger. We've got a little static in the background now."

Two tracking ships, *Redstone* and *Mercury*, are stationed northeast of Australia between the Solomon Islands and Hawaii. The translunar injection burn will begin during the *Redstone* pass.

Shutdown will occur over *Mercury*. There is some overlap in their coverage. There are no backup stations.

"RTC, MERCURY, Net Two."

"Go ahead."

"MERCURY is unable to command either vehicle—command computer tape unit failure. We are troubleshooting it now."

"Roger, MERCURY. Do you have an estimate?"

RTC, MERCURY, about five minutes."

"NETWORK, RTC, did you copy? If his estimate is good, he should be back on line prior to the scheduled hand over from REDSTONE."

George responds, "We copy, RTC. Keep us posted."

"APOLLO ELEVEN, this is HOUSTON through ARIA THREE. Radio check. Over."

"Roger, HOUSTON, APOLLO ELEVEN. You are much clearer and adequately loud. Over."

"Roger, ELEVEN, You are coming in five-by-five here. Beautiful signal."

"This is a lot better than the static we had previously."

"OK."

"And we got the time base six indication on time."

The Instrumentation Unit computer on the third stage will control the upcoming S-IVB engine burn. The crew has seen the signal indicating that it is beginning its restart preparations.

"This is HOUSTON. Roger. Out."

"RTC, MERCURY. We replaced a card in the tape unit. It is operational but we have been unable to connect to the computer using our computer recovery software. We are still RED cannot support for vehicle commands."

We need that computer. *Redstone* is about to acquire the spacecraft signal. The ship will see the spacecraft for about eight crucial minutes. The flight controllers will monitor the ignition sequence and the first few minutes of the five-minute-and-forty-seven-second burn. *Redstone* will then hand the spacecraft over to *Mercury* for the balance of the burn and engine shutdown. The spacecraft velocity at ignition will be 25,560 feet per second. The maneuver will add almost 10,500 feet per second to the spacecraft velocity

"REDSTONE has AOS CSM, IU."

"REDSTONE is GO for command, CSM, and IU."

"NETWORK, RTC. We think they might solve the problem if they reload the command computer program from the system tape."

"RTC, NETWORK. Are they going to have time to do that?"

"Roger. It should be doable. There's not much to lose. The thing is useless as it is."

"Roger that, RTC. Go for it."

"APOLLO ELEVEN, this is HOUSTON. We just got telemetry back down on your booster, and it is looking good."

"MERCURY, RTC. Reload the command computer and report your status."

"RTC, MERCURY, will do."

The ARIA aircraft had provided voice contact, but no telemetry. The *Redstone* telemetry is critical to the assessment of the spacecraft's readiness for the planned maneuver.

"Roger. Everything looks good here."

"HOUSTON, Roger. Out."

While we sweat out the *Mercury* computer loading, George and I take a final look at our translunar injection contingency procedures. There are two cases—no burn and partial burn. If the third-stage engine doesn't restart, the Houston mission computers will use the existing circular orbit parameters to transmit acquisition messages telling the ground stations where to point their antennas. The messages are supposed to be available prior to acquisition of signal at the Guaymas, Mexico, station. Our main task will be to come up with times for station handovers on the Pacific and Atlantic communication satellites. Those will be minor considerations compared to figuring out what went wrong and how, if at all possible, to recover and save the mission.

The partial-burn case is a little more complicated. RETRO is going to need all of the help he can get as he attempts to save the crew and the mission. Reliable communications will be critical.

To keep the process running smoothly, we will need to adjust the message acceptance pulse waiting period according to the apogee predicted as a result of the partial burn. The ground system is designed to transmit a message and wait for a signal from the spacecraft that the message has been received. If there is no acceptance pulse, the system retransmits the original message. For a normal translunar burn, the system automatically adjusts the wait period depending on the distance from Earth. In the partial-burn case, we send a message directing manual adjustment of the wait period based on expected apogee or maximum distance from Earth in the unplanned orbit. So, for example, we will use a two-second wait for distances between 50,000 and 120,000 miles, and a period of 2.8 seconds for an apogee beyond 120,000 miles.

"APOLLO ELEVEN, this is HOUSTON. Slightly less than one minute to ignition, and everything is GO."

Sixty seconds later the crew confirms, "Ignition."

The flight plan calls for ignition at a ground elapsed time of two hours, forty-four minutes, twenty-six seconds. The S-IVB engine starts at two hours, forty-four minutes, nineteen seconds—close enough for government work.

"FLIGHT, BOOSTER, we have ignition on time. Everything looks good."

McCandless repeats that report to the crew, "We confirm ignition, and the thrust is GO."

Charlesworth runs a status check.

"CAPCOM, we are GO at one minute."

"APOLLO ELEVEN, this is HOUSTON at one minute. Trajectory and guidance look good, and the stage is good. Over."

"APOLLO ELEVEN, roger."

The spacecraft velocity has increased to 27,000 feet per second.

"MERCURY has AOS, CSM and IU."

"MERCURY, RTC—command computer status?"

"Reload still in work."

There's no time for consultation now—Spears does his job. *Redstone* has a functioning command computer. We will stay with them as long as we can.

"REDSTONE, RTC, hold the carrier. Stand by to hand over to MERCURY at my direction."

"REDSTONE, roger."

"MERCURY copies."

McCandless's updates continue to go to the spacecraft through Redstone. "APOLLO ELEVEN, this is HOUSTON. Thrust is good. Everything's still looking good."

The S-IVB engine has pushed the velocity past 29,000 feet per second.

"RTC, MERCURY, our command computer is online."

"REDSTONE, MERCURY, RTC, hand over on my mark. Three, two, one, mark."

Silent seconds pass.

"MERCURY is GO for command, CSM and IU."

Just in time—"REDSTONE has LOS both vehicles."

"APOLLO ELEVEN, this is HOUSTON. Around three and a half minutes. You're still looking good. Your predicted cutoff is right on the nominal."

"Roger. APOLLO ELEVEN is GO."

With one minute left in the burn, the spacecraft has accelerated to a velocity of 33,000 feet per second. Faster than a speeding bullet? Yeah, you bet—more than ten times faster.

"HAWAII has AOS, CSM, IU."

"APOLLO ELEVEN, this is HOUSTON. You are GO at five minutes."

"Roger. We're GO."

Don Webb comes up on Net Two. "MERCURY, TRACK. Your S-band high-speed tracking data is not flagged two-way and we aren't seeing any C-band track."

"TRACK, MERCURY, we are seeing S-band dropouts. It may be the effects of the rocket exhaust plume. We have not acquired with the C-Band radar—cause unknown."

"NETWORK, TRACK. We need to hand over to Hawaii and get some valid high-speed tracking data."

George responds, "RTC, TIC, any problem?"

"Negative, RTC."

"Negative, TIC."

I am on the flight director loop. "FLIGHT, NETWORK, we have a problem with *Mercury* tracking data. We recommend an early handover to Hawaii."

Charlesworth queries his team—there are no objections.

"RTC, NETWORK."

"I copy, NETWORK."

"MERCURY, HAWAII, stand by to hand over the carrier on my mark."

"MERCURY, roger."

"HAWAII, roger."

"Hand over on my mark—three, two, one, mark."

Endless seconds later, "HAWAII is GO for command both vehicles."

The handover is complete. We have solid tracking data.

"APOLLO ELEVEN, this is HOUSTON. We show cutoff and we copy the numbers in NOUN Sixty-two."

There are fifteen or twenty seconds of silence. Does Hawaii have an air-to-ground system problem? If they do we are out of tracking stations—the next one is in California.

"APOLLO ELEVEN, HOUSTON. Do you read?"

"Roger, HOUSTON. APOLLO ELEVEN. We're reading a VI of 35579 and the EMS was plus 3.3. Over."

"Roger. Plus 3.3 on the EMS. And we copy the VI."

The spacecraft is headed to the Moon at a velocity 35,579 feet per second.

"Hey, HOUSTON, APOLLO ELEVEN. That Saturn gave us a magnificent ride."

"Roger, ELEVEN. We'll pass that on. And, it certainly looks like you are well on your way now."

The burn is nominal. We announce the successful burn to the network. The tracking stations adjust their communications procedures to compensate for the steadily increasing distance between Earth and spacecraft. The Command and Service Module separates from the Saturn upper stage, docks nose-to-nose with the Lunar Module, and pulls the landing craft free of the Saturn. Ground controllers reignite the S-IVB engine and send it into solar orbit.

The idea that the *Apollo 11* crew is now "safely" on its way to the Moon changes the mood in the control room. My historian urges me to look up across the rows of consoles and make mental notes for posterity. When I do, I see flight controllers who had been fixed in their chairs with their eyes locked on their console displays standing now in casual attitudes. Some chat with their neighbors. Some exchange pleasantries with their White Team relief, now beginning to show up for the upcoming shift change. Most have smiles on their face. I hear phrases like "no problem," "piece of cake," and "just like the simulations."

As I make my notes for the historian, my other alter ego whispers in my ear with a slightly mocking tone, "No problem? Piece of cake?"

I could have done without the questions. My mood is more ambivalent, more complicated. I come up short when it comes to steely-eyed competence. This thing is not just like the simulations. Simulated ground system anomalies are few and far between. Mostly they mean that the simulation system has screwed up and the simulation guys have invented a ground failure to cover their tracks. There are good reasons for that. The simulations have to focus on the sharpening the guys at the pointy end of this tool, the guys who make life or death calls. The real stuff I saw for the first time today reinforces the notion that we are dealing with enormous complexity, mechanical and human. Even when you think you have the machines in order, the people can still do you in—the Canary air-to-ground fiasco is living proof of that.

In the face of today's realities it's clear that when it comes to this machine, my knowledge and experience might just come up short at some critical juncture. I know, I know, I have a team to help me and they mostly handled today's anomalies. But this is irrational, existential stuff for me. I have always been a control freak. Knowledge has been my instrument of control. If you can't control, you can't succeed. And if you fail, then in some sense, you cease to be. As the spacecraft goes ever farther into the celestial darkness, I hover over a black void of my own creation—the legacy of my desperate efforts to make a connection as I grew up in a family where no connection could be made.

And now, whatever the state of my realizations, there is no choice but to go on. There is no time for doubt. There are no time-outs. In "macho land" you don't even get to talk about stuff like this. Anyway, I signed up to do this job, and perilous or not, it is one hell of an adventure. I can only hope that the technology gods are watching and listening. I need them to see that there is no hubris here, not a shred, not a trace. I need them to look with favor on this thing we are trying to do. The ancient gods looked after blacksmiths, farmers, and even thieves. Do you suppose there's a god who looks out for the guys who maintain the plumbing? We'll find out.

CHAPTER TWENTY-ONE

The Command and Service Module and the Lunar Module, joined nose-to-nose to make a single ungainly spacecraft, coast upward toward their distant rendezvous with the Moon. The journey from Earth orbit to lunar orbit will take seventy-six hours. As the spacecraft moves away from the Earth, the eighty-five-foot S-band antenna stations located on three continents, at Madrid (Spain), Goldstone (California), and Honeysuckle Creek (Australia), take over responsibility for communications and tracking. During the Earth orbit phase the west-to-east velocity of the speeding spacecraft overtakes the rotation of the Earth in the same direction so that handovers from ground station to ground station happen from west to east, from Honeysuckle to Goldstone to Madrid. Soon after the translunar injection burn, though, the spacecraft climbs nearly straight up toward the constellation Virgo while the Earth spins west to east behind it. The handovers are now in the other direction—Madrid to Goldstone to Honeysuckle. It takes some getting used to.

The station view periods increase as the spacecraft gets farther away, expanding from a few hours just after translunar injection to ten hours of continuous contact. The stations watch the spacecraft's long coast up out of Mr. Newton's gravity well. At the end of the translunar injection burn, the spacecraft is 180 nautical miles above the Earth, traveling outbound at more than 35,000 feet per second. Three hours later, as we hand over the control room to Gene Kranz's White Team, *Apollo 11* is an astonishing 28,000 nautical miles from Earth traveling at a much diminished velocity of 11,500 feet per second with a flight-path angle only twenty-two degrees from vertical.

The White Team's first priority is to look at the spacecraft trajectory and evaluate the need for the first of four midcourse corrections to the spacecraft's trajectory. The flight plan calls for the crew to execute the first midcourse correction nine hours after the translunar injection burn. They are to make a second correction twenty-four hours after the translunar burn. At twenty-five and twenty-two hours prior to the spacecraft's entry into lunar orbit, the plan calls for two other corrections. Depending on the size of the correction, the thrusters on the side of the Service Module or the main Service Propulsion System engine would be fired to compensate for any accumulated errors and put the spacecraft on the optimum path to the Moon.

Within thirty minutes of shift change, the White Team FIDO concludes that the current trajectory is very close to nominal—close enough for government work. Midcourse correction number one is not required. The crew settles down into what will become a housekeeping routine. They realign the guidance system to remove any errors that may have accumulated since the initial post-launch alignment. Their next priority is to be sure that their microworld—their encapsulated environment—continues to be habitable. They change out the lithium hydroxide canisters that remove carbon dioxide from the cabin, purge fuel cells to remove contaminants, and charge batteries. The decision to delete midcourse correction number one also allows time for another attempt to test the television link with the Goldstone tracking station. This time the ground station is properly configured. Goldstone records ten minutes of good quality television highlighted by a view of a seven-eighths Earth, fifty thousand miles distant, receding into the void.

When the television transmission is over, the crew gets a two-hour head start on their first rest cycle. Earlier, Charlie Duke, the capsule communicator, had read up a set of angles that the crew will use to put the spacecraft into the proper attitude for passive thermal control. In the vacuum of space, a vehicle kept at a constant attitude would be exposed to the extreme heat of the Sun on one surface and heat-shield-cracking cold on the other. To prevent catastrophic temperature differentials, the NASA engineers developed what they commonly refer to as the "barbecue mode." During sleep periods, or any other period when onboard activities do not constrain the spacecraft to a particular attitude or orientation in space, the crew positions the joined spacecraft so that their long axis is perpendicular to the rays of the Sun. They then set up a computer-controlled rotation around that axis at a rate of three revolutions every hour. The rotation distributes the solar heat and prevents damage to systems or surfaces. Eleven hours after launch, the spacecraft is in the barbecue mode. Twenty minutes later, Charlie Duke advises the crew that they are "cleared for some z's." The spacecraft is 55,522 nautical miles from Earth, traveling at a velocity of 7,920 feet per second.

Back on Earth, the station at Honeysuckle Creek is ready to take over the night watch from Goldstone. The station is located on a radio-quiet fourteen-acre site in the Namadgi National Park, twenty miles southwest of Canberra, Australia's capital city. The Jet Propulsion Laboratory's Deep Space Network station is located at Tidbinbilla, about twelve miles to the north. Each station is equipped with an antenna eighty-five feet in diameter that can track the Apollo spacecraft at lunar distance. The large antenna and the high frequency used by the system produce a narrow radio beam less than one-half degree wide. Each station has dual systems that allow it to communicate with both the Command Module and the Lunar Module if they are within the same beam width. If they are separated, the co-location of the two stations allows one station to track the Command and Service Module in lunar orbit while the other covers the Lunar Module. The Honeysuckle station was built by the Australian government in just eleven months between February 1965 and December 1966. Most of the NASA tracking stations around the world are operated and maintained by American contractors. The Australian Commonwealth Department of Supply operates Honeysuckle with an all-Australian crew. The Australians are good at what they do. They are proud of their role in Apollo.

Four hours earlier, Hawaii had handed over the spacecraft to Goldstone. The thought of the name Goldstone brings a knowing smile to the face of the historian in me. The station is located in the heart of California's high desert at the south end of Goldstone Dry Lake. Three great explorers of the American West—Jedediah Smith, John C. Fremont, and Kit Carson—passed this way along the Mojave Trail on their way to the Pacific coast. Three more explorers are passing by now. They have the same burning ambition to know what lies over the next mountain. They are headed for a far different destination.

At handover, Goldstone establishes two-way lock with the onboard communications system. Their uplink carrier captures the spacecraft receiver. The spacecraft then increases the ground station frequency by a known ratio and transmits that signal back to the ground station. The ground receivers lock up on the spacecraft signal. With the two-way link established, Goldstone can uplink a range code, spacecraft commands, and voice. The spacecraft retransmits the range code and adds vehicle telemetry and voice to its signal. This Goldstone-spacecraft dalliance is a short-term affair. The rotation of the Earth will inexorably drive the spacecraft lower and lower in the western sky until it finally disappears below the radio horizon. Before that happens Goldstone must transfer control of the spacecraft to Honeysuckle without interrupting telemetry or voice communication.

The first step in that process is to find the spacecraft as soon as it appears above Honeysuckle's horizon. A warning buzzer sounds, a yellow light begins to flash, electric motors whine, and the great antenna begins to move. A wallaby looks up and then goes back to his meal. He has seen all of this many times before. Using a predicted flight profile, the station's antenna programmer aims the center of the dish at the point on the surrounding hills where the spacecraft is expected to appear. A small acquisition antenna with a ten-degree beam width is mounted at the center of the large antenna. It will be the first to see the spacecraft. When it does, it will use the spacecraft signal to develop a sum and difference pattern. That pattern gives the antenna pointing error. The system servos drive the large antenna to nullify the error and put its main beam directly on the target. After the antenna main receiver locks up on the signal, the antenna continues to automatically track the target.

Honeysuckle completes spacecraft acquisition about an hour and a half before the planned handover from Goldstone. As the antenna follows the spacecraft, the station's tracking data processor records the antenna's pointing angles. The processor also records the difference between the nominal spacecraft radio frequency and the frequency actually received. The difference between the two gives an indication of the spacecraft radial velocity relative to the tracking station. The station transmits both of these measurements via teletype to the real-time computer complex in Houston. The mission trajectory program, running on an IBM 360/75 computer, combines angle, range, and range rate data from Goldstone, the station that has two-way lock with the spacecraft, with angle and velocity information from the other so-called three-way tracking sites—Hawaii and Guam—to compute the spacecraft's position, velocity, and direction of travel. The computed values will be precise. At lunar distance, more than two hundred thousand nautical miles, the expected errors in spacecraft position and velocity are on the order of ± 1600 feet and ±10 inches per second—not bad for government work.

At twelve hours after liftoff, the planned handover time, a radiation hazard warning sounds. The operator at Honeysuckle turns on the uplink carrier at full power. The spacecraft transponder now sees two uplink signals with slightly different frequencies. The two signals interfere, alternately reinforcing or canceling each other. This interference produces a series of "beats" whose frequency is equal to the difference between the two original signals. Both stations, Goldstone and Honeysuckle, immediately hear the audible beat frequency on the spacecraft downlink. Using the beat frequency as his guide, the Honeysuckle operator slowly changes his uplink frequency until the beat is gone. At that point the two uplinks are at exactly the same frequency. The Goldstone operator shuts down his carrier. The radio frequency duet is over. The Honeysuckle operator adds modulation to the uplink signal. Flight controllers in Houston now see spacecraft tracking and telemetry data. Planet Earth is ready to watch over its sleeping children for the next nine hours until the inevitable handover to Madrid. John Saxon, the Honeysuckle operations manager, makes a brief note in the station log: "H/O GDS→HSK. A/G remote. Status sent. Very smooth H/O."

At fourteen hours ground elapsed time, Glynn Lunney's Black Team relieves the White Team. The four flight control teams will continue to change shifts every eight hours—more or less. Some shifts will be as long as twelve hours and some as short as two hours as each team maneuvers to be on console to support the mission events they trained for. Charlesworth's Green Team supported the launch from the Cape and will support the lunar surface extravehicular activity—the Moon walk. The White Team needs to be on duty for the lunar landing. The Black Team needs to be in place to support the launch from the lunar surface. Our schedule shuffle situation is even more complicated. We started out with the Green Team and now have to get in sync with the Black Team in time to support the lunar launch. At this point, Ernie Randall and his partner, Larry Meyer, are still the network controllers with Black Team. They will rearrange their schedule to make room for us on the

Black Team while they migrate to the White Team to support the Moon walk.

During this schedule shuffling process, the time between successive shifts can vary from as little as eight hours to as much as twenty-four hours or more. Even when you are off duty your head is still in the control room. That makes the longer breaks harder to do than the short ones. They just extend the time between doses of an addictive drug. Home is a place where you try to get some sleep. Walter Cronkite and his cohorts continuously screw up the process. It's way too difficult to turn off the TV and put the head on the pillow. The transit time to and from the control center is car radio time. When I leave the house after dark, headed for a night shift, I look up at the thin sliver of the waxing Moon and try for some profound thoughts. I'm not so good at profound stuff, so I get clichés—clichés that always include an element of wonder at what they are doing up there and what I am trying to do down here.

With the crew asleep, things go quiet in the control room. The VIP viewing room is empty. To maintain communications as the spacecraft rolls around its long axis, INCO sends a command every twenty minutes or so to switch from one spacecraft antenna to another. The flight controllers monitor the spacecraft's trajectory and systems telemetry. Any hint of an off-nominal measurement becomes the subject of intense discussion with backroom system experts. They will gnaw at the off-nominal bone until they are satisfied that they understand it and have recommended any required response. The network controllers and their team wait for and watch each planned antenna switch, anxious to prevent an interruption in data or any other circumstance that might interrupt the crew's rest.

Two hours after shift change, the primary and alternate data circuits that connect Houston to Goddard begin to experience intermittent dropouts. Microwave fades near Greenbelt, Maryland, and a radio unit failure in Jasper, Alabama, are the culprits. The flight controllers don't give a rat's ass about Greenbelt or Jasper. They want their data. Randall and his team work the problem for just over two hours before things stabilize. The crew is still asleep. The impact of the dropouts is minimal—this time.

The Madrid tracking station takes over from Honeysuckle at twenty-one hours mission elapsed time. It will have two-way lock for the next seven and a half hours, supported by its sister station at Robledo and the island stations on Ascension and Antigua. The Madrid station is located in an arid, radio-quiet valley at a place called Fresnedillas, about thirty miles west of Madrid proper. I sometimes imagine Don Quixote and his faithful Sancho coming over one of the surrounding hills and seeing that giant Erector Set of an antenna squatting there below them. I don't know how you say "What the fuck?" in Spanish, but I expect that would be the first reaction.

Two hours after the handover to Madrid, Green Team CAPCOM Bruce McCandless makes a wake-up call to the crew and gives them a morning news summary with their breakfast. He reports that the radio telescope at Jodrell Bank in England that has been tracking Luna Fifteen, a Soviet unmanned Moon shot, has lost contact. The Soviet spacecraft has disappeared behind the Moon. Vice President Spiro Agnew has proposed putting a man on Mars by the end of the century. Immigration officials in Nuevo Laredo, Mexico, announced Wednesday that hippies will be refused tourists cards to enter Mexico unless they take a bath and get a haircut. President Richard Nixon declares a holiday for federal employees next Monday so they can witness the lunar landing. The British House of Lords received assurances that American submarines would not harm the Loch Ness monster.

After breakfast, the crew works at more housekeeping chores. They struggle with poor star visibility to make the navigation updates required for an upcoming midcourse correction burn. Twenty-five hours after launch, the spacecraft reaches the halfway point of its outward coast. It is 104,350 miles from both the Earth and the Moon. An hour and forty-five minutes later, the crew ignites the Service Propulsion System engine for 2.91 seconds. The midcourse correction changes their velocity by 20.9

feet per second and lowers their point of closest approach to the Moon from 175 to 60 nautical miles.

The ground systems function well enough in support of the course correction. Trouble, in the form of more wideband data line dropouts on the primary circuit between Houston and Goddard, shows up an hour and a half after the maneuver. There is no backup line available so there are some uncomfortable periods without a Goddard connection. After hours of troubleshooting, the problem is traced to the primary line modem in Houston—a device that encodes and decodes signals for transmission on the wideband circuit. A backup modem is put into the circuit while the primary unit is repaired. No harm, no foul—this time.

The Madrid tracking station hands the spacecraft over to Goldstone. The crew enjoys a lunch of salmon salad. In the control room a clock begins to display the time until the first lunar landing. At twenty-nine and a half hours after launch, it shows seventy-three hours, twenty-six minutes, and thirty seconds. This thing is beginning to look like it might happen.

Gene Kranz and his White Team relieve the Green Team. *Apollo 11* is 121,158 nautical miles from Earth, traveling at a speed of 4,613 feet per second. The flight crew turns on their television camera to test their onboard equipment in anticipation of a broadcast scheduled for later in the day. They run in place and send the picture down to Goldstone. The television circuit between Houston and Goldstone hasn't been called up, so no one in the control room can see what is going on. The Goldstone operations supervisor describes the video quality. Everything checks out OK.

As the spacecraft slowly passes from east to west across North America, the crew fills the time by providing a space-based weather report. There is a frontal system building three hundred miles north of Cuba. It has just rained at the Cape. There are thunderstorms around Houston. Except for a few clouds north of Bakersfield, California has clear skies. Using one of the spacecraft telescopes, Buzz Aldrin picks out a jet fighter taxiing along the runway at Edwards Air Force Base.

The planned television broadcast begins at thirty-three hours and fifty-nine minutes and goes on for thirty-six minutes. A worldwide audience sees the view from the spacecraft window—a ghostly half-Earth, 130,000 miles distant, floating in the cosmic darkness. They are treated to a visual tour of the spacecraft interior—the onboard computer display, sleeping arrangements, and a pantry with bacon bites, fruit juice, and chicken stew, oh my! When the broadcast finishes, the crew cleans up a few more household chores, and tries without success to see a laser being beamed into space from west Texas. Finally at thirty-six hours after launch, the CAPCOM tucks the crew in for their second sleep period in space. *Apollo 11* is 137,219 nautical miles from Earth, traveling at a speed of 4,132 feet per second.

The Black Team shift begins about two hours into the crew's rest cycle. Gerry Griffin is sitting in for Flight Director Glynn Lunney. George and I have rejiggered our sleep-work cycle to be more or less present here tonight with the Black Team. The changeover briefing we get from George Ojalehto and Doug Wilson, the White team network controllers, widens our sleepy eyes. Halfway through their watch, the mission operations computer experienced a problem in updating the flight controller's console television displays. The problem caused the loss of all real-time television displays of spacecraft status for approximately one hour and fifteen minutes. The problem was eventually isolated to a bad card in the 2701 line adapter, a device that acts as an interface between the mission operations computer and the display equipment.

This is scary as hell! If this had happened at a critical mission decision point, the upcoming mission phase might have been aborted. The abort would not have been for want of an electronics card costing a few hundred dollars. We have replacement parts. It would have been the direct result of having different contractors, IBM and Philco-Ford, on the two sides of the display interface. Neither would admit a fault—both pointed their fingers across the interface and said, "It's their problem—not ours!"[5]

George and I digest this tale of near-catastrophe and try to settle in for the remainder of this night watch. The public affairs officer makes the oxymoronic observation that, "Here in Mission Control, things have settled down into a rather quiet nighttime routine." Say what? A routine coast to the Moon? Certainly the mood is different than it was during launch and translunar injection. But "routine" is too simple a descriptor. I know, and everyone else knows, that the Moon is coming at us at more than four thousand feet a second. I think about what we might do, beyond all that we have already done, to be ready. This is not routine. It

---

[5] The display problem is scary enough that shortly after the end of the *Apollo 11* mission the director of flight operations, Chris Kraft, puts out the word that potentially mission-ending control center failures will never happen again. For reasons that I do not understand, that prohibition comes to rest squarely on my desk. My bosses tell me I can have whatever resources I need. That's the good news. The bad news is that whatever solution we dream up has to be in place before *Apollo 12* flies in November. I reach out to the "good guys" I came to know during my stint in the operations scheduling office. I recruit representatives from each of the major control center contractors—people from IBM, Philco-Ford, and UNIVAC. We decide that the biggest threat comes from failures like the last one—failures that occur at the interface between equipment supplied by different contractors. That's where territorial instinct poses the greatest danger. These guys are good. We build a list of these critical connection points. Now what? John Baker, the lead UNIVAC guy, suggests the solution. We set out to develop a set of agreed-upon procedures for troubleshooting problems at the critical interfaces. Each procedure is a set of information-gathering and decision steps designed to isolate the problem. If these logic flow diagrams point to a culprit, then all will have agreed that we have in fact found the culprit—regardless of which side of the interface it happens to be on. The procedures replace finger-pointing with structured communication. But building them is not enough. The people who operate the equipment—the guys likely to be on duty when stuff happens—have to understand these new communication protocols. We put them on paper and organize a series of training sessions. The trainees are busy getting ready for the next mission. They cannot come to us. We go to them—talking to people on midnight and swings—whenever we can collect some of them in one place for an hour or two. We get the job done. There are no more major unresolved control center problems. Serendipity? Maybe, but we are happy to take the credit.

is simply a lull in the fighting. The shift change briefing I have just heard does not improve my outlook.

As we try to settle in for this shift *Apollo 11* is 150,000 miles, more or less, above the western Pacific. Honeysuckle Creek is prime, maintaining two-way lock with the spacecraft. The Tidbinbilla station and the stations at Carnarvon and Guam are providing three-way tracking data. A couple of hours into our shift, the Carnarvon operations supervisor reports that he has an amplifier in the antenna main tracking circuit that is "red can support." The device increases the strength of the minimal signal received from the spacecraft to the level needed to operate the station antenna's automatic tracking function. This one has become unstable. It is providing only about half of the normal signal strength increase. The antenna continues to track, along a ragged edge where the angle information it provides is in constant danger of dropping out.

Two hours later we have a more serious incident at the Tidbinbilla site. In addition to providing three-way tracking support, Tidbinbilla is our backup site. It's assigned to take over two-way lock from Honeysuckle in the event of a failure at that station. A short circuit has caused a fire that destroys one of the station's transmitter power supplies and damaged the other. There are no injuries, but the station can no longer send a signal to the spacecraft. We are left without an eighty-five-foot backup antenna until the spacecraft comes over Madrid's horizon almost two hours later.[6]

---

6   The fire does extensive damage. The Tidbinbilla team, with support from Honeysuckle, makes a heroic effort to rebuild the damaged systems. The systems are operational within twelve hours. Some components are rebuilt from scratch using whatever parts are available. They work. But they are what the engineers call a "kluge." No one knows how reliable they might be. Under existing plans, Tidbinbilla is to be the prime station to support lunar extravehicular activity, including reception of critical biomedical telemetry from Armstrong's and Aldrin's Portable Life Support System backpacks. Project managers at Goddard and Houston decide not to trust the crew members to the jury-rigged equipment. Honeysuckle inherits the lunar surface assignment. Tidbinbilla will support the orbiting Command and Service Module.

When the Green Team shows up to relieve us, we are more than happy to give up our seats. We go away, but the tracking station blues keep playing. The Deep Space Network station at Robledo, about five miles from the Manned Space Flight Network station at Madrid, has two-way lock with the spacecraft. The Madrid station and the stations at Ascension Island and the Canary Islands are three-way.

The air temperature in the pine-studded hills surrounding Robledo is 105 degrees Fahrenheit. Two hours after the station establishes two-way lock with the spacecraft, the main circuit breaker for the generator supplying power to the transmitters trips. The station cannot transmit—the Green Team hands the spacecraft over to the Madrid station. The breaker cools and is reset. Robledo resumes the prime station role—at least for an hour. A breaker on another generator trips again, disabling the station transmitters. Houston makes another unscheduled handover to Madrid. The station crew provides additional cooling to the hydromechanical building housing the generators. The transmitters come back online and operate until the scheduled handover to Goldstone at fifty-five hours after liftoff. The failures cause brief losses of tracking data. The impact is minimal. The tracking data already in hand indicate the velocity value for midcourse correction three, scheduled at a mission elapsed time of fifty-three hours, fifty-four minutes, is only eight-tenths of a foot per second. The current velocity is once again close enough for government work—the flight director cancels the planned maneuver.

The crew sleeps undisturbed through the two ground system failures. Even so, the whole sequence is more than a little disconcerting. Robledo is scheduled to be the primary tracking station for the Lunar Module during the launch from the Moon. When its problems are coupled with the earlier Carnarvon and Tidbinbilla problems, I begin to feel that the Fates may be leading us into an electronic ambush. Continuing data losses due to modem problems on the primary circuits between Houston and Goddard add to my growing discomfort. I hope the wizards at both places are working the problems. I don't have the time or the resources to do that. I have to be on station at the appointed times and do the business at hand.

The cancellation of midcourse correction number three allows the crew an extra hour of rest. Capsule Communicator Bruce McCandless delays his first call to the spacecraft until fifty hours and forty minutes mission elapsed time. *Apollo 11* is 166,135 miles from Earth, moving toward the Moon at 3,404 feet per second. The usual housekeeping chores are the first order of business on this the third day of translunar coast. Houston transmits an updated position and velocity report to the spacecraft computer. Batteries are charged. Fuel cells are purged.

Midway through the day, McCandless delivers what has now become the standard daily news update—a mixture of the pedestrian with the downright banal that strikes someone in the Public Affairs Office as appropriate. Houston has had some badly needed rain. "Mayor Louie Welch promises a lifting of lawn-watering restrictions if the rains continue." On the international scene, the Norwegian explorer Thor Heyerdahl says that "the crew of his papyrus boat, the *Ra*, will sail into Bridgetown, Barbados, despite damage from heavy seas." In sports, the St. Louis Cardinals beat Philadelphia 11–3. "And in Corby, England, an Irishman, John Coyle, has won the world's porridge-eating championship by consuming twenty-three bowls of instant oatmeal in a ten-minute time limit from a field of thirty-five other competitors."

Madrid hands the spacecraft over to Goldstone. The Green Team hands over to the White Team. The major business of the day begins when Aldrin and Armstrong take their television camera into the Lunar Module for a two-hour inspection. Audiences in the United States, Japan, Western Europe, and South America watch the live broadcast. Everything is in order. Aldrin reports that the interior is "very clean" with "very few loose particles of bolts, nuts, and screws and lint and things." The spacecraft is 177,000 miles from home.

Two hours after the crew closes the Lunar Module hatch, Charlie Duke gives them a "good night from the White Team."

As the crew settles in for their rest period, they pass a major milestone. Since the translunar injection burn, they have been struggling upward from the Earth at an ever-decreasing velocity. At sixty-one hours, thirty-nine minutes, and fifty-five seconds, the Moon's gravity becomes the dominant factor. They begin to fall toward the Moon now with ever increasing velocity. The spacecraft is 186,437 nautical miles from Earth and 33,822 nautical miles from the Moon. The velocity with respect to the Earth is 2,990 feet per second, and about 3,272 feet per second with respect to the Moon. The displays in the control room switch from Earth-centered to Moon-centered.

Twenty minutes after the spacecraft starts its plunge toward the Moon, we relieve the White Team on the consoles. Honeysuckle takes over from Goldstone. We get to cover another sleep shift. They call us the "Black Watch" for a reason. Jay Green, our duty FIDO, recommends to the flight director that he cancel midcourse correction four. The velocity change would be a miniscule one-half foot per second. INCO switches spacecraft antennas as the vehicle rotates about its long axis out there in the void. We listen and watch for any sign of trouble. The shift passes with frequent trips to the coffeepot and the head.

The Green Team relieves us at seventy hours into the mission. *Apollo 11* is 13,638 nautical miles from the Moon. Velocity is 4,047 feet per second relative to the Moon. The Green Team watch is going to be way more active than ours. The crew wakes up at seventy-one hours. The first order of business is for Bruce McCandless to read up the maneuver PAD[7] for the engine firing that will slow the spacecraft down enough to put it into orbit around the Moon. The ignition time for that burn is seventy-five hours, forty-nine minutes, and forty-nine seconds. The duration

---

7   Pre-advisory data. The detailed information that the crew would need to execute an upcoming maneuver is entered on a preprinted form by the flight dynamics team and read up to the crew by the CAPCOM. In most cases, the crew then reads it back for confirmation. Information for an upcoming maneuver would include, for example, the time of ignition and the length of the burn.

of the braking maneuver will be six minutes, two seconds, and the change in velocity will be a minus 2,917.3 feet per second. The expected orbit following that maneuver is 169.2 by 61 nautical miles. The burn will take place on the far side of the Moon. We will lose signal with *Apollo 11* at seventy-five hours, forty-one minutes, twenty-three seconds, as it goes behind the Moon. If the lunar orbit insertion burn is successful, we will acquire the spacecraft signal at seventy-six hours, fifteen minutes, twenty-nine seconds. If for some reason *Apollo 11* cannot perform the burn, we will acquire the spacecraft ten minutes earlier than planned at seventy-six hours, five minutes, thirty seconds.

The Black Team is not due back on shift until ninety-three hours—but no one goes very far from the control room. I make a quick call home to say that I won't be there anytime soon. I get something to eat. I head back to my desk in the other wing of the control center. I shuffle through the papers that have piled up on my desk. Shuffle is the operative word. At this point those papers can't have anything to say that could compete with the theater happening in the other wing of this building. Shuffling complete, I head back to the control center to plug in my headset so I can wait and watch with the rest of the world.

Fifteen minutes before the spacecraft is due to disappear behind the Moon, the Green Team flight director makes a final status check with his controllers. Bruce McCandless passes the verdict to the crew, "ELEVEN, this is Houston. You are GO for LOI. Over." Two minutes prior to loss of signal, McCandless confirms, "*Apollo 11*, this is Houston. All your systems are looking good going around the corner, and we'll see you on the other side. Over."

"Roger. Everything looks OK up here."

"Roger. Out."

Luna has come between the Earth and her children. Where once there was reassuring voice contact and system telemetry there is only silence and static display screens. Flight controllers look up from their video screens seemingly unsure about what to do. The intermission is awkward. The players look nervously at the parts they are meant to play in the next act. They hope that they will get to play them as written. The Fates can always insert alternative tragic endings. Above the heads of the actors, a clock at the front of the control room counts down to the planned ignition time for the orbit insertion burn. Another clock counts down to the time when Madrid is expected to see the spacecraft if the maneuver is a success.

There is nothing to do now but to wait, to hope, and to have faith—faith in Kepler's laws of planetary motion, faith in Robert Goddard's liquid fuel propulsion technology, and faith in the dedication, intelligence, and craftsmanship of the tens of thousands who helped to make these machines and send them on their way. As the expected acquisition time approaches, a half dozen astronauts find seats in the first row in the viewing room. Deke Slayton and the *Apollo 11* backup crew, Lovell, Anders, and Haise, join CAPCOM Bruce McCandless at his console. The mission clock counts up past the no-burn-acquisition time of seventy-five hours and five minutes. There is no signal from the spacecraft. The silence confirms that something has slowed it down—a catastrophic failure—a partial burn—a sweet, perfect engine firing. Ten minutes will tell, ten more minutes.

The ground elapsed time clock counts up to seventy-six hours, fifteen minutes, and thirty seconds. The acquisition clock counts down to zero.

"GOLDTONE has AOS CSM."

"FLIGHT, NETWORK, Goldstone has AOS."

"APOLLO ELEVEN, APOLLO ELEVEN, this is HOUSTON. Do you read? Over."

"APOLLO ELEVEN, APOLLO ELEVEN, this is HOUSTON. Do you read? Over."

"GOLDSTONE is GO for command CSM."

"HOUSTON, APOLLO ELEVEN. Over."

"APOLLO ELEVEN, APOLLO ELEVEN, this is HOUSTON. We are reading you weakly. Go ahead. Over."

"Roger. Burn status report follows."

Armstrong describes a perfect burn that put the spacecraft into an elliptical orbit around the Moon: apolune 168.5 nautical miles, perilune 61.2 nautical miles. It will make a complete circuit around the Moon in two hours, eight minutes, thirty seconds. The ground stations will see the spacecraft for an hour and twenty-eight minutes of that time before it disappears behind the western limb of the Moon for forty minutes. The spacecraft has traveled from Earth to Moon in just over seventy-six hours with a single 2.91-second midcourse correction maneuver that changed its velocity by 20.9 feet per second—not bad for government work.

During this initial pass across the visible side of the Moon, the crew gets its first view of their intended landing site. Armstrong reports, "The pictures and maps brought back by *Apollo 8* and *10* have given us a very good preview of what to look at here. It looks very much like the pictures, but like the difference between watching a real football game and watching it on TV. There's no substitute for actually being here."

Thirty minutes into the pass, Eris, the goddess of strife, strikes again. The Deep Space Network station at Goldstone, which is tracking the spacecraft, experiences a power amplifier failure. The station switches to its backup system. Disruption is minimal. This is Goldstone's third power amplifier failure in three days.

After emerging from behind the Moon for their second orbit, the crew downlinks television through Goldstone. From ninety-two miles above the lunar surface they take millions of viewers on a tour of the landmarks that will guide them to a landing. As the transmission ends, Bruce McCandless reads up the parameters for a second lunar orbit insertion burn that the crew will make while the spacecraft is behind the Moon after loss of signal on this current pass. The first insertion burn put the spacecraft into an elliptical orbit. This second burn will circularize the orbit at an altitude that is right for the landing attempt. Safety dictates this two-burn approach. At this point in the program there is still uncertainty about the exact gravitational field of the Moon. In the single burn case, any major miscalculation of the maneuver parameters could have serious consequences—reducing the spacecraft altitude to a negative value is one of them. This iterative approach provides the opportunity to confirm the effects of one step before the next one is taken. The crew will take that second step at eighty hours and eleven minutes. It will be a short burn, only seventeen seconds. If all goes well, the spacecraft will end up in a roughly circular orbit that it will maintain for the duration of the lunar stay. After copying another maneuver PAD that will allow the crew to make a return to Earth in the event of some malfunction, the spacecraft disappears behind the western limb of the Moon.

When Goldstone acquires the spacecraft signal as it reemerges to start its third orbit, Armstrong again reports a near perfect burn. With the spacecraft in a stable orbit at the required altitude, the crew starts the next major step in their progress toward a landing—they pressurize the Lunar Module. Buzz Aldrin goes aboard the lunar landing craft to power it up for the first time and make a series of system checks. Just prior to loss-of-signal on this orbit, Milt Windler's Maroon Team takes over the control room duties. Charlie Duke sits at the CAPCOM's console for the upcoming orbits. A new display appears on the large screen at the front of the room—a map of the lunar landing site.

When the spacecraft crosses the Moon's east limb to start its fourth pass, there are three Goldstone antennas searching for it. The eighty-five-foot *Apollo* station dish stands by to track the Command and Service Module frequency. The eighty-five-foot deep-space antenna and the 210-foot Mars antenna guard the Lunar Module frequency, waiting for the first critical tests of the lander's communication systems. The Mars antenna is a three-thousand-ton insurance policy. Mission rules for powered descent initiation—the maneuver that will slow the Lunar Module down for its final approach to landing—require that TELCOM, the flight controller responsible for the Lunar Module electrical, environmental, and communications systems, be able to see high bit-rate telemetry, which can only be downlinked using the vehicle's steerable antenna. If that antenna fails, only the Mars dish has enough gain to receive high bit-rate telemetry transmitted by the Lunar Module's low-power omnidirectional antennas. There had been problems with the steerable antenna during the *Apollo 10* low pass over the lunar surface. Backup is critical. You need to have a Plan B—the Mars antenna is Plan B.

Forty minutes into the pass, "HOUSTON, APOLLO ELEVEN—APOLLO ELEVEN/EAGLE. Over.

"Roger, EAGLE. This is HOUSTON. We read you. Over."

"Roger. I read you about four-by-four. Could you give me a short count, please?"

"Roger, EAGLE. Coming in with the short count: 1, 2, 3, 4, 5; 5, 4, 3, 2, 1. HOUSTON out. Over."

"Roger. Are you copying my low bit rate? Over."

"Roger. We got some beautiful data here, EAGLE. We're—all those guys are looking at it—systems guys. We'll have some word for you in a minute how everything looks."

The Lunar Module is powered up. It can communicate with the home planet. It has a call sign. Aldrin checks out the very high frequency link with the Command Module. He steps through the various S-band configurations that will connect him with Houston during the lunar descent. After seventeen minutes, Duke reports, "EAGLE, this is HOUSTON. We're happy with all our data in all modes. You can power down the comm now. Over." The two spacecraft are at an altitude of 54.3 nautical miles, streaking across the near side of the Moon at 5,376 feet per second.

At eighty-three hours and forty-five minutes, *Apollo 11* disappears behind the Moon. When it reappears to begin its fifth pass, Goldstone still has the duty. During the pass, Houston begins to believe that there is a problem with the Command and Service Modules' steerable antenna, with its ability to automatically re-acquire the ground station carrier after an interruption. The Goldstone carrier is turned off and then back on twice during the pass. The antenna does what it is supposed to do.

Just after acquisition of signal by Honeysuckle on revolution number six, Charlie Duke reports to the crew, "APOLLO

ELEVEN, HOUSTON. We believe we've tracked down the reacquisition problem we had on the previous REV. It looks like it was a receiver power supply here on the ground and no problems in the spacecraft at all. Over."

"OK. Glad to hear it."

"ELEVEN, that really winds things up as far as we're concerned on the ground, for the evening. We're ready to go to bed and get a little sleep. Over."

"Yes. We're about to join you."

The duty public affairs officer captures what all of us are thinking and feeling at this point, and puts it out to his worldwide audience:

"This is Apollo Control, Houston; at eighty-seven hours, thirty-one minutes now into the flight, *Apollo 11*. The *Apollo 11* spacecraft continues on its front-side pass above the Moon. We're now less than ten minutes away from Loss of Signal. The *Apollo 11* crew is currently in their rest period. We've received no indication yet that any of the three crew members are actually sleeping, although all three appear to be in a very restful mode. This will be the final sleep period for the crew, now at the threshold of their prime mission objective, for the final sleep period prior to landing on the lunar surface and returning. The next scheduled rest period will in fact take place on the surface of the Moon. We're now past midnight Central Daylight Time. It is now July 20, the day scheduled for lunar landing."

CHAPTER TWENTY-TWO

Another sleep shift—I am beginning to feel paranoid. Could it be that no one trusts us with any serious mission events? Then again it might be better to quit whining. Just be grateful for the quiet time. It is about to end. It is 6:00 a.m. (CDT) on Sunday, July 20. We are ninety-three hours and thirty minutes into the mission. The spacecraft is near the end of its ninth pass across the near side of the Moon. It is in a sixty-four by fifty-five nautical mile orbit moving at nearly 5,400 feet per second. In about five minutes, Honeysuckle will lose the spacecraft signal as the ungainly combination of lunar landing craft and mother ship passes behind the Moon. Black Team spacecraft communicator Ron Evans has been standing by to wake the crew just before occultation. "APOLLO ELEVEN, APOLLO ELEVEN. Good morning from the Black Team."

"Good morning, HOUSTON."

"Good morning. We got about two minutes to LOS here, Mike."

"…You…Yes, you're about two minutes early on the wakeup."

"Looks like you were really sawing them away."

"You guys wake up early."

"ELEVEN, HOUSTON. Looks like the Command Module's in good shape. Black Team has been watching it real closely for you."

"We sure appreciate that. Because I sure haven't."

"APOLLO ELEVEN. Thirty seconds. AOS will be ninety-four plus twenty-one."

Madrid has the duty when the spacecraft starts its tenth pass. The *Apollo* station locks up on the Command Module. The deep-space station at Robledo waits patiently for the Lunar Module to power up. The crew is eating breakfast and running their post-sleep checklist. They report that the commander had five and a half hours of sleep during the night. The Command Module pilot had six hours. The Lunar Module pilot had five hours. Considering the day ahead, you have to wonder how they got so much sleep. You wonder, at the same time, if it will be enough. While the crew eats, Ron Evans tells them that the "Black Bugle" just arrived with some morning news briefs. With a captive audience he relates the usual foolishness. He advises the crew to "watch for a lovely girl with a big rabbit. An ancient legend says a beautiful Chinese girl called Chang-o has been living there for four thousand years. It seems she was banished to the Moon because she stole the pill of immortality from her husband. You might also look for her companion, a large Chinese rabbit, who is easy to spot since he is always standing on his hind feet in the shade of a cinnamon tree."

Shift change is still an hour away. Some members of the White Team are already drifting into the control room.

Figure 5: Flight Director Gene Kranz (sitting on the console) and his White Team. Captain George Ojalehto, the White Team network controller, stands just to the right of the flight director in this photo. (NASA photo courtesy of George Ojalehto)

They compare notes with their Black Team counterparts and then set to work putting together numbers for maneuver attitudes, times, and durations. There are plenty of numbers to get ready. In the next ten hours, the crews of the two spacecraft will perform three maneuvers. After undocking from the Lunar Module, the Command Module will make a brief separation burn. It will open a safe distance between the two spacecraft while keeping them close enough for Collins to make a visual examination of the Lunar Module. An hour later, with the spacecraft out of view behind the Moon, the Lunar Module crew will begin their descent to the lunar surface. This first maneuver, the descent orbit insertion burn, will bring the low point of their orbit down to just fifty thousand feet. The powered descent initiation burn, the maneuver that will take the crew the rest of the way to the surface, will begin at that low point. It will slow the craft down for its final approach to the surface.

Minutes before loss of signal on this tenth revolution, Aldrin reminds our CAPCOM that our next meeting will be more eventful, "Black Team, we'll be looking for an interesting day with you all tomorrow."

"Roger. We'll be going off here shortly, and we'll pick you up in the morning for sure."

We finish our shift change briefings and give up our chairs to Gene Kranz and his White Team flight controllers. Astronaut Charlie Duke is the capsule communicator on this shift.

As the spacecraft disappears behind the Moon, the Lunar Module pilot glides through the docking tunnel, makes a visual check of his flying machine, and starts the vehicle activation checklist. He turns on power and activates the subsystem that distributes electric current from the vehicle batteries to the onboard equipment. He verifies that the circuit breakers for the equipment are in the proper positions. He switches on and tests the primary guidance and navigation system, the PGNS or "pings" in NASA-speak, that will control the vehicle during its flight. The primary guidance and navigation system provides data on Lunar Module position, velocity, and attitude. The primary system uses the same basic setup as the Command Module version. It has two major parts: an inertial measurement unit and a computer. The inertial measurement unit is the navigation sensor, incorporating accelerometers and gyros to sense changes in velocity and attitude. It sends this information to the computer, which contains pre-programmed logic for display of information to the crew, for navigation, for calculation and execution of guidance commands, and for processing of landing radar measurements of range and velocity during the powered descent to the lunar surface.

An abort guidance system, or AGS, backs up the primary system. The abort guidance system is a stripped-down version of the primary system. It is not meant to duplicate the full functioning of the primary system. Instead it is just good enough to control the spacecraft if the primary system fails and the crew is forced to abort the lunar landing approach.

Armstrong joins Aldrin in the Lunar Module and begins his sequence of checks. He turns on and checks the environmental control system that will keep the vehicle habitable during its expedition to the surface and back. After a call to the Command Module checks out the very high frequency radio link, he turns his attention to the primary guidance system. He tells it the time and lets it know which way is up. He pressurizes and checks the small reaction control system thrusters that will control the spacecraft attitude as it maneuvers toward the surface. He deploys the Lunar Module landing legs that have been tucked up under the ascent stage since launch. He activates and runs tests on the craft's two radar systems—the landing radar that will give them altitude and velocity during the landing phase, and the rendezvous radar that will bring them back to their mother ship when the expedition is done. In parallel, Aldrin verifies the functions of the S-band communication system. He also activates and configures the abort guidance system.

The checks go on through lunar revolutions eleven and twelve. They go quickly—the crew is ahead of the flight plan schedule. In the control room, flight controllers monitor and analyze every bit of data generated during the activation. They have trouble keeping up. They fall behind in providing the data that the crew needs to continue their activation sequence.

During revolution twelve, the CAPCOM checks status, "EAGLE, HOUSTON. Could you give us an idea where you are in the activation? Over."

Aldrin responds, "We're just sitting around waiting for something to do."

The flight controllers catch up. Ten minutes before loss of signal on revolution twelve, Charlie Duke makes the call, passing the expected, carefully considered, minutely massaged verdict to the crew through the Madrid deep-space station, "APOLLO ELEVEN, Houston. We're GO for undocking. Over."

Forty minutes after the spacecraft disappears behind the Moon, Duke anticipates its reappearance, "Hello, EAGLE. HOUSTON. We're standing by. Over."

"EAGLE, HOUSTON. We see you on the steerable. Over."

"Roger. EAGLE is undocked."

"Roger. How does it look, Neil?"

"The EAGLE has wings."

The network is tracking two vehicles now. The Madrid *Apollo* station has the Command and Service Module. The other Spanish station at Robledo has locked up with the Lunar Module's steerable antenna. The antenna is a parabolic dish, twenty-six inches in diameter, mounted on the top of the spacecraft just to the right of the vehicle access hatch. It can be pointed either manually or automatically and provides coverage of 174 degrees in azimuth and 330 degrees in elevation. The crew moves the antenna by hand to point it at the ground station. Once it locks on to the uplink signal, it is designed to automatically track the ground station signal to maintain two-way lock.

That two-way automatic tracking will be critical during the approach to the landing site. The Lunar Module transmits measurements that describe the operation of its onboard systems at two data rates—1,600 bits per second and 51,200 bits per second. To make sure that flight controllers have what they need to monitor the performance of critical systems, the mission rules require that the high bit-rate Lunar Module telemetry be available during the descent. More bits per second require more signal power. More signal power means that the small omnidirectional antennas mounted fore and aft on the Lunar Module cabin cannot do the job, even when they are coupled with one of the eighty-five-foot ground antennas. These omni antennas have a hemispherical transmit pattern. Their limited power output is spread over the entire hemisphere. The steerable antenna can do the job, because its shape creates a narrower twelve-to-fourteen-degree antenna pattern that concentrates the twenty watts of transmitted power. The solid checkout during the Lunar Module activation sequence and the ease of this acquisition are reassuring.

With the air-to-ground connection in place, the crew and flight controllers work their way through the flight plan sequences that will get *Eagle* safely to the surface. Charlie Duke reads up the numbers for the descent orbit insertion and the powered descent initiation maneuvers. The crew reads them back for confirmation. Kranz and his controllers pore over the data from both spacecraft. They are satisfied with what they see. Twenty minutes into the pass, Duke notifies the crew, "APOLLO ELEVEN, HOUSTON. You are looking good for separation. You are GO for separation, COLOMBIA, over."

The Command and Service Module backs away from the Lunar Module at a foot per second. By the time that the Lunar Module ignites to put the craft into its descent orbit, Collins will be a safe one thousand feet away. With the vehicles separated, Armstrong activates and tests the landing radar that will provide continuous input on Lunar Module altitude during the descent. Duke reads another maneuver PAD. Mike Collins copies this one—these are the numbers he will need if he has to go to the rescue of his comrades.

Fifteen minutes before loss of signal on this thirteenth pass, Kranz warns his flight controllers to look carefully at their data one more time. He is about to ask for a GO/NO-GO for the descent orbit insertion maneuver. I'm not sure anyone needs that heads-up. Everyone has been locked on to their displays, working with their backroom experts to dissect anything that they even suspect is suspicious. When Kranz does make his status check, he gets a thumbs-up from each critical position. Duke passes the word, "EAGLE, HOUSTON. You are GO for DOI. Over."

"Roger. GO for DOI. Do you have LOS and AOS times?"

"Roger. For you LOS at 101 28. AOS 102 16. Over."

The spacecraft disappear behind the Moon. The Lunar Module descent engine will ignite seven minutes, and forty seconds into this dark-side pass. It will burn for almost thirty seconds, to slow the spacecraft and put it into a 57.2 by 8.5 nautical mile orbit. When the tracking network next acquires the Lunar Module, it will be at an altitude of about eighteen nautical miles on its way down to the low point of its orbit, about fifty thousand feet, where the powered descent to the lunar surface will begin. When the spacecraft do emerge, the Madrid *Apollo* station will go active on the Command Module. The Goldstone deep-space station will lock on to the Lunar Module. Antigua, Canary Islands, the Madrid deep-space station, and Ascension Island will contribute three-way high-speed tracking data to mission computers in Houston. That data will allow the flight controllers to monitor *Eagle*'s path to the surface of the Moon.

The first three rows of the control room empty as some of the controllers head across the hall for a precautionary pee. A few of those who remain sit at their consoles reviewing their landing procedures for the ten billionth time. Most of the others stand around talking, hands in their pockets, glancing up at the countdown-to-acquisition-time display, like kids waiting for the school bell to ring. The VIP viewing room fills up. The NASA hierarchy is there—Dr. Thomas Paine, the NASA administrator, Dr. Abe Silverstein, director of NASA's Lewis Research Center; Rocco Petrone, director of launch operations at Kennedy Space Center; Dr. Wernher Von Braun, director of the Marshall Space Flight Center; along with Dr. Kurt Debus, director of the Kennedy

Space Center. Secretary of the Air Force Robert Seamans represents the Defense Department. The astronaut corps is there too: Tom Stafford, Gene Cernan, Jim McDivitt, and John Glenn, among others.

The control room itself is beginning to get top-heavy. Management row, the back row of consoles closest to the VIP room window, is filling up. Dr. Robert Gilruth, director of the Manned Spacecraft Center; General Sam Phillips, director of the Apollo Program; Chris Kraft, director of flight operations at the Manned Spacecraft Center; and George Low, the Apollo Spacecraft Program manager are all on board. Astronauts Pete Conrad, Fred Haise, Jim Lovell, and Bill Anders, along with Deke Slayton, director of flight crew operations at the Manned Spacecraft Center, are beginning to gather around the CAPCOM's console.

I am as determined as any of the big guys to be present when this bit of history is made. My knothole is more distant, but it will have to do. When our short shift ends and the spacecraft goes behind the Moon during lunar orbit ten, I gather up my headset and three-ring binders and get out of the control room. But I don't go very far. Going home is not an option. The mission managers have decreed that once the *Eagle* lands, the Black Team must be on-site in case the crew has to get off the surface in a hurry. I take my gear over to the bunk room on the second floor between the admin and operations wings of the building. I pick out a lower bunk. Sleeping is going to be tough enough—the thought of having a climb between me and the head in the dark of the night would not help. I drop my stuff and head across to the cafeteria for a quick meal.

After eating, I still have time to kill. I go across to my office and do some more meaningless paper shuffling. Finally, as the time for acquisition of the spacecraft signal approaches, I head back to the control center. I make my way up to the Network Staff Support Room on the second floor. I find a communications panel, pull up a chair, and plug in my headset. I push the monitor buttons for the comm loops where the action will be—Net

One, the air-to-ground circuit; Flight Director, the channel Kranz will use to manage this landing; Net Two, the tracking network channel, and Network, the internal channel that the duty network controller will use to respond to whatever contingency might arise out there in the global tracking and communications systems. And then, along with half of the population of planet Earth, I watch the clock and wait.

A flashing white light on the communications panel distracts me from my dedicated clock watching. The light indicates a telephone call coming in from outside the control center. That's kind of odd at this juncture. I look around. Everyone is ignoring the light. I am just about to decide that that is a good idea when Type A takes control. I punch the button, "Network Staff Support Room."

"This is the Public Affairs Office. I have Mrs. Harriet Grew on the line from Clinton, Iowa. She would like to relay a concern about the upcoming landing."

"Are you sure you have the right number? This is the Network SSR."

"The PAO people in the control room gave me this number. They were too busy to take the call. Go ahead, Mrs. Grew, you have mission control on the line."

A tentative, grandmotherly voice asks, "Is this mission control in Houston?"

OK, OK, now I get it. This is one of those practical jokes that these guys are famous for. I look around the room to see who is looking my way and laughing into their headset microphone. No one is paying me the least bit of attention. Could there really be a concerned citizen on the line?

"This is mission control. Go ahead, Mrs. Grew."

"Oh, young man, I'm so glad I reached you in time. You must do something to stop those boys from trying to land on the Moon."

"Why is that, ma'am?"

"The dust, young man, it's the dust. The whole place is covered in dust so deep that it will swallow them and their machine."

I don't know much about lunar dust or Lunar Module design, but I give it a go with what little I have. "Ma'am, the engineers who designed the lunar lander were very aware of the dust problem. If you look at a picture of the spacecraft you can see those, those great big pie plates at the end of each of its legs. They're designed to spread the weight of the machine across a wide area so it won't sink into the dust."

"Young man, all of your science and your engineers and your arrogance will not prevail against the prophecy of doom!"

"The prophecy, ma'am?"

"It's there, young man, right there in Genesis Three Nineteen. 'For dust you are and to dust you will return.'"

I could argue that Mrs. Grew is wildly misinterpreting that passage. But my qualifications in biblical exegesis are even shakier than my Lunar Module design expertise.

"Yes, ma'am—dust."

"You have to do something, young man. You have to stop this now."

"Ma'am, I don't think that there's much I can do at this point."

"Do something, young man. Lives hang in the balance. You must promise to do all that you can."

"Yes, ma'am, I'll do whatever I can. Have a nice day."

As I hang up, I can't help but wonder if I have just been listening to a midwestern version of the Trojan Cassandra—prophesying an unlikely cause for a likely outcome—her predictions doomed to be disbelieved by all who hear them. The road to catastrophic failure may not be covered with dust, but there are a whole lot of more likely hazards waiting for the crew of *Apollo 11*—and they are just about to come up against the worst of them.

When I refocus on the clock, the descent orbit insertion burn is underway. Or at least it should be. With the spacecraft behind the Moon we have no way of knowing. We wait some more—wait for the Command and Service Module to appear from behind the eastern limb of the Moon. If the burn is successful, Eagle will be in a lower orbit, just fifteen miles above the surface, and moving faster than *Colombia*. Relative to the lunar surface, the Lunar Module is about a minute ahead of the Command Module. But *Colombia*, traveling at sixty miles above the surface, will be visible before it comes around the lunar corner—visible a full two minutes earlier than *Eagle*.

As the acquisition time approaches, an expectant silence replaces the usual chatter on the control room communication channels. The flight director breaks the silence. "OK, all flight controllers, about fifteen seconds to CSM acq."

There are thirty merciless minutes left before the planned landing. The tracking network has to supply the control center with data on the Lunar Module's position and condition—enough data to allow the flight control team and the crew to decide that it is safe to go ahead with this first-ever attempt to land on another celestial body. Heart rates go up. Assholes pucker.

"GOLDSTONE has CSM AOS."

"MADRID, AOS CSM."

Captain George Ojalehto, the White Team network controller, comes up on the flight director's loop and confirms Command and Service Module acquisition. "George O" is a short man, more round than angular, with closely cut light brown hair. His competence and his self-control have put him in this particular room on this particular day. His Philco-Ford partner is Doug Wilson, whose strong, unhurried Southern drawl adds to the deserved impression that this team is cool, calm, and collected. Today they may just need all of the coolness, calmness, and collectedness that they can come up with—no one has ever done what they are about to do.

Madrid brings up its carrier and establishes two-way lock with the spacecraft. "MADRID, GO for command, CSM.

Charlie Duke tries to hurry things along, "COLUMBIA, HOUSTON. We're standing by. Over."

"COLUMBIA, HOUSTON. Over."

"HOUSTON, COLUMBIA. Reading you loud and clear."

"Roger. Five-by, Mike. How did it go? Over."

"Listen, babe. Everything's going just swimmingly. Beautiful."
Two minutes later, "GOLDSTONE has LEM AOS."
"GOLDSTONE GO for two-way."
"GOLDSTONE has high-gain LEM."

OK. This is the end-to-end communications hookup they need to maintain if this thing is going to work. The Lunar Module pilot comes up on the air-to-ground voice circuit, "HOUSTON, EAGLE. How do you read?"

"Five-by, EAGLE. We're standing by for your burn report, over."

"Roger. The burn was on time. The residuals before nulling: minus 0.1, minus 0.4, minus 0.1, X and Z nulled to zero… nulling…"

"GOLDSTONE has LOS LEM."

"COLUMBIA, HOUSTON. We've lost all data with EAGLE. Please have him reacquire on the high gain. Over."

"GOLDSTONE, NETWORK, Net Two."

"GOLDSTONE."

"Roger, are you attempting to reacquisition at this time?"

"That's affirmative."

"EAGLE, this is COLUMBIA. HOUSTON would like you to reacquire on the high gain. They've lost your data. Over."

"FLIGHT, TELCOM, we may have locked up on a side-lobe. Request you try to reacquire. They are at attitude."

Don Puddy, White Team TELCOM, is an Oklahoma native who has been with the spaceflight program since 1964. He is the flight controller who worries about Lunar Module electrical, life support, and communications systems. He thinks that there may be a ground station problem. Most of the radiation from the Lunar Module steerable antenna is concentrated in a narrow beam that can reach the ground station with enough energy to allow high bit-rate telemetry. But Mother Nature never allows perfect designs. The narrow main beam of an antenna is always flanked on both sides by a series of low-power beams called "side-lobes." TELCOM suspects that the ground station has locked up on one of these nuisance beams, a beam whose energy level is too low to support the required telemetry rate. The remedy is to break lock with the side-lobe and reacquire on the main lobe.

George has anticipated the request, "They're reacquiring at this time, FLIGHT."

"EAGLE, did you copy COLUMBIA?"

"GOLDSTONE has AOS LEM."

George confirms the signal, "AOS LEM."

"EAGLE, HOUSTON. Did you call?"

"EAGLE, HOUSTON—HOUSTON, EAGLE. How do you read?"

"GOLDSTONE GO for two-way LEM."

TELCOM verifies a solid connection, "Looks good, FLIGHT."

"Roger. Five-by, Neil. We copied up to the AGS residuals. Would you please repeat the AGS residuals in the trim—correction—the Sun check? Over."

Armstrong completes the report on the descent orbit insertion burn. The onboard estimate of the new orbit gives a high point of 57.2 nautical miles and a perilune of 9.1 nautical miles.

We are about thirteen minutes away from the start of the powered descent. It is a three-phase operation. Each phase is controlled by one of three sequential computer programs. Phase one, controlled by P63, is a braking maneuver. It begins about 260 nautical miles from the intended landing site at an altitude of 50,000 feet. The Lunar Module is oriented with the descent engine pointing in the direction of travel. The cabin windows are facing down to allow the crew to make a rough navigational check during the initial part of the maneuver. The descent engine fires for about eight and a half minutes, bringing the spacecraft down to an altitude of about seven thousand feet at a range of approximately 4.5 nautical miles from the landing site. As the burn progresses, the spacecraft yaws so that the spacecraft windows are facing up.

The approach phase, P64, starts at seven thousand feet. The spacecraft pitches to a windows-forward attitude providing the crew visibility of the landing area. During the one-minute-and-forty-second approach, the altitude decreases from seven thousand to five hundred feet, and the range to the landing site decreases from about 4.5 nautical miles to two thousand feet.

When the spacecraft reaches 500 feet, the approach phase terminates and the landing phase begins under the control of P65. Between 500 feet and 150 feet, the Lunar Module has 60 feet per second of forward velocity, 16 feet per second of vertical rate, and an attitude of approximately 16 degrees off the vertical. The automatic vertical descent from an altitude of 150 feet is at a 3-feet-per-second vertical downward altitude rate. These conditions are designed to allow the crew to take over manual control at any point during the landing. When probes that extend six feet below the Lunar Module landing pads make surface contact, a light signals the crew to shut down the descent engine. The spacecraft settles into the lunar surface dust.

"PROCEDURES from FLIGHT. Would you make sure the doors get secured now, please?"

No one gets in or out until this thing is over—one way or another.

"GOLDSTONE, NETWORK, Net Two."

"Station calling GOLDSTONE, go ahead."

"This is NETWORK GOLDSTONE. Can you verify whether we are processing eighty-five data to Houston or MARS data to Houston?"

"You have MARS, NETWORK."

"Roger, thank you."

"FLIGHT, NETWORK. Data from Goldstone is from the two ten foot dish."

The flight controllers and their backroom support teams understand that in about six minutes, the flight director is going to ask for a GO for powered descent.

They scrutinize every bit of the Lunar Module onboard system status. After just about two and a half minutes of good data, "FLIGHT, TELCOM."

"TELCOM."

"We've lost data. For some reason or another I think we may be locking up on a side-lobe."

"NETWORK, FLIGHT."

"FLIGHT, NETWORK."

"See if you can get that squared away, please?"

George doesn't think this is a ground station problem.

"We have a very weak signal on the LEM at this time—minus 140 [dBm]."

The minus 140 dBm compares the power of the signal being received by the Goldstone 210-foot antenna to a reference power. That reference signal is one-thousandth of a watt—.001 watts. The minus 140 dBm indicates that the received signal is only a tiny fraction of the already tiny milliwatt. Pre-mission calculations predicted a value between minus 90 dBm and minus 100 dBm for the 210-foot antenna at this point in the mission. Even at those values, the received signal would be a whisper barely distinguishable above the roaring torrent of galactic radio noise. Minus 140 dBm measures a whisper thousands of times less audible than the predicted value.

To an apprentice plumber like me, this whole business of communication link power is black magic. I mean, how the hell do they make that work? However they do it, they need to do it now. The continuation of this mission depends on whether TELCOM, the Network Control team, and the crew at Goldstone can restore this fragile connection.

"GOLDSTONE, NETWORK. Are you attempting reacquisition at this time?"

"That's negative. We're still two-way."

"Thank you, GOLDSTONE."

"GOLDSTONE, TIC. Are you remoting two ten?"

"That's affirmative. We have no telemetry at this time, however."

"Roger, understand."

Based on Goldstone's report that they are still "two-way," I am guessing that the station is still radiating its uplink signal. The Lunar Module appears to be receiving the signal and transmitting a signal in response. That downlink signal is being detected by Goldstone's receivers, but it is too weak for the telemetry equipment to process it.

The flight director takes control, "TELCOM, do you want the spacecraft to try and reacquire us?"

"Rog."

"Rog. OK, go ahead CAPCOM."

"COLUMBIA, HOUSTON. We've lost EAGLE again. Have him try the high gain. Over."

George comes up on the flight director's voice loop.

"GOLDSTONE reports they still have uplink lock, but the downlink, they have no lock on downlink."

"OK."

There seems to be confusion about the exact status of the link and the best approach to a fix.

"TELCOM, NETWORK."

"Go, NETWORK."

"Yeah, Goldstone says they still have uplink lock, but they have no downlink. It looks like they're coming back in—"

"OK, all flight controllers. Keep watching your data. I'm still gonna be asking for a GO/NO-GO in about four minutes."

The data that the flight director wants his controllers to watch is intermittent at best.

"EAGLE, this is COLUMBIA. Houston lost you again. They're requesting another try at the high gain."

CAPCOM tries to work the problem with TELCOM. He seems to suspect that the problem is with the uplink from Goldstone to the Lunar Module.

"How does the signal strength look?"

"It's about eighty-eight. It's higher than it has been."

Eighty-eight dBm at the spacecraft receiver should be more than enough to do the job. The data continues to drop in and out.

"GOLDSTONE, NETWORK."

"Do you have solid two-way lock at this time—on the LEM?"

"That's affirmative."

"Roger copy, thank you."

There still seems to be enough signal power to maintain lock but not enough to support high-bit rate telemetry.

Augie Degner, the White Team telemetry instrumentation controller, comes up on the network controller's voice circuit, "NETWORK, TIC."

"Go ahead."

"Did he ask him if he was on the 210 or not?"

"Negative."

"GOLDSTONE, NETWORK, Net Two."

"NETWORK, GOLDSTONE."

"Are we still sending 210 data to Houston at this time?"

"That's affirmative."

As if it had been summoned by the question, the telemetry data is suddenly solid and certain.

"EAGLE, HOUSTON. We have you now. Do you read? Over."

"Loud and clear."

With data online, the flight director starts to worry other critical pre-landing checklist steps.

"GUIDANCE, FLIGHT. AGS initialization and alignment?"

"Standing by, FLIGHT."

Besides providing an emergency backup system, the abort guidance package plays another critical role during the lunar landing. The flight controllers continually compare the Lunar Module velocity components computed by the primary guidance and navigation system with those computed by the abort guidance system and with those computed on the ground using Manned Space Flight Network tracking. A two-out-of-three voting comparison logic is used to determine if either of the on-board systems is degrading. Detecting a potential failure in its early phase gives the flight controllers the time to consider fixes that could save the mission and maybe even the lives of the crew.

"FLIGHT, NETWORK. We're still on 210 data."

The Goldstone 210-foot antenna is *Apollo 11*'s three-thousand-ton lucky charm. Everyone knows that it will do the job—at least they hope it will. Twenty seconds after George's reassuring report, the Lunar Module telemetry is again intermittent. Received signal levels are way below expected values, even on the 210-foot Mars antenna. The vehicle must be flying at an angle that makes it difficult for the steerable antenna to stay pointed at the ground station.

Kranz is still working the backup guidance problem. "See if we can get this alignment and initialization in."

"GOLDSTONE NO-GO for command LEM."

"Roger, GOLDSTONE."

"—am reacquiring."

Ten seconds later, " GOLDSTONE GO for two-way LEM."

There is a dance going on here. A dance that is delicate under the best of circumstances. These are far from the best of circumstances. I'm a novice plumber, not a choreographer, but this thing is feeling dangerously disorganized. The training people have never simulated the intermittent communications that the crew is seeing here. In simulations things are either on or completely off. This on again–off again scenario has to be disconcerting in more ways than one. The task of manually pointing the antenna has been crammed into the crew's already crowded job jar. Maybe even more difficult to deal with is the damage that the situation is doing to the crew's confidence in their connection with their ground support. They depend on the flight controllers to sort the phantoms from the real failures—to exorcise mechanical and digital demons.

Lines from Shakespeare's *Henry IV* run through my head. Glendower challenges his rival Hotspur, "I can call spirits from the vasty deep."

Hotspur responds, "Why, so can I, or so can any man; But will they come when you do call for them?"

TELCOM, CONTROL, GUIDANCE, and FIDO are the crew's guardian spirits. Will they be there when the crew calls for them?

For the moment, at least, the data is solid enough for GUIDANCE to make a call on the status of the backup guidance system.

"FLIGHT, GUIDANCE. We're GO on the initialize."

"Rog, GO on initialize."

"EAGLE, HOUSTON. The AGS initialization looked good to us. Over."

George is still working the communications problems, "TELCOM, NETWORK."

"GO."

"This looks like reflections?"

"It sure does."

Puddy seems to have another idea about the cause of the communications problems. The steerable antenna, in its attempts to keep pointed at the Earth, may be pointing at or close to parts of the Lunar Module structure. The resulting reflections would distort the signal and account for the dropouts we are seeing. The onboard computer has a map of the Lunar Module structure. Theoretically the map is meant to avoid a situation where the antenna tries to look at the Earth through the vehicle structure. Theory and practice may have become disconnected. They often do.

"You don't suspect a ground problem then, do you?"

An altitude report from *Eagle* wipes out TELCOM's response. Given TELCOM's comment about reflections, I am positive that the response to George's question is negative. No one suspects a ground station problem. I try to imagine what is going through George's mind. I may be in a similar situation not many hours from now. I'm certain that he has the communications troubleshooting diagram spread out in front of him. The key to using that diagram is coordination between TELCOM and NETWORK. Unilateral changes to either the spacecraft or ground configuration or both would lead straight down the road to a mission abort or worse. But when the whole world is watching there is a temptation to do something—anything—that looks right from your limited perspective. George is resisting that temptation.

"Hey, FLIGHT, suggestion—would a little yaw help this high gain any?"

Only the CAPCOM would start a transmission with "Hey, FLIGHT."

Kranz checks with his expert. "What do you think, Don?"

"Sure would, FLIGHT."

Eagle is flying backward along its orbital path, anticipating the powered descent initiation burn which will slow it down for the approach and landing phases. The crew is looking straight down at the lunar surface. The CAPCOM is suggesting that a slight rotation from that face-down attitude might give the steerable antenna a better view of the Earth.

The telemetry signal becomes intermittent.

"How much? What direction?"

"Ten degrees right, FLIGHT."

"You want them to roll about ten degrees right?"

"Yaw-yaw ten degrees right."

"Yaw, roger."

After getting a correct understanding of the proposed maneuver, Kranz reminds his troops to look carefully at the on again, off again Lunar Module data.

"OK, all flight controllers, we've got forty seconds to the GO/NO-GO."

Charlie Duke gets on with the proposed corrective action.

"EAGLE, HOUSTON. We recommend you yaw ten right. It will help us on the high-gain signal strength. Over."

"OK, all flight controllers—GO/NO-GO for powered descent."

"RETRO? GO."

"FIDO? GO."

"GUIDANCE? GO."

"CONTROL? GO."

"TELCOM? GO."

"G&C? GO."

"EECOM? GO."

"SURGEON? GO."

Intermittent or not, the data had been sufficient to make the call.

"CAPCOM, we're GO for powered descent."

Seconds later George reports, "LOS for the LEM downlink, FLIGHT."

Goldstone has lost spacecraft telemetry one more time. The air-to-ground channel is noisy. The CAPCOM tries to get the message through.

"EAGLE, HOUSTON. If you read, you're GO for powered descent. Over."

Transmitting in the blind to confirm a go-ahead for the first lunar landing—that cannot be a good sign!

"FLIGHT, TELCOM, go omni."

"Want to go omni, TELCOM?"

"That's affirmative—aft omni before yaw, forward thereafter."

Theoretically the 210-foot antenna can handle high bit-rate data transmitted by the omnidirectional antennas, but to an apprentice plumber this call feels like a "Hail Mary" pass.

"EAGLE, this is COLUMBIA. They just gave you a GO for powered descent."

"COLUMBIA, HOUSTON. We've lost them on the high gain again. Would you please—we recommend they yaw right ten degrees and reacquire."

The flight director tries for a correction. "Break, break, CAPCOM. Break, break, CAPCOM. We'd like to go forward OMNI."

TELCOM corrects the correction.

"Aft omni, FLIGHT."

"Sorry."

Mike Collins heard Duke's earlier transmission and tries to help, "EAGLE, this is COLUMBIA. You're GO for PDI and they recommend you yaw right ten degrees and try the high gain again."

The request to switch to the omni antenna seems to have gotten lost in this shuffle.

"FLIGHT, NETWORK. We've got data again, FLIGHT—dropping in and out."

"Don, you want to try the yaw first?"

"That's affirm, FLIGHT."

"OK."

Mike Collins tries again, "EAGLE, you read COLUMBIA?"

Aldrin responds, "Roger. We read you."

"EAGLE, HOUSTON. We read you now. You're GO for PDI, over."

"FLIGHT, CONTROL. Guidance stream in AGS looks good."

"You're saying the alignment's good, CONTROL?"

"That's affirm."

"Alignment's GO, CAPCOM."

"EAGLE, HOUSTON. Your alignment is GO on the AGS. On my mark, three thirty until ignition."

"Mark, three thirty until ignition."

With just over three minutes to go before the descent burn ignition time, Wilson makes a check on the Earth–Lunar Module connection.

" GOLDSTONE, NETWORK."

"Give me a signal strength on the LEM, please."

"Roger, wilco."

"Negative one one nine."

"Copy, NETWORK?"

"I copy, thank you."

The value is still disconcertingly low—Lunar Module telemetry is dropping in and out.

"FLIGHT, TELCOM."

"Go, TELCOM."

"May be able to pick up the steerable if you desire to try—pitch 212, yaw 37."

"Pitch 212, yaw 37."

"That's affirm, FLIGHT."

"CAPCOM, why don't you try them?"

"Rog. Are we on the omnis now?"

TELCOM responds, "That's affirm."

The crew seems to have switched to the omni antenna even though the request was never relayed to them.

"EAGLE, HOUSTON. If you'd like to try high gain, pitch 212, yaw 37. Over."

Aldrin responds, "Roger. I think I've got you on high gain now."

In the last thirty seconds TELCOM said "omni" and Aldrin said "steerable." George is confused. So am I, but my confusion doesn't count—his does.

"TELCOM, NETWORK."

"Go."

"Are we on omni or high, huh, steerable still?"

Before TELCOM can answer, the flight director tries for his own clarification. "Got us locked up there, TELCOM?"

"OK, it's just real weak."

"OK, how are you lookin'? All your systems GO?"

"That's affirm, FLIGHT."

"How about you, CONTROL?"

"We look good."

"GUIDANCE?"

"GO."

The responses are delivered without hesitation based on intermittent data on critical systems delivered across a quarter of a million miles in an electromagnetic whisper. Aldrin is still looking to improve that tenuous connection. "Say again the angles, though."

"FIDO, how about you?"

"We're GO, FLIGHT."

"I'll set them in to use them before we yaw around."

"Roger. Pitch 212, yaw plus 37."

Augie Degner, the White Team telemetry instrumentation controller, is still hoping for a 210 miracle.

"GOLDSTONE, TIC."

"GOLDSTONE."

"Are you remoting two ten data or wing?"

The Goldstone operations supervisor has heard this question more than once in the last thirty minutes. He tries to take that bit of wishful thinking off the table. "Two ten always."

The Lunar Module pilot reports, "Omni's in."

I have no idea which antenna they are using. I hope they do.

"OK, all flight controllers, thirty seconds to ignition."

The telemetry is still a sometime thing. The air-to-ground voice is noisy.

"HOUSTON COMM TECH, GOLDSTONE COMM TECH."

"Go ahead GOLDSTONE."

"He's coming down broken."

Goldstone is sending what they are receiving. The problem isn't with the circuits between the station and Houston.

At 102 hours and 33 minutes ground elapsed time, 2 minutes and 8 seconds before the pre-mission predicted time, the descent propulsion engine ignites. Aldrin confirms the event. "Ignition...ten...ten percent..."

The Lunar Module is fifty thousand feet above the lunar surface. The three-phase burn will take eleven minutes and fifty-eight seconds. Sixteen seconds after ignition,

"GOLDSTONE has LEM LOS."

"COLUMBIA, HOUSTON. We've lost them. Tell them to go to aft OMNI. Over."

Collins relays the message.

"They've lost you. Use the OMNIs again."

"GOLDSTONE GO for two-way LEM."

The high bit-rate telemetry is back online and stable—at least for the moment.

"EAGLE, HOUSTON. Everything is looking good here."

The Lunar Module is approaching an altitude of forty-five thousand feet. At that point it will begin to rotate from a windows-down to a windows-up attitude. Windows-up will allow the landing radar to update the guidance computer's estimates of position and velocity. The crew will be able to monitor their approach to the landing site. Duke gives the crew the antenna angles they will need to use after the maneuver.

"EAGLE, HOUSTON. After yaw around, angles: S-band pitch minus 9, yaw plus 18."

Aldrin acknowledges the angles and reports, "AGS and PNGS agree very closely."

That's a good thing. The telemetry stream continues to hold for a minute or so and then goes unstable—dropping in and out.

Duke lets the crew know that the flight controllers are watching the progress of the descent maneuver.

"Stand by, looking good. You're still looking good at three, coming up three minutes."

The flight director is worrying the start of the spacecraft re-orientation. "OK, CONTROL, let me know when he starts his yaw here."

He's worrying the quality of the tracking data. "How's your MSFN looking now, FIDO?"

"FLIGHT, FIDO, we do have—filter. We're GO."

MSFN is shorthand for the ground tracking data that measures changes in the spacecraft's velocity. FIDO's filter is a software routine run on the Houston mission operations computer that smoothes the noisy velocity data provided by the ground stations and gives the most precise estimate of the Lunar Module's position and velocity.

The conversation on the internal control room communications circuits is overlaid with the crew's running air-to-ground commentary. They no longer have time for the niceties of call signs.

Armstrong has been integrating the information displayed by the guidance computer with his own "look-out-the-window" estimates. "Our position checks downrange show us to be a little long."

Kranz confirms the crew commander's estimate. "How about you, GUIDANCE?"

"Holding at about eighteen foot. We're gonna make it to a position downrange, so it will be a little long."

The descent engine has been firing for almost four minutes. It appears that *Eagle* will overshoot the landing site. No one seems to be worried about that. Telemetry drops out one more time—the air-to-ground voice circuit goes noisy.

"OK, all flight controllers, thirty seconds to our next GO/NO-GO."

"FLIGHT, NETWORK. LOS LEM TM."

"OK, all flight controllers, I'm going to go around the horn. Make your GO/NO-GOs based on the data you had prior to LOS. I see we have it back."

The flight controllers' response to the flight director poll is unanimous.

"CAPCOM, we're GO to continue PDI."

Duke relays the message—multiple times—no room here for misunderstanding.

"Roger. You are GO—You are GO to continue powered descent. You are GO to continue powered descent."

Eagle's yaw maneuver will allow the crew to start using their landing radar. The flight director is anxious to have that additional input to confirm the spacecraft's altitude and velocity.

"OK, everybody, look for the landing radar."

"And, EAGLE, HOUSTON. We've got data dropout. You're still looking good."

"OK, we got data back."

GUIDANCE reports, "Radar, FLIGHT! Looks good."

"Rog, two thousand feet DELTA-H?"

"Let me know when they accept it, GUIDANCE."

The initial inputs from the landing radar show a two-thousand-foot altitude difference between the radar measurement and the primary guidance and navigation system computer value. The difference is within limits. Had it been on the order of ten thousand feet, an abort would be required. When the crew puts this data into the computer, it will adjust the trajectory until its altitude estimates converges to the radar reading. The guidance officer and his backroom guys are all over the telemetry data, making sure that the radar input is reasonable before the crew feeds it to the onboard computer.

"HOUSTON, you're looking at our DELTA-H?"

Duke responds to Armstrong's question.

"It's looking good to us. Over."

The Lunar Module computer sounds an alarm.

Armstrong reports, "It's a 1202."

"FLIGHT, RETRO, throttle down at six plus two five."

Armstrong and Aldrin have no idea what this alarm means. They have never seen it before. Armstrong asks for help.

"Give us a reading on the 1202 PROGRAM ALARM."

Steve Bales, the guidance officer, and his backroom crew, do know what the alarm means. The computer is reporting that it is overloaded, but it is continuing to perform its normal processing. As long as the alarm is intermittent, the computer should be OK. Within seconds of Armstrong's request, Bales responds, "We're GO on that, FLIGHT."

Duke relays the message.

"Roger. We got—we're GO on that alarm."

The Lunar Module is less than thirty thousand feet above the surface moving at two thousand feet per second. Communications are holding up. This is the way the system is designed to work. The flight controllers supply the in-depth information that no Lunar Module crew could access as they plunge toward the surface—they supply it and they do it right now!

Bales expands his report. "If it doesn't reoccur we'll be GO."

"He's taking in the DELTA-H now."

Reassured by Bale's report, Kranz turns his attention to the next major milestone in the landing sequence. The onboard computer has been running the descent engine at full throttle since shortly after ignition. It is about to reduce the throttle setting below 60 percent so it can make small trajectory adjustments during the final minutes of the braking phase.

"Did you get the throttle down, CAPCOM? Six plus two five."

Duke reads the numbers to the crew. Aldrin acknowledges.

"FLIGHT, FIDO, converging on DELTA-H."

The spacecraft is at 27,000 feet. Aldrin reports another 1202 alarm. "Same alarm, and it appears to come up when we have 1668 up."

GUIDANCE responds to the second alarm. He appears to think that the computer routine used to monitor the altitude difference between the landing radar and the onboard computer is the culprit.

He proposes to take on some of the crew's workload. "OK, we'll monitor his DELTA-H, FLIGHT. I think that's where he's getting it."

"EAGLE, HOUSTON. We'll monitor your DELTA-H."

A minute and a half later GUIDANCE reports, "DELTA-H is beautiful."

Duke starts to repeat the message to the crew.

"DELTA-H—"

Aldrin finishes his sentence, "—looks good now."

"OK, all flight controllers, hang tight—should be throttling down pretty shortly."

Aldrin confirms the event. "Ah! Throttle down…throttles down. Better than the simulator."

Eagle is at 21,000 feet descending at 1,200 feet per second.

"FLIGHT, CONTROL. Everything looks good."

"FLIGHT, GUIDANCE."

"Go, GUIDANCE."

"The Noun Sixty-eight may well be the problem and we can monitor DELTA-H."

"FLIGHT, FIDO, looks real good."

"At seven minutes, you're looking great to us, EAGLE."

The spacecraft has yawed to a face-up attitude with the crew looking at the lunar sky. It is about to pitch up and forward in preparation for the approach and final descent phases of the landing. Aldrin wants to be sure they maintain communications.

"OK. I'm still on SLEW so we may tend to lose as we gradually pitch over. Let me try AUTO again now and see what happens."

"OK. Looks like it's holding."

Duke confirms, "Roger. We got good data."

The spacecraft altitude is 16,300 feet. Kranz anticipates the final call for landing.

"OK, everybody hang tight—seven and a half minutes."

"FLIGHT, GUIDANCE, this landing radar has fixed the velocities—it's beautiful."

"FLIGHT, CONTROL, descent two fuel."

"Descent two fuel crit."

A voice I don't recognize breaks in.

"Descent two fuel only, not critical. He didn't want to say critical."

"Rog. Descent two fuel."

"EAGLE, HOUSTON. It's descent two fuel to MONITOR. Over."

The descent stage propellant tanks have two independent quantity measurement systems. Either one can be monitored by the crew. The flight controllers can monitor both. As the descent progresses, the controllers watch both systems. They make the judgment that the crew should depend on system two for the remainder of the descent. The spacecraft is at 13,500 feet, descending at 760 feet per second.

"FLIGHT, FIDO, looking real good."

Aldrin anticipates the start of the P64 approach phase. "Give us an estimated switchover time please, HOUSTON."

"Roger. Stand by. You're looking great at eight minutes."

"Got an estimated—what's our TGO, GUIDANCE?"

"Thirty seconds to P64."

"EAGLE, you've got thirty seconds to P64."

"OK, we've still got landing radar, GUIDANCE?"

"Affirm."

"OK, has it converged?"

"It's beautiful!"

The flight director is not interested in aesthetics.

"Has it converged?"

"Yes."

"OK."

"EAGLE, HOUSTON. Coming up eight thirty; you're looking great."

The spacecraft is at 7,000 feet. The descent rate is now less than 150 feet per second. Aldrin reports the start of the approach phase, "P64."

The data is solid—solid—solid. Altitude is just 5,200 feet.

"EAGLE, you're looking great. Coming up nine minutes."

"OK, all flight controllers, GO/NO-GO for landing."

The responses are delivered in controlled, steely-eyed missile-guy tones touched this time by just the slightest hint of awe.

"RETRO?"

"GO."

"FIDO?"

"GO."

"GUIDANCE?"

"GO."

"CONTROL?"

"GO."

"G&C?"

"GO."

"EECOM?"

"GO."

"SURGEON?"

"GO."

"CAPCOM, we're GO for landing."

Four-thousand two-hundred feet and continuing the descent.

"EAGLE, HOUSTON. You're GO for landing. Over."

Aldrin acknowledges, "Roger. Understand. GO for landing. Three thousand feet. Program alarm."

He adds and Armstrong repeats, "Twelve-oh-one."

"Twelve-oh-one alarm, guys."

Bales is on the case. "Same type—we're GO, FLIGHT."

In less than ten seconds, Duke has the response on its way to the crew.

"Roger. Twelve-oh-one alarm. We're GO. Same type. We're GO."

"FLIGHT, FIDO, real good, right on."

Aldrin begins to call out altitude and landing point designator angles. "Two thousand feet, two thousand feet. Into the AGS, 47 degrees."

The landing point designator is a simple but effective landing aid. Lines indicating angles from zero down to sixty degrees are scribed on the inner and outer panes of the commander's window. When he positions himself so that the lines on the two panes coincide, he simply looks out at the angle read from the computer by Aldrin and he is looking at the intended landing site.

"EAGLE, looking great. You're GO."

Another computer alarm goes off. The computer ignores it and gets on with the landing task.

"How are you doing, CONTROL?"

"We look good here, FLIGHT."

The voice and telemetry data quality are just what the entire planet Earth needs them to be[8]—close to perfect. Aldrin adds the descent rate, twenty-three feet per second, to his call-outs.

"Thirty-five degrees. Seven hundred and fifty. Coming down at twenty three."

Kranz continues his status check.

"How about you, CAPCOM?"

"GO."

"GUIDANCE, you happy?"

"GO."

"FIDO?"

"GO."

"Seven hundred feet, twenty-one down, thirty-three degrees."

"Six hundred feet, down at nineteen."

Hang on Goldstone—keep the connection—almost there.

"Five hundred and forty feet, down at minus thirty. Down at fifteen."

Concerned that the Lunar Module is headed toward a landing in a boulder field, the crew switches to a manual guidance

---

8   Post-mission analysis would show that the onboard computer's map of Lunar Module body blockage of the steerable antenna line-of-sight needed correction. At some points the antenna was trying to look through the Lunar Module body to see the Earth. After the yaw maneuver that brought the spacecraft face up, the antenna-look angles were such that body blockage and reflection were avoided. The antenna operated in the automatic mode through touchdown.

program—P66. Armstrong takes control of the vehicle's attitude while the computer regulates the descent engine thrust to control the vertical speed—the rate of descent. Using a hand controller, Armstrong adjusts the attitude and therefore the horizontal speed of the craft. Using a switch, he can also make small incremental changes to the computer-controlled rate of descent. In effect Armstrong can now hover the spacecraft like a helicopter.

"At four hundred feet, down at nine."

"Three hundred feet, down three and a half, forty-seven forward."

"Three and a half down, two hundred twenty feet, thirteen forward."

We have solid high-bit rate telemetry—it looks like a simulation.

"One hundred feet, three and a half down, nine forward. Five percent."

A light comes on, warning the crew that they have just over 5 percent of their propellant remaining. Two men in a flimsy spacecraft, 250,000 miles from home, connected to their support team by an electromagnetic whisper, have 94 seconds to decide whether to put their machine down on an alien surface or to abort to orbit by firing the ascent stage engine.

"OK. Seventy-five feet. And it's looking good. Down a half, six forward."

Duke reminds the crew that mission control is counting down to the land-abort decision point, "Sixty seconds."

"Forty feet, down two and a half. Kicking up some dust."

Dust. I hear Mrs. Grew's voice in my ear!

"Thirty feet, two and a half down. Faint shadow."

The Lunar Module is landing with the low morning Sun behind it. Aldrin can see its shadow moving toward them.

"Four forward. Four forward. Drifting to the right a little. OK. Down a half."

"Thirty seconds."

Aldrin calls "contact light" as one of the six-foot probes attached to each of the Lunar Module landing pads strikes the surface.

"OK. Engine stop."

Duke looks for confirmation of what he thinks he just heard. "We copy you down, EAGLE."

Armstrong comes up on the circuit using a call sign that signals the transition from flying machine to isolated outpost on an alien surface.

"HOUSTON, TRANQUILITY BASE here."

"The *Eagle* has landed."

His message come through loud and clear—Goldstone is on the job.

Duke's voice reflects the relief he feels. "Roger, TRANQUILITY. We copy you on the ground. You got a bunch of guys about to turn blue. We're breathing again. Thanks a lot."

Aldrin responds with a simple, "Thank you."

The people around me in the network staff support room look up from their communication panels. Thumbs-up and broad grins are the order of the day. My historian reminds me to take careful note of the directness, simplicity, and, yes, even the eloquence of these first exchanges between Houston and Tranquility Base.

I can imagine that the people in the control room are in the same celebration mode. Kranz tries to get things under control. These guys have work to do. "OK, all flight controllers, about forty-five seconds to T1 STAY/NO-STAY."

A couple of seconds later he's back with a more authoritative tone. This time it is not an alert—it's an order. "OK, keep the chatter down in this room!"

The flight plan has three preplanned liftoff times as a hedge against a post-landing emergency. All of them allow a Command Module rendezvous within the electrical lifetime of the Lunar Module. The first of them is just two minutes after landing. The flight controllers put their heads down and make a double-quick assessment of the vehicle's condition. A minute and twenty seconds after landing, Duke notifies the crew that they are "STAY for

T-1." The next planned liftoff is at eight minutes after landing. The verdict is the same—stay. The third decision point is two hours away. Again the decision would be to stay. Now the flight plan calls for the crew to eat and then rest for four hours. The Black Team needs to do the same. We need to be ready for any emergency launch from the surface. I unplug my headset and head out for a meal and some rack time. Like everyone else on planet Earth, I am happy that this act in our drama has come to a successful conclusion. The intermittent communications have made it more dramatic than anyone had anticipated. Tomorrow, when our turn comes, I fervently hope that the gods will dispense with the special effects.

CHAPTER TWENTY-THREE

Eagle has reached the lunar surface in one piece. For the next two hours, the crew take a quick series of lunar surface photos, align their guidance systems, load ascent data into the onboard computer, and run a simulated launch countdown. At this point, the crew have been on very active duty for about ten hours. The flight plan calls for a meal followed by a four-hour rest period before the start of the first-ever walk on that hostile, cratered lunar terrain.

Just prior to the start of the eat-rest period, Aldrin comes up on the air-to-ground circuit. "Roger. Our recommendation at this point is planning an EVA with your concurrence, starting about eight o'clock this evening, Houston time. That is about three hours from now."

Duke responds with an appropriate, "Stand by."

Aldrin understands the need to run the recommendation past the flight control hierarchy. "Well, we will give you some time to think about that."

About twenty-five seconds after the initial recommendation, Duke has their answer. "TRANQUILITY BASE, HOUSTON. We thought about it; we will support it. You're GO at that time."

The crew will have a quick meal and then start their extravehicular activity preparations.

After the landing, I find some cafeteria food and then head back to the "bunkhouse" for a shower and some rack time. Our bunkhouse has three main spaces—a television lounge, a shower room, and a bunk room—literally a room filled with two-tier bunk beds.

I am just stepping out of the shower when someone sticks his head through the doorway and says, "They are going to skip the rest period and get out early." Thoughts of sleep vanish. I get dry, put on some skivvies, and head for the television lounge. As I walk in the door, a strange feeling of unreality creeps up my spine. The room has a television against one wall. Armchairs and small sofas are scattered around the room facing the television. The furniture, with its motel modern ersatz wood frames and plastic-covered cushions, might have been teleported here from the dayroom on the second floor of the Bachelor Officers Quarters at Bunker Hill Air Force base. I have often wondered why I am here in Texas and not back there in South Dakota or Indiana. I have the unnerving sensation that I have never left those places—the sensation that I have been wandering in a dream and have now been dumped without ceremony right back where I started.

I shake off my mobile nightmare and look around the room. A bunch of the Black Team controllers are already there, sprawled on the chairs and couches. It's kind of strange to see T-shirts where you usually see short-sleeved white shirts with skinny ties.

A couple of hundred feet away from where we are sitting, Cliff Charlesworth and his Green Team are monitoring the preparations for Armstrong's first steps on the Moon. The capsule communicator is Bruce McCandless. The duty network controller is Ernie Randall. His partner is Larry Meyer, another one of the Philco-Ford crew whose job is to keep us out of trouble. As *Apollo 11* approached, Ernie lobbied hard to cover the lunar walk. His preference for that shift probably has a lot to do with my working the two launch shifts.

I find a space on the tile floor where I can sit and lean back against the wall. The historian is beside himself with anticipation.

My butt is cold. We are about to witness the first steps on the Moon in a room filled with experts—with guys who invented a lot of the stuff we are watching. As I look up at the television screen I can't see anything but fuzzy black and white shapes. Slowly one of the blobs resolves itself into a Neil Armstrong. He is descending the ladder to the surface. Reaching the bottom rung he drops down onto the Lunar Module's footpad. To confirm that he can get back up he jumps up to the lower rung. "OK, I just checked—getting back up to that first step, Buzz. The strut isn't collapsed too far, but it's adequate to get back up."

McCandless responds, "Roger. We copy."

"It takes a pretty good little jump."

"I'm at the foot of the ladder. The LM footpads are only depressed in the surface about one or two inches, although the surface appears to be very, very fine grained, as you get close to it. It's almost like a powder. The ground mass is very fine."

I hope Mrs. Grew is watching.

"I'm going to step off the LM now."

"That's one small step for man, one giant leap for mankind."

This adventure on the Moon captures the Black Team flight controllers' full attention. The room is eerily quiet. To my surprise and the historian's disappointment, it will mostly stay that way. After his historic step, Armstrong sets off about his otherworldly business. He begins by amplifying his description of the surface. He reports that "There seems to be no difficulty in moving around." Using a custom-made tool, he scoops up a "contingency sample"—a small amount of material that will provide something for the earthbound geologists to examine if the *Eagle* has to make an early escape from the surface.

Aldrin joins Armstrong and comments on the "magnificent desolation." Armstrong describes a plaque attached to the front landing gear of their craft.

"First there's two hemispheres, one showing each of the two hemispheres of Earth. Underneath it says, 'Here Men from the planet Earth first set foot upon the Moon, July 1969 A.D. We came in peace for all mankind.' It has the crew members' signatures and the signature of the president of the United States."

Armstrong then moves the television camera from a storage bay on the Lunar Module to a point about sixty-five feet away—showing a first-time panorama of their desolate new world. It has an unreal quality that makes it look like something they would dream up on a back lot at Warner Brothers. While Armstrong works the camera, his partner gets on with the first science project planned for their lunar stay—deployment of the solar wind composition experiment. It consists of a long strip of aluminum foil mounted on a pole. Exposed to the rays of the Sun and then returned to Earth, it will give scientists a look at the stream of particles constantly emitted by that star.

Both crew members then stick another pole in the ground. This one will display the American flag. They seem to spend an inordinate amount of time fooling around with a mechanism designed to make the flag look as if it is fluttering in the nonexistent lunar breeze. Following the flag-raising, Aldrin does an evaluation of surface mobility. He lopes back and forth across the surface in view of the camera and provides a commentary on the dynamics and effort involved. He does a "kangaroo hop" that looks like fun.

McCandless interrupts the crew's activities to say that the president is on the line from the White House. Armstrong and Aldrin stop what they are doing to listen. I don't pay much attention to Nixon's remarks—not a lot of creativity or eloquence there. But a couple sentences catch my attention. "For one priceless moment, in the whole history of man, all the people on this Earth are truly one. One in their pride in what you have done. One in our prayers that you will return safely to Earth."

I am not a praying man, but I catch myself hoping that those praying Earthlings have some effect. In a few hours, we are going to need all of the help we can get. When the president finishes his remarks, Armstrong makes a graceful and appropriate response. Both men then give the president a hand salute and get back to what they were doing.

Armstrong begins to collect scoopfuls of surface material for the geologists back home. Aldrin inspects and photographs *Eagle*'s landing gear. When Armstrong finishes with the bulk sample, the two men open the scientific equipment bay on the Lunar Module landing stage. They remove and start to deploy the Early Apollo Surface Experiment Package. It contains two instruments. The Passive Seismic Experiment will detect lunar "moonquakes" and provide information on the internal structure of the Moon. The Laser Ranging Retroreflector will allow measurement of the distance between the Earth and Moon with great precision. As copilots the world over always do, Aldrin does the heavy lifting. He carries the two experiments to their deployment site and puts them in position.

The tracking station at Carnarvon, Australia, is standing by for the first signals. When the crew turns the seismometer on, the signal produced by the impact of their footsteps is downlinked to the thirty-five-foot antenna and relayed back to Houston. Joe Vice, one of our NASA network controllers, coordinates the data reception and transfer from a new surface-experiments area on the first floor of the control center. In the coming months, all of us will pull our share of incredibly boring shifts as we watch the experiment packages deliver their data around the clock.

After an hour and forty-one minutes on the lunar surface, Aldrin climbs back on board *Eagle*. Armstrong follows a few minutes later, after transferring the lunar samples up to Aldrin. The crew closes *Eagle*'s hatch at 11:11 p.m. (CDT) to end their lunar surface stay. They will try to rest and be ready for the next day's liftoff.

I try to do the same. I crawl into my lower bunk. I listen as the bedtime preparation noises are replaced by a chorus of snores. The room is dark now, but I keep seeing sleep-defeating visions of tomorrow morning. A form comes alongside my bunk. The voice of one of our flight surgeons asks if I'm having trouble sleeping. I answer with a definite yes. He offers me a pill. I take it—grateful that he appeared when he did.

By 9 a.m. (CDT), the Black Team is relieving the Maroon Team. Glynn Lunney is our flight director. Ron Evans is the capsule communicator. George and I are replacing Dave Young, my in-house math tutor, and Captain Ron De Cosmo, another member of the air force detachment. They brief us on the status of the tracking network and the control center. Everything is working the way it is supposed to—at least for the moment. As soon as George and I sit down, we get on the net with our own team to make a check on the status and configuration of the specific sites that will support this first-ever launch from the Moon. The deep-space station at Robledo, Spain, will be prime on the Lunar Module for the launch. The station on Ascension Island in the middle of the South Atlantic will back up the Spanish station. The station at Madrid will be prime on the Command and Service Module, with the Merritt Island station at Cape Kennedy as backup. They are reporting all of their systems as "green—can support." George and I hope that it will stay that way.

Evans starts the day's serious business. "TRANQUILITY BASE, TRANQUILITY BASE, HOUSTON. Over."

"Good morning, HOUSTON. TRANQUILITY BASE. Over."

"Roger. Loud and clear. And how is the resting standing up there? Did you get a chance to curl up on the engine can?"

"Roger. Neil has rigged himself a really good hammock with a waste tether, and he's been lying on the ascent engine cover, and I curled up on the floor. Over."

"Roger. Copy, Buzz. Got a couple of changes to your surface checklist here. And, in general, what we're going to want you to do is P22, tracking the Command Module for one last hack on your position there. And this will be…In other words, P57, P22, and then to press on with the checklist."

The first order of business is basic. The Lunar Module landed long. It went beyond its designated landing point. No one knows exactly where it is. Dave Reed, the ascent FIDO, and his team need a better position so they can pick a liftoff time that minimizes propellant usage and gives the proper phasing for rendezvous. They will try for a better fix on the *Eagle*'s position by using its rendezvous radar in Program 22, the rendezvous radar lunar surface navigation program. The Houston computers have a pretty good idea of where *Columbia* is. During *Columbia*'s next pass, *Eagle* will track Collins's spacecraft. The ground computers can then use that data to work backward to a better location for *Eagle*.

The position update is the first item on a crowded agenda. Evan's made his wake-up call to Tranquility Base at 121 hours and 32 minutes ground elapsed time. If things go as planned, the *Eagle*'s ascent engine will ignite at 124 hours, 22 minutes, 0 seconds. When that engine ignites, *Eagle* will go straight up for just about fifteen seconds. With no atmosphere to battle, the only requirement is to get high enough to clear the stark, forbidding terrain. Once clear of the terrain, *Eagle* will pitch over so that the thrust of its engine will be used as efficiently as possible to gain the horizontal velocity needed to achieve orbit. The spacecraft will go from zero to more than six thousand feet per second in seven minutes and eighteen seconds. One hundred and sixty-eight miles downrange from the launch point and sixty thousand feet above the surface, it will be back in lunar orbit coasting toward an apolune of about forty-five nautical miles half a revolution later, on the far side of the Moon.

During ascent, the crew members are passengers in a vehicle controlled by the onboard computer. Once in orbit, they will become directly responsible for their own fate. To get home they have to rendezvous and dock with the Command and Service Module. They will chase the *Columbia* for the next four hours through two lunar revolutions, executing three maneuvers using the small reaction control system thrusters. After coasting to the apolune of their orbit, the crew will initiate the coelliptic sequence initiate, or CSI burn, to circularize the *Eagle*'s orbit. They can then begin tracking Collins's spacecraft using the Lunar Module rendezvous radar. The direction, duration, and timing of each of their maneuvers will be computed by the crew based on that tracking data. The Houston flight dynamics machine will compute those same values using ground tracking data as a "sanity check" on the onboard values. But the real work will be done in lunar orbit.

Half a revolution after the circularizing burn, the *Eagle* crew will execute a second maneuver—the constant delta height or CDH maneuver. This maneuver will put *Eagle* into an orbit that is a constant distance below the Command Module orbit. Again, the basic objective is to provide the tracking data the crew needs to finalize their terminal initiation, or TPI burn. The TPI burn will put *Eagle* on an trajectory such that it will intercept its target after about 130 degrees of orbital travel. After this burn, there will be opportunities to make small midcourse corrections to precisely control *Eagle*'s final approach to *Columbia*.

Twenty-six minutes after the wake-up call to Tranquility Base, *Columbia* comes out from behind the Moon on its twenty-fourth lunar revolution.

Collins has turned on the beacon that will respond to interrogation by the *Eagle*'s rendezvous radar. He reports, "HOUSTON, COLUMBIA. My rendezvous radar transponder is operating."

Evans completes the connection, "TRANQUILITY, HOUSTON. Request rendezvous radar breakers in about now."

The Lunar Module rendezvous radar locks up on *Columbia*'s radar beacon. Thirteen minutes later, Houston has enough data and asks both spacecraft to terminate the rendezvous radar tracking. Collins reports that he had "about five hours good sleep." Tranquility Base makes a hot-fire check of the reaction control thrusters that will control spacecraft attitude during the ascent burn and provide the thrust needed for the rendezvous maneuvers. Evans confirms that, "The RCS check looked mighty fine to us." With the check complete, Evans reads the ascent pre-advisory data to *Eagle*'s crew. He follows with data for coelliptic sequence and terminal phase maneuvers. The rendezvous maneuver information is the ground system's best guess. The crew will make it specific once they are in orbit and tracking their target.

George and I make careful note of the ascent engine ignition time. We coordinate the time with our team in the control center and pass it to the tracking stations. We make another check of their support status. They all report no change from our earlier check. "Green—can support" has a reassuring sound as it is repeated by each station in turn.

We have about one hour and twenty minutes before ignition. George and I take the opportunity to make another pass through the "Ascent Work Schedule General Ground Rules" we have put together and coordinated over the two months or so. When things begin to happen, there won't be time for review. We work our way through the rules:

1. Voice communications and high bit-rate telemetry have maximum priority during the Ascent Phase.

2. There are no Lunar Module command requirements during the Ascent Phase, therefore:

    a. A failure of the Madrid command computer after completion of the last required Lunar Module Guidance Computer and Command Module Computer uplinks (approximately 123:00:00 GET) will not be grounds for an automatic handover to Ascension. Such a handover will be made only <u>at the specific direction of TELCOM.</u>

    b. In the event of a complete telemetry computer failure at Madrid, the remaining computer will be loaded with the telemetry program for ascent.

3. In the event of a failure which prevents the transfer of high-speed tracking data from Bermuda, Antigua, or Ascension, a site previously configured for Command and Service Module support will not be reconfigured for Lunar Module support. In the event of two such failures, TRACK, in coordination with SELECT SUPPORT, will designate a third high-speed tracking station for the Lunar Module (probably Merritt Island), <u>provided that the selection does not jeopardize communications with the Command and Service Module.</u>

4. Before requests are made for Lunar Module reconfiguration to by-pass communications difficulties, every attempt will be made to determine whether or not the ground station is the source of the problem.

5. In the event of voice or telemetry problems during Ascent Phase, every attempt will be made to maintain Madrid-X (eighty-five-foot antenna) as the active station before a hand over is made to Ascension (thirty-foot antenna).

6. If a complete failure is experienced at Madrid and Madrid-X, handover will be made to Ascension for the Lunar Module and Merritt Island for the Command and Service Module.

7. If Ascension fails Bermuda will be designated as the back-up station for the Lunar Module.

8. In order to prevent fifty kilobit-per-second line overflow [between Goddard and Houston] TIC will turn on *Apollo* [telemetry] data from two stations only and EASEP data from one station only during the period that high-speed tracking data is online from four stations.

We have backups for the backups—no one has ever done this before.

"TRACK, NETWORK, my loop. Confirm high-speed tracking data from the following stations."

"MADRID WING?"

"Roger, MADRID WING high speed."

"ASCENSION?"

"Confirm ASCENSION."

"BERMUDA?"

"Roger BERMUDA."

"ANTIGUA?"

"Confirm ANTIGUA high speed."

"MILA?"

"MILA data is good."

"Copy all stations configured, thanks, TRACK."

"FLIGHT, NETWORK, your loop, confirm all high-speed tracking stations are configured."

Lunney looks over and gives us a nod as he acknowledges the report, "Roger, NETWORK."

George picks up the next checklist sequence. "COMM CONTROL, NETWORK. Can you confirm your circuit restoral priorities for me?"

I am not a praying man—at least so far. But the confident demand-response sequence of these checklist call-outs has a reassuring liturgical feel. The issues involved in these checks aren't complex. We just need to ensure that everything is in place when the ascent engine ignites. My historian repeats his mantra, "Leave nothing to chance—no one has ever done this before."

"Roger, NETWORK. Restoral priorities are Net One, Four, Six, Two, Five, Three."

"Concur. Pass those to GODDARD COMM MANAGER and confirm."

"Roger that, NETWORK."

Columbia emerges from behind the Moon on its twenty-fifth revolution. Ignition is less than thirty minutes away. Evans provides a position update based on the rendezvous radar data collected on the last revolution.

"HOUSTON, COLUMBIA on OMNI Delta. Over."

"COLUMBIA, HOUSTON. Roger. Loud and clear."

"And if you would like to take it down, we have the latest position of Tranquility Base. Over."

"Go ahead."

"Roger. It's just west—at west crater, Juliett 0.5, 7.7, over."

"Understand that it is just west of the crater Juliett 0.5 and 7.7. Is that correct?"

"COLUMBIA, HOUSTON. That is correct."

"OK. Thank you, Ron."

I have my head down—staring at my checklist steps one more time to make sure I won't miss anything.

"It looks like it's showtime."

I look up at the sound of George's voice, and he nods toward the front of the room. The display on the center plot-board has changed. Since the landing, we have been looking at a plot showing a horizontal strip of the visible lunar surface extending forty degrees north and south of the lunar equator. The orbital ground tracks of the Command and Service Module are plotted in red against that background. A spacecraft symbol travels the orbital ground track from east to west as the spacecraft makes its transit across the near side of the Moon. Now it has been replaced by a flight dynamics plot that shows *Eagle*'s nominal ascent trajectory. When the ascent engine ignites, plotters will scribe the actual trajectory based on three sets of data—the Lunar Module onboard primary and abort guidance systems and the ground network tracking. We have seen this display dozens of times during our ascent phase training runs. No one has ever seen the real thing.

"NETWORK, CPC, your loop. We have an instruct fault on CP Alpha. We switched to Bravo and we're recycling Alpha out of sync."

George takes the call. "Roger, CPC. Let us know when you're ready to recycle both machines to get in sync."

One of the two UNIVAC 494 communications-processing computers that receive data from the outside and route it to its internal destination has had a momentary failure. The UNIVAC computer controllers are in the process of correcting the problem and bringing the machine back online. When that happens the two computers will be out of sync. They will be in slightly different parts of their scripts—an unacceptable condition when the backup may be called on to instantaneously take over as prime. To get them in the same place, the communications processor troops will have to restart them at the same time. That recycle operation will interrupt data flow into the control center.

Less than a minute later, "NETWORK, CPC. We're ready for a recycle."

George responds, "Roger, CPC. Stand by."

Before George finishes his response, I am pressing my transmit switch. The recycle will interrupt data flow for a minute or so.

"FLIGHT, NETWORK, your loop. We need to recycle the communications processors when it's convenient."

Lunney gives me a look that says, "That's never convenient."

He speaks to the room at large, "Anyone have a problem with that?"

No response.

"Go ahead, NETWORK."

Two minutes later the lunar umbilical is restored—almost.

"NETWORK, TRACK. COMPUTER SUP reports that the mission operations computer was trying to send site acquisition messages during that recycle. He's not sure they all went out. They are going to retransmit."

The site acquisition messages tell the tracking stations, based on the latest trajectory projections, the time that they will have acquisition of signal from the spacecraft. They are the critical element for tracking station planning. In just a few minutes those predictions have to include the orbit-bound *Eagle*. Retransmitting is a good idea.

"NETWORK, TRACK. We'll keep an eye on this and let you know if they have any problems. If we have to, we'll come up on Net Two and pass the data that way."

"Roger all of that, thank you."

"COLUMBIA and TRANQUILITY, I'll give you a mark at twenty minutes to go, and that's in about twenty seconds."

"Stand by."

"Mark."

Twenty minutes until ignition and liftoff from the lunar surface. Time to get on with our checklist. "MADRID, ASCENSION, NETWORK on Net Two. Confirm Jump Key Number One down on both computers."

The operational telemetry and command processing software run on two UNIVAC computers at each tracking station. The programs are designed so that when a fault occurs, the computer stops and performs a core memory dump to magnetic tape. The idea is to make it easier to troubleshoot software problems post-pass. After the dump, the tape rewinds and the computer reloads itself and restarts. Depending on the circumstances, this whole process can take a lot of seconds. At this point, software troubleshooting doesn't even show up on our list of mission priorities. The "program jump" switch allows the software dump routine to be manually bypassed without affecting normal operation. That's what we are going to do.

"TRANQUILTY BASE, HOUSTON."

"Roger. Go ahead."

"Roger. Our guidance recommendation is PGNS, and you're cleared for takeoff."

"Roger. Understand. We're number one on the runway."

Ascent engine ignition minus seventeen minutes—battle short time. "MADRID, NETWORK, Net Two. Enable the battle short function at the wing station and verify."

"Stand by, NETWORK."

A lot of the equipment at the tracking stations, especially the transmitter equipment, operates at high voltage. Circuit breakers protect that equipment from excessive voltage or current. The battle short mode bypasses those protective devices. We will let millions of dollars worth of equipment burn before we give up any critical data. No one has...

Aldrin comes up on the air-to-ground circuit. "HOUSTON, TRANQUILITY. We're not sure that we got number two tank to fire. It's still showing a high pressure."

"Roger. We confirm that. Try it again."

I give George a puzzled glance. He shrugs his shoulders. Are we about to be stuck in the middle of a major problem? We have no idea. The Lunar Module flight controllers seem calm enough.

"OK. We'll go to number two this time."

"Roger. We concur."

"Roger. No fire."

Whatever didn't happen earlier has not happened again.

"NETWORK, MADRID. The battle short function is enabled."

"Roger, MADRID."

The Lunar Module backup station will operate in the same mode.

"ASCENSION, NETWORK, Net Two. Enable the battle short function and verify."

"Stand by, NETWORK."

"NETWORK, ASCENSION, battle short enabled."

"We copy, ASCENSION."

"FLIGHT, NETWORK. Battle short enabled at Madrid and Ascension."

"Roger, battle short."

Aldrin comes back up on the circuit to talk about the tank problem, "HOUSTON, looks like there's very little difference between the two."

"We've got number two reading 3050 and number one is reading—3000 and it drops down to 2990. So I'm not sure that it's really indicative that it didn't go. Over."

"Roger. We copy and we agree."

I still don't know for sure what is going on. I stand up and look down at the consoles just below ours. I see the backs of some very busy Lunar Module guys. Talking to them is not an option. They are too busy working the problem. I look over at my console partner. He makes a guess, "I think maybe they're talking about one of the helium tanks that pressurize the ascent propulsion fuel and oxidizer tanks. They need to pressurize the tanks so that the propellants flow smoothly through the engine. Sounds like one of the explosive squibs that they fire to open the line from the tank didn't work."

"Is that serious stuff? They have two tanks."

"I don't know. We'll find out soon enough."

Aldrin responds to Evans last input, "OK. I assume we're—we're GO for liftoff, and we'll proceed with the ascent feed."

"Roger. That's correct, and we'll go ahead and watch tank two. If it doesn't—tank two doesn't decrease, we'll tell you to close the ascent feeds and open the shutoffs. Over."

"OK. Ascent feeds are open and shutoffs are closed."

The clock display at the front of the room shows that we are ten minutes from ignition. We have two checklist steps to work. The first one reads, "NETWORK confirm with TELCOM that the Lunar Module steerable antenna has been transferred from SLEW to AUTO mode."

I press the transmit switch. "TELCOM, NETWORK, can you confirm AUTO mode?"

Just as I transmit, Ron Evans has the same question for the crew.

"TRANQUILTY BASE, little less than ten minutes here. Everything looks good, and we assume the steerable's in track mode AUTO."

"Roger. It is in track mode AUTO."

"Let's hope it stays that way," George mutters *sotto voce*.

"NETWORK, TELCOM, did you copy TRANQUILITY?"

"Roger that, TELCOM. Thanks."

The contingency procedures that we will use if we have Lunar Module loss of signal during the launch are based on the antenna being in the automatic mode. In that case, the crew is not involved. If it is in SLEW mode, Aldrin has to add the additional task of manually pointing the antenna to his already crowded to-do list.

I pass the antenna status to our team on the first floor to make sure we are all on the same page of our contingency plan if something goes wrong. George follows up with the next step in our pre-launch checklist—confirming with the telemetry controller that he has the required telemetry formats selected at Madrid and Ascension, formats that focus on critical launch system measurements. Check, and check again. No one has ever done this before.

The Lunar Module guys are still working what we think is a helium tank problem.

"FLIGHT, CONTROL."

"Go."

"OK, we reviewed this in the back room, SPAN, Building 45. They concur on their recommendation that bottle number two did not blow, to open the mains, terminate ascent feed."

"At a couple of minutes after—"

"We confirmed that it did not blow when everything settled down."

"OK, we're on ascent batteries?"

"That's affirmative and they look real good."

"Anything else you need now, FLIGHT?"
"Nope."

We are about seven minutes from liftoff. There is a problem with the ascent propulsion system. There also seems to be a workaround. The clock at the front of the control room continues to count down. The crew continues to work their way through the pre-launch checklist.

Lunney makes a status check. "Four minutes to liftoff. Crew's standing by at TIG minus two in the checklist. FIDO, status?"
"We got it all, FLIGHT. Green and GO."
"CONTROL?"
"GO, FLIGHT."
"TELCOM?"
"GO, FLIGHT."
"SURGEON?"
"GO, FLIGHT."

We also have everything we need. The plumbing is all in order. We wait with the rest of the world for ignition of the ascent engine. As we wait, my inner historian contrasts this first launch from another planetary body with the launch from the home planet. There are no test conductors, no towering gantries, no rescue forces on standby. Range safety is not a problem—there is no range. We are reduced now to two cold, tired men[9] in a

---

9   "*Apollo 11* Mission Report": "<u>Lunar rest period</u>. The rest period was almost completely unsatisfactory. The helmets and gloves were worn to relieve subconscious anxiety about a loss of cabin pressure, and they presented no problem. But noise, lighting, and a lower-than-desired temperature were annoying. The suits were uncomfortably cool, even with the waterflow disconnected. Oxygen flow was finally cut off, and the helmets were removed, but the noise from the glycol pumps was then loud enough to interrupt sleep. The window shades did not completely block out light, and the cabin was illuminated by a combination of light passing through the shades, warning lights, and display lighting. The Commander rested on the ascent engine cover and was bothered by the light entering through the telescope. The Lunar Module Pilot estimated that he slept fitfully for perhaps 2 hours, and the Commander did not sleep at all, even though body positioning was not a problem. Because of the reduced gravity, the positions on the floor and on the engine cover were both quite comfortable."

flimsy machine that has no backup—a machine that may have a problem that is still unresolved. And no one has done this before—ever.

As we wait for ignition, my historian has a look of excited anticipation on his face. My own expression is one of serious macho cool. A hint of "auto-shake" in my left hand suggests the abject terror that I am trying to conceal. I strike a pose of competent concentration, leaning forward in my chair and extending my left hand to grip a small handle to the left of my television display—one of two handles the maintenance people use to install or remove the television module. If the guys worrying the plumbing are having this kind of problem, can you imagine the stress on the crew and the controllers who really have to make this thing work?

Evans relays the status check results to the crew. The change to the in-flight call sign foreshadows what we all hope is about to happen.

"EAGLE, HOUSTON. You're looking good to us."

"CAPCOM, FLIGHT."

"CAPCOM, go."

"Just a reminder. The order is open RCS, close ascent feed."

"Open main shut-off valves, close ascent feed, right."

"CONTROL, FLIGHT."

"This is CONTROL. If we did that we'd also want to close the cross-feeds."

"At what step?"

"That will be the last thing he did."

I wish CONTROL had picked different words. There seems to be some confusion about how to deal with the tank problem.

Lunney reminds his team, "Coming up on TIG minus two."

Evans passes the same message to the crew. "Mark. TIG minus two."

Aldrin reports, "Roger. Guidance steering in the AGS."

FIDO confirms the report, "We see it, FLIGHT. Looks good."

"OK."

The abort guidance system is initialized and ready to back up the primary guidance system. After almost a minute of near silence marred only by background noise on the air-to-ground link, Aldrin continues his narrative on launch preparations. "OK. Master arm, on." Armstrong has armed the explosive devices that are about to break the spacecraft in half.

FIDO confirms, "Roger, we see it, FLIGHT."

"OK."

Continuing through their checklist the crew members put on their helmets and gloves.

Lunney makes one more check with the Lunar Module controllers, "Still up for you, Don?"

"Looks good, FLIGHT."

"CONTROL? CONTROL?"

"Say again, FLIGHT."

"Still lookin' good?"

"Lookin' good."

"GUIDANCE?"

"GO both systems."

Aldrin reports, "DSKY blanks." The guidance computer display has gone blank and then is reilluminated to signal that the computer has calculated the average acceleration needed to put the spacecraft into orbit. He picks up the launch countdown. "Nine, eight, seven, six, five, abort stage, engine arm, ascent, proceed."

Explosive bolts separate the ascent and descent stages. Other explosive charges drive guillotine blades that sever the electrical cables and plumbing connecting the stages. The engine controller opens the engine valves. The computer displays "Verb 99." Armstrong responds by pressing the proceed button on the computer. The ascent engine ignites. Data and voice signals disappear.

"MADRID has LM LOS."[10]

---

10   "*Apollo 11* Mission Report": "The performance of the communications system during the ascent and rendezvous phases was nominal except for a fifteen second loss of down-link phase lock at ascent engine ignition. The data indicates that this loss can be attributed to rapid phase perturbations caused by transmission through the ascent engine plume."

"ASCENSION has LM LOS."

Oh shit, oh dear. Not now! Please, not now!

I fumble with my contingency checklist. Loss of signal at both prime and backup sites. That's Attachment Three. My fingers aren't working very well. I finally open to the procedure. I am looking at a terrifying logic diagram covering an entire page. That shouldn't be a surprise. We made the damn thing that way. But I see now that there's some considerable difference between building it and using it. I look at the first entry: "Wait thirty seconds." Even I can do that. But when do I start the thirty seconds? How much time elapsed while I fumbled?

George comes to my rescue.

"Twenty seconds," he says almost to himself with his eyes locked on the mission clock at the front of the room.

Five seconds later, "MADRID has AOS LM."

We hold our collective breath.

"MADRID has two-way lock LM."

Without thinking, I come up on Net Two, "MADRID you're beautiful."

The Madrid operations supervisor responds without missing a beat, "We try to do our best, NETWORK."

We hear Aldrin again, his voice readable through moderate static, "—twenty-six, thirty-six feet per second up. Be advised of the pitch-over. Very smooth."

I picture the Robledo antenna tracking the Moon as it slowly descends toward the horizon. I mentally offer some encouragement to the tracking system operators, *Keep it locked up, you guys. Please, keep it locked up.*

The Lunar Module has completed its short vertical ascent. It pitches down about fifty degrees and begins to gain some of the five-thousand-feet-per-second horizontal velocity it needs to reach orbit.

CONTROL comes up on the flight director's voice net, "Bottle two is going down, FLIGHT."

"Tank two is good, CAPCOM."

The problem with the helium tank seems to have been a false alarm.

"FIDO, how are you looking?"

"Looking good, FLIGHT."

"GUIDANCE?"

"Looking good, FLIGHT."

"One minute, looking good, CAPCOM."

"EAGLE, HOUSTON. One minute and you're looking good."

The Lunar Module is once again a flying machine—call sign EAGLE.

"TELCOM, how are you?"

"Looks good, FLIGHT."

Aldrin reports, "A very quiet ride, just a little bit of slow wallowing back and forth. Not very much thruster activity."

"SURGEON?"

"Good, FLIGHT."

Aldrin supplies a velocity and altitude update. "Seven hundred [feet-per-second horizontal velocity], 150 [feet-per-second vertical velocity] up. Beautiful. Nine thousand [feet altitude]. PGNS and AGS agrees within a foot per second."

FIDO confirms, "Looking good, FLIGHT. There all together."

"Good at two, CAPCOM."

"EAGLE, HOUSTON. You're looking good at two. PGNS, AGS, MSFN [ground tracking] all agree."

"And that's a thousand, one seventy up. Beautiful. Fourteen thousand. And a foot per second again, AGS to PGNS."

Once again FIDO confirms. "We see that, FLIGHT. GO both systems."

"Roger."

"CONTROL?"

"Looking good, FLIGHT."

"TELCOM?"

"Looks real good."

"FIDO, all sources on the money?"

"Roger, that."

"S-band looks like it's holding good, HOUSTON."

Grinning like Alice's Cheshire cat, I turn toward George, "We'll take all of that we can get."

He holds up his right index finger in a standby-one gesture. He goes up on Net Two.

"MADRID, NETWORK. Can you give us the Lunar Module signal strength?"

"Stand by, NETWORK."

"NETWORK, MADRID, minus 105 dBm."

The predicted performance for an eighty-five-foot antenna is minus 105 dBm.

George gives me a thumbs-up, "It don't get no better than that!"

Aldrin reads the horizontal and vertical velocities, "Fifteen hundred [feet per second], one eighty-five [feet per second]."

"EAGLE, HOUSTON. You're GO at three minutes. Everything looks good."

Thirty seconds later CONTROL gives continuing confirmation. "Still looking good, FLIGHT."

"APS looking good to you?"

"That's affirmative."

"Helium tracking?"

"Coming right on down. Looking good."

"OK. Normal usage, huh?"

"Is that right?"

"Roger."

We hear Armstrong come up on the air-to-ground, "We're going right down US 1." The spacecraft passes through 32,000 feet.

Lunney runs his circuit. "GUIDANCE?"

"Go both systems."

"Real tight, huh?'

"Better than ever."

"OK."

"FIDO? FIDO? Status?"

"Real good, FLIGHT."

"OK. All of them together."

"At four, CAPCOM, all GO."

"EAGLE, HOUSTON. Four minutes; you're going right down the track. Everything's great."

The spacecraft is moving at nearly 2,500 feet per second. Aldrin and Armstrong identify the craters below them as they streak through the lunar sky—Sabine, Ritter, Schmidt. The flight director makes another status check with his flight controllers at five minutes into the maneuver—everything is working as planned. Downlink data is steady. Spacecraft voice is loud and clear. Armstrong captures the moment, "Looking good here. It's a pretty spectacular ride."

The only continuing worry seems to be the suspect helium tank. Lunney makes one more check with CONTROL, "Two minutes to go."

"Still good, FLIGHT."

"Roger. Helium tracking all right there?"

"Comin' on down."

"Tracking right?"

"Affirmative."

"Good."

"We're a little above our predicted."

"Good."

On the trajectory display at the front of the room, the data from the two onboard computers and the tracking stations is plotting directly along the nominal predictions.

"Rates look good there, CONTROL?"

"Affirmative.'

"FIDO?"

"Green and GO, FLIGHT."

"GUIDANCE?"

"GO both systems."

"CONTROL?"

"We're GO."

"TELCOM?"

"GO."

"CAPCOM, six."

"EAGLE, HOUSTON. You're still looking mighty fine."

Aldrin responds and then begins to countdown the velocity *Eagle* still needs to gain before engine cutoff. "Roger. Good agreement in DELTA-V to go in both AGS and PGNS."

"Eight hundred [feet per second] to go."

"Seven hundred to go. OK, I'm going to open up the main shutoffs."

"—three fifty to go."

"Stand by on the engine arm. Ninety [feet per second], OK, OFF, fifty [fifty feet per second]."

"Shutdown."

"We got 5337.3 [feet-per-second horizontal velocity], 32.8 feet per second [vertical velocity], 60,666 [feet altitude]."

"EAGLE. Roger. We copy. It's great. Go."

"Roger, HOUSTON. The *Eagle* is back in orbit, having left Tranquility Base and leaving behind a—a replica from our Apollo 11 patch and the olive branch."

"EAGLE, HOUSTON. Roger. We copy. The whole world is proud of you."

"We had a lot of help down there."

Eagle reaches orbit seven minutes, fifteen seconds after lift-off from the Sea of Tranquility. The predicted time was seven minutes and eighteen seconds. Not bad for government work. Perilune is 9.1 nautical miles, and apolune is 47.2 nautical miles. The trajectory plot on the center display at the front of the room is replaced by a graphic that shows the orbital tracks of the two spacecraft—the Command and Service Module in the lead, chased by the Lunar Module twenty degrees of lunar longitude behind it.

The orbital chase goes on for three hours and forty minutes. The first order of business after orbit insertion is to compute the velocity, duration, and direction of the first maneuver, coelliptic sequence initiation, or CSI. Aldrin realigns *Eagle*'s guidance system so that the onboard computer knows exactly where it is. Armstrong initiates the rendezvous navigation program and turns on the rendezvous radar to track the Command and

Service Module. Collins, on *Columbia*, computes the mirror image maneuver in the event that he has to go to *Eagle*'s rescue. Four minutes before loss of signal on *Columbia*'s twenty-fifth lunar revolution, Evans gives both vehicles a "GO for CSI." To complete the maneuver, the onboard computer must fire the reaction control thrusters to increase the craft's velocity by 51.5 feet per second as *Eagle* reaches apolune ten minutes after loss of signal. That velocity increase will have its effect 180 degrees after the burn—raising *Eagle*'s perilune from 9.4 nautical miles to 45 nautical miles. As *Eagle* emerges from behind the Moon on revolution twenty-six, Aldrin reports a successful burn. The perilune change is greater than expected but that doesn't seem to pose a problem. *Eagle*'s orbit is now 56.6 nautical miles by 62.5 nautical miles. The two spacecraft are just over one hundred miles apart, closing the gap at a rate of ninety-nine feet per second.

The next burn, the constant differential height maneuver, is due to take place on this near-side pass. The maneuver will twist the *Eagle*'s orbit so that it remains at a constant distance below *Columbia*'s orbital track. Madrid is tracking *Columbia* with Ascension as backup. The station at Robledo is two-way on *Eagle* with Merritt Island as backup. Thirteen minutes before the maneuver, things get complicated. A cooled amplifier failure at Madrid interrupts the Command and Service Module's downlink signals. The station crew tries to replace it with an uncooled amplifier. The output from that amplifier is too weak and noisy to be readable. *Columbia* can hear Houston, but Houston cannot hear *Columbia*—all of this during the run-up to a critical maneuver. Madrid speculates that the problem is with the downlink voice. We let them know that both Ascension and Merritt Island are receiving good voice signals. We are caught up in our own incredible stupidity for fourteen endless minutes. At that point, INCO quietly suggests that since we have good voice from Ascension we might just switch to Ascension and solve the problem. We do and it does. George and I stare intently at our console displays as if avoiding eye contact would help us avoid the "dumb shit" label we fully deserve. The fact that we are in a kind of territorial pissing contest with those guys doesn't help.

In spite of our feeblemindedness, the maneuver takes place as scheduled. A few minutes after the burn, Evans delivers a message, "COLUMBIA, HOUSTON. Our comm problem was traced to a ground station here."

"OK. Glad to hear it."

"Roger. You're mighty fine now."

At least he has the good grace not to add "and a ground crew screwup."

The crews of both spacecraft make navigation updates in preparation for the next burn—the terminal phase initiation maneuver. Planned ignition time is 127 hours, 3 minutes, and 39 seconds ground elapsed time. The ignition time is 6 minutes and 39 seconds later than planned. At the appointed time, just before loss of signal on this the twenty-sixth lunar revolution, *Eagle* thrusts along the line of sight to *Columbia*. As the two spacecraft go behind the Moon they are 38 miles apart, closing at a rate of 110 feet per second.

When the spacecraft come out from the Moon on revolution twenty-seven, the plan calls for the Goldstone Apollo station to track *Columbia*. The Goldstone deep-space station will be two-way with *Eagle*. Part two of that plan works just fine. At the expected acquisition of signal time, Evans makes his call.

"EAGLE and COLUMBIA, HOUSTON. Standing by."

Five seconds later Armstrong responds, "Roger. We're station-keeping."

And part two—how does it work out? Not so good. An equipment operator at the Goldstone Apollo station makes a procedural mistake. For six and a half minutes, we have no voice or data from *Columbia*. The two spacecraft can talk to each other on their very high frequency radios—that's the important thing as they approach each other to dock. But Houston is blind—unable to monitor the status of *Columbia*'s systems. By the time we sort out the problem, the two spacecraft are docked.

Collins reports that the docking had its hairy moment. "That was a funny one, you know. I didn't—I didn't feel a shock, and I thought things were pretty steady. I went to retract there, and that's when all hell broke loose. Were you guys—did it appear to you to be—that you were jerking around quite a bit during the retract cycle?"

Armstrong responds, "Ah yeah. It seemed to happen at the time I put the plus-X thrust to it, and apparently it wasn't centered, because somehow or other I accidentally got off in attitude and then the attitude hold system started firing."

"Yeah. I was sure busy there for a couple of seconds."

With the spacecraft connected, the crew of *Eagle* begins the process of cleaning up themselves, their equipment, and their precious sample containers in preparation for the transfer to *Columbia*. They are still working that problem when the spacecraft goes behind the Moon on its twenty-seventh orbit. That transfer should take place after the spacecraft comes into view on its twenty-eighth orbit.

We won't be here to see that. During the dark-side pass, we are relieved by the White Team network controllers, George Ojalehto and Doug Wilson. We relate our tale of electromagnetic mishaps. When we complete our shift-change briefing, Wilson summarizes what he heard, "It sounds like y'all were all eat up with the dumb shit!"

We can't disagree. We grab our headsets and notebooks and try to disappear as fast as we can.

The transfer to *Columbia* takes place earlier than planned—while the spacecraft is behind the Moon. The crew jettisons *Eagle*, leaving it to orbit and eventually crash into the Moon. Seven hours and twenty minutes after docking, behind the Moon at the beginning of *Columbia*'s thirty-first revolution, the crew starts their journey home. They fire the Service Module engine for two minutes and twenty-eight seconds and head for Earth at almost six thousand miles per hour. Everyone is more relaxed—not much—just a little bit more—during the trans-Earth coast. The crew makes one midcourse correction about fifteen hours after the trans-Earth injection burn.

About two hours after the midcourse correction, the crew gets ready for a rest period by putting *Columbia* into its passive thermal control mode. With its long axis perpendicular to the Sun's rays, the spacecraft will rotate three times each hour to ensure even solar heating of onboard systems. Because the spacecraft is rotating and the crew is resting, someone has to periodically switch omni antennas. Our friend the INCO is supposed to do that. At one point he doesn't. We lose all contact with the spacecraft for forty-eight minutes. We have no data—tracking or telemetry—and no voice capability. The spacecraft disappears for almost an hour. The Goldstone station tracks along the spacecraft's predicted path until the active antenna comes into view and they can regain two-way contact. Once the situation is safely resolved, it provides the opportunity, through the remainder of the mission, for the guy on the NETWORK console to glance over at the guy on the INCO console with a shit-eating grin on his face.

Besides midcourse corrections, the only scheduled activities are three television broadcasts. The first starts at 177 hours and 30 minutes ground elapsed time. Goldstone receives and relays the television signal. In the course of the broadcast, Mike Collins thanks everyone who contributed to the mission: the rocket and spacecraft builders, and all the people in Houston, including management, mission planners, flight controllers, and crew-training folks. I am surprised that he makes no mention of the people at the tracking stations around the world and at Goddard who made this thing work.

As the spacecraft continues its coast toward Earth, those people manning the network deal with the usual array of problems. Power amplifiers fail at Robledo and Bermuda. There is a continuing series of problems with the wide-band data circuits between Goddard and Houston due to microwave fading, unstable weather conditions, and misbehaving data modems at the Houston end of the circuits. The crews on duty make good use of redundant circuits and terminal equipment. There are no major data losses.

Fourteen hours before splashdown, the mission managers decide to use the *Apollo* spacecraft's lifting capabilities to stretch the entry path 215 nautical miles farther downrange toward Hawaii to a new landing point because of thunderstorms forecasted in the primary recovery area in the mid-Pacific. At 195 hours, 3 minutes, and 7 seconds ground elapsed time, *Columbia* slams into the atmosphere at more than 36,000 feet per second. For the next three and a half minutes, communications are cut off by a fiery sheet of plasma that surrounds the spacecraft. After the spacecraft emerges from the blackout, the drogue parachutes deploy, followed by the main parachutes. Five minutes after the main parachutes deploy, *Columbia* touches down on planet Earth. The pre-mission flight plan touchdown time is 195 hours, 18 minutes, 59 seconds. The Command Module splashes down in the Pacific at 195 hours, 18 minutes, 35 seconds after liftoff from the Kennedy Space Center. Not bad for government work.

PART VI
CURTAIN CALL

CHAPTER TWENTY-FOUR

I am sitting on the step behind the NETWORK console and just in front of the Department of Defense representative's console. A jubilant crowd swirls around the flight director's console in a thick fog of victory cigar smoke. The flight directors exchange handshakes and high fives with each other and with an ever-shifting crowd of flight controllers and mission support people who have emerged from all parts of the building. In the row above me, Chris Kraft's face is covered by a nonstop "I told you we could do it" grin.

Figure 6: A beaming Chris Kraft celebrates the safe recovery of *Apollo 11*. Just behind him are George Low, manager of the Apollo Spacecraft Program, and Dr. Robert Gilruth, Manned Spacecraft Center director. (NASA photo)

The floor space between the front row of consoles and the group displays in the front of the room is filled with excited people who alternate their attention between exchanging congratulations and watching themselves exchange congratulations on the projection TV screen at the right front of the room. The *Apollo 11* mission patch, a graphic of an eagle touching down on the Moon with the Earth hovering in the black space above it, lights up the display screen at the front center of the room. Above the mission emblem are the words "Task accomplished . . . . . July, 1969." Handheld American flags bob up and down on the surface of a roaring wave of jubilant sound.

Just to my right, the flag-waving crowd that packs the hallway in front of the Recovery Control Room parts before the metallic clanging that heralds the incongruous appearance of an aluminum extension ladder. Dutch and one of his workmates carry the ladder to a spot about fifteen feet from the right front corner of the network controller's console. Some of the controllers in the room take the ladder and raise it so that it reaches up to a spot high on the wall. The crowd, which had momentarily shied away from the long metal structure looming above it, surges back expectantly to surround the foot of the ladder.

Deep in an adrenaline-depletion fog, I wonder what all of that fuss is about. What the hell are they all excited about? I look up from my momentary refuge on the step, looking up past the hips and elbows of flag wavers and hand shakers. The top end of the ladder rests on the wall maybe twenty feet above the floor. It is just to the right of the *Apollo 10* mission plaque. Mission plaque—oh shit, oh dear—there's supposed to be another mission plaque high, high up on the wall—the *Apollo 11* plaque.

The startling realization that the plaque has to be hung on the wall is accompanied by the terrifying awareness that I have to do the hanging. The lead network controller always hangs the damn plaque. It's anxiety city now. My stress tolerance reservoir is dead empty. This is the one part of the mission we never trained for—no checklists, no simulations. You need me to climb up a steeply pitched ladder in front of television cameras

Figure 7: Up against the ceiling of the Mission Control Room: the infamous *Apollo 11* mission plaque. (NASA photo)

broadcasting the event to tens of millions viewers? Then I fumble around and try to snag a fastener of unknown configuration onto some sort of hook whose configuration is equally mysterious? A split-second vision anticipates hours of slow-motion attempts to put the thing where it belongs. The vision ends sadly with plaque and plaque hanger tumbling into the muttering, restive crowd. I see the headline on the front page of the next edition of the *New York Times*: "Lunar Landing Mission Ends with Single Fatality."

"Time to get this thing up."

Dave Young's voice interrupts my apocalyptic vision. He shoves the blue and gold mission plaque into my reluctant hands. Seeing my hesitation and the I-don't-really-think-I-want-to-do-this look on my face, he applies the ultimate stimulus, "Ernie Randall said he'd be glad to do this if you don't."

"OK, OK."

I grab the plaque in sweating palms and start toward the foot of the ladder. I put my right foot on the first rung and hope I don't slip. A burst of cheers and applause accompanies my first shaky step up the ladder. I imagine the avuncular measured tones of Walter Cronkite voicing over the background cheers, "NASA management informs us that this inept-looking young man has no real idea of what he is doing. His auto-shake mode seems to confirm that assertion. We will stand by to see the outcome, but the outlook is not optimistic. This situation may produce the major embarrassment that NASA has so far avoided on the *Apollo 11* mission."

As Walter's words beam out over the airwaves they are translated in midair into Spanish, French, Swahili, and Christ knows what all. When this disaster happens, the whole world will be witness.

My second step is so shaky that a young woman standing near the foot of the ladder says, "You better let me help," as she instinctively reaches out to give me a little shove in the middle of my lower back. Pushed up by that sympathetic touch, I finally reach plaque-placing altitude. I take a quick glance at the back of the plaque and then at the wall to see what I have to hang on what. Reaching out with trembling hands, I slide the plaque down the wall toward the intended hanger until I feel what I think is a contact. Gingerly I release my grip on the plaque. Dumb luck prevails—the thing stays in place on the wall. The cheers of the crowd drown out my murmured prayer of thanks to the gravity gods. I back down the ladder and plant my feet on the deck. My part of this mission is done. No one told me that I would be running on empty when it was done. No splashdown parties for me—home to bed.

END NOTE

The last page of the "Apollo 11 *Mission Report*" lists nine conclusions relating to the conduct of the mission. Conclusion number nine reads, "The Mission Control Center and the Manned Space Flight Network proved to be adequate for controlling and monitoring all phases of the flight, including the descent, surface activity, and the ascent phase of the mission."

My personal claim to fame does not go beyond "adequate." I had played my small role in making history. Mostly I had done it without major embarrassment. That NASA experience would alter the rest of my life. I had started to study mathematics during my tour in Houston—it was an attempt to learn the local language. I completed a mathematics degree about a year after leaving Houston. With that degree in hand, I spent the rest of my air force career doing leading-edge engineering development work.

My family and I made our next stop at Wright-Patterson Air Force Base in Dayton, Ohio. The air force gave me twenty million dollars and a one-sentence task: "Develop a pilotless aircraft that will carry 1,500 pounds of payload above 55,000 feet for twenty-four hours without refueling." With the help of the Boeing Company and the Teledyne-Ryan Company, we did that. We met that goal. The "we" includes a very skilled and patient aeronautical engineer named Orin Brenning. The descendants of our Compass Cope pilotless aircraft now operate all over the world. The ready-made family-friendly infrastructure that you find on any military installation also meant a better experience for my wife and children.

After a tour at the Pentagon, I was assigned to a joint navy–air force development program in Crystal City, Virginia, as deputy director of the Ground Launched Cruise Missile Program. We built and tested these missiles within budget against an unmoving deadline. When the time came to deploy the missiles in Europe, we volunteered to go to Ramstein Air Base in Germany to do that job. It was well underway when the time came to activate a cruise missile unit on the island of Sicily. We volunteered again and accepted the job of commanding that unit. My wife was one of two air force wives on base. The other 1,500 people assigned to our unit were without their families because of a lack of facilities. We lived in porta-cabins in the middle of a dusty construction site and shopped in the local *supermercato*. Despite the hardships, the people in my command met the NATO deadline for activating the unit. I have never served with a more dedicated group of men and women than those in the 487th Tactical Missile Wing.

Post–air force I helped the Boeing Company design and launch satellite systems. These days I combine training in mathematics and history to write about the history of science. And maybe best of all, I get to tutor fifth-grade kids in math at the local elementary school. Any experience that ultimately lets you be ten years old again can't be all bad. And it all started with a whimsical invitation to see how a "liberal arts puke" would make out in the land of rocket scientists!

APPENDIX A: THE MANNED SPACE FLIGHT NETWORK

Size does matter—at least when you're trying to get to the Moon. That's why Manned Space Flight Tracking Network stations come in three sizes: large, larger, and huge. The large and larger sizes do basically the same thing. The primary difference between them is the size of the main antenna they use to track and communicate with the *Apollo* spacecraft. We will talk about antenna size in a minute. But first we need to talk about the services that these ground stations and their antennas have to provide.

When you send a spacecraft and its crew to the Moon, you need to know some stuff. You need to know where they are and where they are going. You need to know the status of the machine and its crew. The crew and the spacecraft also need information that large ground-based computers can generate more precisely than the systems onboard the spacecraft.

Projects Mercury and Gemini both used separate systems to carry out each of these information exchanges. The Gemini spacecraft carried two beacons that allowed ground tracking stations to determine its position, direction, and velocity. The beacons received and retransmitted a signal generated by ground radar. The total time from broadcast of the signal to receipt of the spacecraft return signal could be divided by two to give the distance, or range, to the spacecraft. Changes in the frequency of the signal gave the velocity of the spacecraft relative to the ground station, the range rate. An increase in frequency meant the spacecraft was moving toward the ground station. A lower frequency indicated motion away from the ground station. The spacecraft distance and velocity combined with the radar antenna pointing angles fix the spacecraft's position in space.

A variety of sensors measured the status of both the *Gemini* spacecraft and its crew. Three telemetry transmitters sent information provided by the sensors to ground stations by radio frequency link. The most important information link, air-to-ground voice, was handled by two ultra-high-frequency transmitter-receivers. Another pair of ultra-high-frequency receivers processed commands uplinked from ground control to the spacecraft. The commands controlled specific switch functions and also provided updates for the onboard computer. The combination of uplink and voice information was critical to the execution of the maneuvers needed to get the spacecraft where it needed to go.

If you have been keeping count, information exchange with a *Gemini* spacecraft in Earth orbit required nine electronic assemblies. Apollo needed a better answer. To get to the Moon, you have to climb out of a deep gravity well that exacts a penalty of nearly one hundred pounds for every pound that you add to the Command and Service Module. And you need to make the same information exchanges as you do in Earth orbit at something like one thousand times the distance.

Not only did the Apollo Program need a better system than the one that supported *Gemini,* they needed it in a hurry. The program had less than seven years to develop and field a worldwide tracking network. Fortunately, NASA's Jet Propulsion Laboratory had already pioneered a concept they called Unified S-band. The S-band part is the easiest to explain. It means that the system operates in the part of the radio frequency spectrum lying between 2,000 and 4,000 megahertz. In fact, the Command Module frequency is 2106.4 megahertz, and the frequency used by the Lunar Module and the third stage of the Saturn V is 2101.8 megahertz.

The unified part takes a little more explaining. We can begin by pointing out that the Unified S-band system is a range and range rate system. Range is measured by transmitting a code that is 5.4 seconds long—a code that does not repeat within that time interval. The spacecraft receives the code and retransmits it to the ground station. The ground station tracking computer matches the received and transmitted code to determine range. At 186,000 miles per second, the 5.4-second interval provides time for signal transmission and return from distances well beyond the Moon. As explained earlier, range rate or the radial velocity is measured using the frequency shift of the returned signal. OK, so far, so good.

But what about the voice and command signals that also need to be sent up to the Command and Service Module? Good question—that's where the unified concept comes into play. Voice intended for uplink is first frequency-modulated onto a thirty-kilohertz electromagnetic wave called a subcarrier. The command signals phase-modulate a seventy-kilohertz subcarrier. The range code we discussed a minute ago modulates a one-megahertz subcarrier. The three signal types—voice, command data, and ranging code—are then combined to produce a wave form that phase-modulates the main carrier. In other words, the single uplink radio frequency at 2106.4 megahertz for the Command Module carries three distinct types of information simultaneously—hence the descriptor "Unified S-band." A power amplifier increases the power of the modulated S-band spectrum to twenty kilowatts and feeds the resulting signal to the station antenna for transmission up to the spacecraft.

A processor on board the Command Module extracts the subcarriers from the composite received signal. It detects and extracts the uplink voice for monitoring by the astronauts. It also recovers the digital commands and feeds them to the onboard computer, which converts them into instructions for the onboard systems. The processor preserves the ranging code, which it then combines with the downlink voice and telemetry information. The combined signals then phase-modulate the main carrier, which conveys the information to the ground tracking receiver. The downlink carrier operates at a slightly higher frequency (2287.5 megahertz) to prevent interference with the uplink carrier. An amplifier increases the power of the downlink carrier to a maximum of twenty watts. Omnidirectional or steerable antennas then transmit the signals to a ground station. The communications processing system on board the Lunar Module operates in the much the same way as the Command and Service Module system we have just described, except that there is no requirement for uplink of command data.

How do you make twenty watts work across a distance of two hundred thousand miles? You need five times that amount to make a decent light bulb. Well it turns out that you can make it work if you have an antenna with enough of something called "gain." Antenna gain is a measure of the ability of the antenna to focus scattered radio frequency waves into a narrower, useful plane, thereby increasing signal strength at the ground station receiver.

The three variables in the equation for calculating gain are the wavelength of the carrier wave you use, the efficiency of the antenna, and, yes, the size of the antenna. Up to a point, shorter wavelengths are better than longer ones. Shorter wavelengths mean higher frequencies. But after you get to about 12,000 megahertz, the carrier wave begins to suffer severe attenuation from gases, precipitation, and cloud particles in the atmosphere. S-band is a good compromise. The possible range of antenna efficiency is limited, being in the range of 70 to 80 percent for a well-designed system. The only variable left that can be altered over a wide range is the area of the antenna. For the *Apollo* mission, ground system designers settled on steerable parabolic dish antennas with diameters of eighty-five feet and thirty feet.

The ground station antennas have to provide coverage of six mission phases: launch and insertion into Earth orbit, Earth orbit and injection into translunar flight, lunar orbit and landing, and reentry. The eighty-five-foot antennas cover the lunar phase. Given the distance between the Earth and the Moon, one of three stations located 120 degrees apart on the Earth's surface always has the Moon in view. One of the three stations is located at Goldstone in California's Mojave Desert. A second is thirty miles west of Madrid, Spain. The third is at Honeysuckle Creek about twenty miles from Canberra, Australia. In each case, the newer Apollo station is adjacent to an existing eighty-five-foot station that is a part of the Jet Propulsion Laboratory's Deep Space Network, a system designed to track unmanned satellite missions at planetary distances. The co-located deep-space stations provide backup for the Manned Space Flight stations.

Figure A-1: The 210-foot Goldstone Mars antenna that tracked *Apollo 11* down to the lunar surface. (NASA photo)

Two other antennas, supersized 210-foot structures, support the lunar phases of the mission by receiving television, voice, and telemetry. One of them is the Mars antenna, part of the Jet Propulsion Laboratory's deep-space Goldstone station.

Completed in 1966, the Mars station began tracking operations by acquiring signals from the *Mariner* Mars mission spacecraft across a distance of 205 million miles. The second giant backup antenna is the Parkes radio telescope, operated by the Commonwealth Scientific and Industrial Research Organization, Australia's national science agency. Both of these giant antennas are steerable—they can acquire a radio source and track it across the sky. To do that, the antenna control systems point six million pounds with an accuracy of 0.006 degrees.

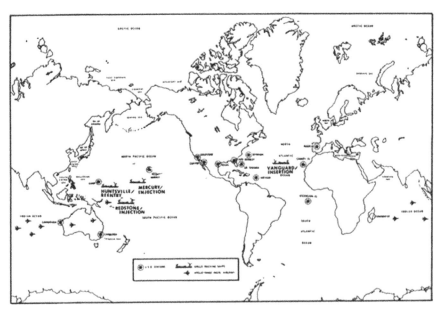

Figure A-2: The worldwide *Apollo* Manned Space Flight Network. (NASA illustration)

A combination of Unified S-band ground stations with thirty-foot antennas, instrumented ships, and instrumented aircraft provide coverage of the near-Earth phases of the mission. Range safety constraints, orbital dynamics, vehicle operational considerations, geography, and sometimes international diplomacy determine the location of these resources. To keep pieces of rocket from falling on unsuspecting citizens in the event of a malfunction, the Air Force Easter Test Range limits the launch azimuth (the launch direction) to headings between 72 degrees and 108 degrees. For the nominal launch azimuth of seventy-two degrees, coverage of launch and insertion into Earth orbit is provided by three land stations: Merritt Island, Florida; Grand Bahama Island, located seventy miles east of Palm Beach, Florida; and the island of Bermuda, 1,100 miles northeast of the launch site. If the launch azimuth shifts toward the south because of Earth-Moon orbital geometry, the station on Antigua, an island in the British West Indies, can provide launch coverage. Regardless of the launch azimuth, NASA runs out of islands before the Saturn upper stage completes its burn into orbit. To fill that gap and also provide coverage for other critical events that occur in mid-ocean, NASA acquired three ships and converted them into sea-based tracking stations equipped with most of the systems common to the land stations. One of these three, USNS *Vanguard*, is stationed one thousand miles southeast of Bermuda to supplement the coverage provided by Bermuda and Antigua and to monitor Earth orbit insertion.

Figure A-3: The tracking ship *Vanguard* was positioned in an area of the Atlantic Ocean where there are no island stations. It provided tracking, telemetry, and voice coverage during the insertion into Earth orbit. (US Navy photo)

After insertion into orbit, the spacecraft traces out a track on the Earth's surface that resembles a sine wave with its maximum and minimum amplitudes at about thirty-two degrees north and south of the equator. For the seventy-two-degree launch azimuth, the spacecraft passes directly over a station in the Canary Islands, just off the coast of Africa north of the equator. Canary provides the first confirmation of Bermuda and *Vanguard* orbital predictions. The spacecraft's ground track then continues to the southeast over the African continent, passing just to the north of a station near the city of Tananarive on the island of Madagascar in the Indian Ocean. Tananarive provides very high frequency air-to-ground voice coverage of the *Apollo* spacecraft and C-band radar tracking of the S-IVB upper stage of the Saturn.

The orbital ground track continues to the southeast, where it reaches its most southerly point at about 115 degrees east longitude. As the spacecraft approaches the west coast of Australia, it is under the watchful electronic eye of a thirty-foot S-band station at Carnarvon, a small community about five hundred miles north of Perth at the mouth of the Gascoyne River. Heading northeast now, the *Apollo* crew has a brief encounter with the eighty-five-foot station at Honeysuckle Creek just before leaving Australia and heading northwest across the vast expanse of the Pacific Ocean.

Minutes later the *Apollo* spacecraft makes electronic landfall in North America, coming over the radio horizons of the thirty-foot antenna at the Guaymas tracking station located in the Mexican state of Sonora, and the eighty-five-foot Goldstone antenna. The Guaymas site provides S-band tracking and telemetry from the S-IVB stage and very high frequency voice contact with the crew. Goldstone provides S-band support for the Command and Service Module.

S-band coverage is continuous across the rest of the United States, and the Command and Service Module is handed off from Goldstone to a station at Corpus Christi, Texas, and then to the Merritt Island station at the start of the second revolution. Because of the rotation of the Earth under the spacecraft orbit, the ground track of the second revolution is displaced to the west of the revolution-one ground track. Despite the offset, the space vehicle stays within the coverage of the same set of stations that covered revolution one, as it travels southeast across Africa, the Indian Ocean, and western Australia.

East of Australia, the coverage changes dramatically. On this pass over the western Pacific, the engine of the S-IVB upper stage fires for almost six minutes to propel the Command and Service Module into an elongated orbit that will allow it to be captured by the Moon's gravity. To cover this critical event, NASA deploys two *Vanguard*-class tracking ships, *Redstone* and *Mercury*, and the Apollo Range Instrumented Aircraft (ARIA). The aircraft is an air force version of the Boeing 707 airliner. Operated by air force crews, the aircraft transmits and receives voice traffic and records spacecraft telemetry for later processing on the ground.

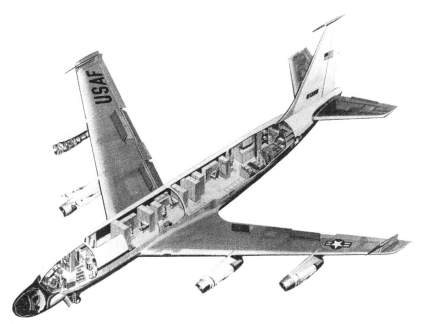

Figure A-4: A cutaway view of the ARIA. The aircraft supplied voice and telemetry coverage for the *Apollo* spacecraft during those parts of Earth orbit that were beyond the reach of the ground stations. (NASA illustration)

Because the crew must spend orbit number one checking out their onboard systems, the translunar injection event is scheduled for orbit number two. If there are problems, the burn can be delayed until the third orbit, but not beyond, because of limitations on the Saturn upper-stage attitude-control propellant and battery power. If the third orbit is required, it is once again displaced to the west by the Earth's rotation. That displacement forces changes in the tracking station roles. Antigua comes on stage in place of Bermuda. A site located on the rocky British island of Ascension replaces the Canary Island station to track the spacecraft as it transits the South Atlantic. After a successful translunar burn, the thirty-foot station on Kauai in the Hawaiian Islands tracks the spacecraft until it is far enough away to be turned over to the eighty-five-foot stations for coverage of the lunar phases of the mission. For the reentry phase of the mission, the stations in Australia, Carnarvon, and Honeysuckle, and the station on the island of Guam, track the spacecraft as it plunges down toward the western Pacific. The final minutes of the fiery descent are covered by mobile assets, including three *Apollo* aircraft and the tracking ships *Redstone* and *Huntsville*. The *Huntsville* is a converted Victory ship equipped with a sixteen-foot Unified S-band system.

At the S-band stations, a small acquisition antenna mounted on the main antenna dish initially detects the radio frequency signal from the spacecraft. When the signal is detected—for example, when the Command and Service Module signal is first received at Carnarvon—the station operations supervisor announces, "Carnarvon, AOS, CSM," on the network communications channel. Guided by signals from the acquisition antenna, the main antenna then acquires the target and begins to track it. The ground station then begins to transmit the S-band carrier with no range code. Onboard the spacecraft, a transponder locks to the ground carrier frequency. The transponder multiplies the ground frequency by a known multiplier and retransmits it to the ground station. A ground station main carrier tracking loop locks to the spacecraft frequency, achieving what is called two-way coherent lock. With two-way lock complete, both the uplink and the downlink carrier can be modulated with ranging, voice, command, and telemetry data. When two-way lock is achieved, the operations supervisor announces, in our example, "CARNARVON, go for command, CSM."

The signal from the spacecraft is then run through signal processing units that strip out the telemetry, ranging code, and voice from the composite signal. A UNIVAC 642B computer arranges the telemetry data into pre-stored formats that can then be selected for transmission to HOUSTON. A second UNIVAC 642B stores digital commands that can be selectively called up by controllers in HOUSTON for transmission to the space vehicles. Another onsite processor collects tracking information including range, range rate, and the angles that show which way the antenna is pointing, and formats it for transmission. The Unified S-band tracking system measures range with a resolution of about five feet, velocity to about four inches per second, and angles with an accuracy of 0.025 degrees.

Crew voice transmissions and the processed telemetry and tracking data are then transmitted over long-line communications circuits to the Goddard Space Flight Center in Greenbelt, Maryland. Depending on its capabilities, each station in the tracking network might be connected back to Goddard by as many as six circuits. The highest priority circuit, naturally enough called Net One, carries air-to-ground voice communications between the CAPCOM in the control center and the flight crew. The circuit that carries telemetry down from the space vehicles and ground commands up to those vehicles is designated Net Four and has the next highest priority. (I know, I know, Net Four with priority two. I don't know why that is—it just is.) Net Two, with priority three, is used by the duty network controller to coordinate network support operations. Net Five, priority four, carries the high-speed tracking data used to measure the current positions of the spacecraft and predict their future trajectories. Net Six with—yup, you guessed it—priority five, carries biomedical data such as crew members' heartbeats and respiration rates. Net

Three, with the lowest priority, is used by Goddard to coordinate site readiness in preparation for upcoming support periods.

Goddard's charter is to operate NASA's worldwide tracking network in support of both manned and unmanned space missions. Consequently, data to and from the remote tracking stations and the actual mission control center, be it in Houston or at the Jet Propulsion Laboratory in Pasadena for an unmanned probe, is switched at Goddard to the final destination. For a manned space mission, data from a site such as Carnarvon, Australia, is uplinked to an Intelsat communications satellite over the mid-Pacific, down-linked to a ground station in Brewster Flat, Washington, and then sent on to Goddard and on to Houston by landline.

Nineteen land-based stations, four ships, eight instrumented aircraft, and the communication networks that connect them support the *Apollo 11* mission. This Manned Space Flight Network is the largest and most complex of all the machines that make America's lunar landing mission possible.

APPENDIX B: SATURN V LAUNCH VEHICLE

The Saturn V is the second most complex machine supporting America's lunar landing program. Given that it carries a three-man crew and millions of pounds of fuel and oxidizer, its failure modes tend to be considerably more critical and dramatic than those of the Manned Space Flight Network.

The *Apollo* spacecraft, which includes the Command Module, Service Module, and Lunar Module, sits atop the Saturn launch vehicle (Figure B-1). The complete assembly, including the *Apollo* spacecraft and the Saturn launch vehicle, stands 363 feet tall and weighs over six million pounds. The Saturn is the largest and most powerful US expendable launch vehicle ever built. It can place more than 130 tons in Earth orbit, or send 50 tons to the moon. It employs three stages:

First Stage (S-IC): The first stage has five F-1 engines, each one of which produces 1.5 million pounds of thrust. One engine is rigidly mounted on the stage centerline. The four outer engines, mounted in the shape of a square, can be maneuvered in any direction to control the direction of the rocket's flight. The five engines gulp 15 tons of liquid oxygen and kerosene per second, generating a total of 7.5 million pounds of thrust. The first-stage engines ignite at liftoff and burn for about 2.5 minutes, taking the vehicle and payload to an altitude of 43 miles and a velocity of about 8,000 feet per second. The first stage then separates and falls back into the ocean.

Second Stage (S-II): The second stage uses five J-2 engines that burn liquid hydrogen and liquid oxygen. After the first stage is discarded, the second stage burns for approximately 6 minutes, taking the vehicle and payload to an altitude of 109 miles and a velocity of almost 23,000 feet per second. The second stage separates and is also discarded.

Third Stage (S-IVB): The third stage contains one J-2 engine. This engine burns for 2.5 minutes, boosting the spacecraft to orbital velocity of about 26,000 feet per second at an altitude of 119 miles. The third stage is shut down with fuel remaining and remains attached to the spacecraft in Earth orbit. During Earth orbit number two, the J-2 engine reignites to propel the spacecraft into translunar trajectory at a velocity of 36,000 feet per second.

Instrument Unit: The Instrument Unit is a ring-shaped structure fitted to the top of the Saturn V rocket's third stage. It is just below the Spacecraft/Lunar Module Adapter that contains the Lunar Module. It contains the guidance system for the Saturn V rocket, including a digital computer, an analogue flight control computer, an inertial guidance platform, control accelerometers and control rate gyros, and an emergency detection system.

Launch Vehicle Instrumentation and Communication: The first stage and third stages each carry two very high frequency telemetry transmitters. The second stage has three. They downlink a total of over 1,100 measurements to the engineers monitoring the progress of launch. Each propulsive stage also has an ultra-high-frequency command destruct receiver. In the event of an in-flight emergency, the Range Safety Officer transmits a command that shuts down all engines. A second command detonates explosives that rupture the fuel and oxidizer tanks to disperse the propellants.

The Instrument Unit downlinks the results of just over 220 measurements via two very high frequency transmitters and one S-band transmitter. The S-band uplink enables transmission of command data and a range code for tracking. The Instrument Unit also carries a C-band radar tracking transponder.

Spacecraft Lunar Module Adapter: The Spacecraft Lunar Module Adapter is an aluminum structure built in the shape of a truncated cone. It supports the Command and Service Module above the Saturn third stage. It houses the Lunar Module during launch and protects the Service Propulsion System engine nozzle. The adapter has two sections. The lower section consists of four fixed 7-foot-tall panels bolted to the Instrument Unit on top of the S-IVB stage. Above the fixed panels there are four 21-foot-tall panels. Hinges connect these large panels to the fixed panels and allow them to open like the petals of a flower to allow extraction of the Lunar Module after the translunar injection burn.

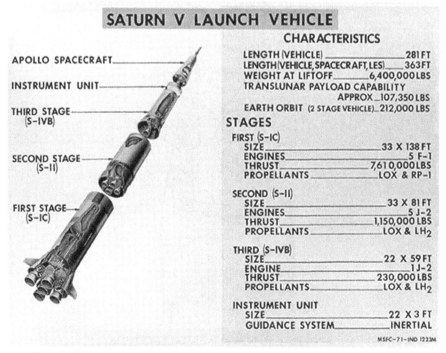

Figure B-1: The Saturn V launch vehicle and *Apollo* spacecraft. (NASA illustration)

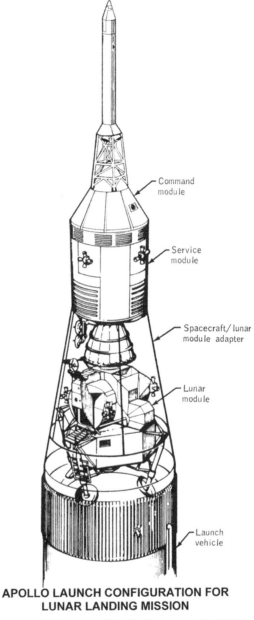

APOLLO LAUNCH CONFIGURATION FOR LUNAR LANDING MISSION

Figure B-2: The Saturn third stage and the *Apollo* spacecraft. (NASA illustration)

Launch Preparation: The Boeing Company builds the S-IC at the Michoud Assembly Facility in New Orleans. North American Aviation at Seal Beach, California, builds the S-II. Douglas Aircraft Company builds the S-IVB third stage at Huntington Beach, California. After the contractor completes construction and ground testing of a stage, NASA ships it to the Kennedy Space Center. The first two stages are so large that the only way to transport them was by barge. The third stage and Instrument Unit are carried by a specially designed aircraft.

On arrival at the space center's Vertical Assembly Building, technicians check out each stage in a horizontal position before moving it to a vertical position. NASA stacks the Saturn V on a Mobile Launcher Platform, a two-story steel structure that supports both the launch vehicle and its Launch Umbilical Tower. The tower has nine swing arms, a "hammerhead" crane, and a water suppression system that is activated prior to launch. The swing arms support umbilical connections that provide consumables such as air, power, and propellant until the moment of liftoff. The highest swing arm, number nine, provides crew access to the *Apollo* spacecraft.

After crews complete assembly of the booster, they move the Mobile Launcher Platform with its massive load from the Vertical Assembly Building to the launchpad using the Crawler Transporter. The transporter runs on four double-tracked treads and is the world's largest tracked vehicle, weighing in at three thousand tons.

The transporter keeps the rocket level as it travels the three miles to the launch site and climbs a 3 percent grade to deposit its cargo at the launchpad. After delivering the Saturn, the transporter moves a Mobile Service Structure into place. The Mobile Service Structure stands on the opposite side of the Saturn from the umbilical tower. It has five work platforms that allow technicians access to the rocket until shortly before launch, when the transporter moves it away to a safe distance.

Figure B-3: The Mobile Service Structure (on right) being moved away from the launchpad. (NASA photo)

APPENDIX C: COMMAND AND SERVICE MODULE

The *Apollo* spacecraft has four segments: the Launch Escape Assembly, the Command Module, the Service Module, and the Lunar Module. This appendix describes the first three segments. Appendix D deals with the Lunar Module.

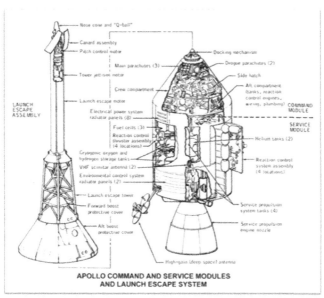

Figure C-1: Apollo Command and Service Modules and Launch Escape System. (NASA illustration)

The Launch Escape Assembly is a rocket mounted above the Command Module. The rocket carries the module containing the astronauts away from the launch vehicle in case of an emergency on the pad or shortly after launch. It carries it far enough from the launch vehicle so that the Earth Landing System parachutes can operate. The rocket is connected to the Command Module by a latticework tower. A boost protective cover is attached to the tower and covers the Command Module. The cover protects the crew module from the heat generated by launch vehicle boost through the atmosphere and from the rocket exhaust if an abort is required. It remains attached to the tower and is carried away when the Launch Escape Assembly is jettisoned at about 295,000 feet, or about thirty seconds after ignition of the second stage of the Saturn V.

The Command Module designers selected a truncated cone shape for the spacecraft. It is about 10.5 feet tall and almost 13 feet in diameter across the base. The cone encloses three compartments (Figure C-2). The forward compartment surrounds the docking tunnel. Below the aft compartment is the pressurized crew compartment with an interior volume of 210 cubic feet. That works out to seventy cubic feet per crew member, versus forty cubic feet in the Gemini spacecraft. Below that, the aft compartment provides structural mounting points for the heat shield that protects the spacecraft during reentry.

The Service Module is a cylinder about 24.5 feet long with the same diameter as the aft end of the Command Module. The cylinder encloses a central tunnel that is surrounded by six pie-shaped sectors. Three stainless-steel straps connect the cylinder to the Command Module heat shield. Just before entry into the Earth's atmosphere, it separates from the Command Module and exposes the heat shield that protects the spacecraft during its fiery descent. Between them, the Command and Service Modules provide all of the systems and mechanisms required to maintain the crew and accomplish the lunar mission.

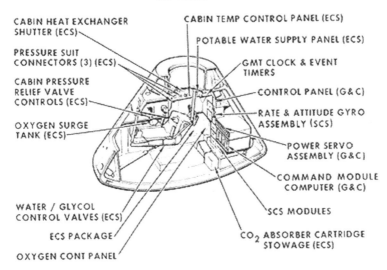
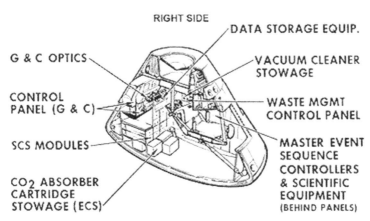

Figure C-2: Command Module. (NASA illustration)

Environmental Control System: This system maintains a safe haven for the crew. It manages cabin atmospheric pressure, temperature, and water supply. The system uses two oxygen tanks carried in the Service Module. After Service Module separation, the system uses a small oxygen tank located in the Command Module. The water is a by-product of the operation of the Electrical Power System fuel cells also located in the Service Module, and is stored in a potable water tank in the Command Module. A water and glycol cooling system dumps waste heat from the spacecraft using two large radiators built into the skin of the Service Module.

Electrical Power System: Three fuel cells located in the Service Module generate electrical power by combining hydrogen and oxygen. They also produce potable water as a by-product. Three batteries in the Command Module provide power after Service Module jettison.

Guidance, Navigation, and Control System: This system provides the crew with information on where they are, where they are going, and how fast they are going there. It includes an Inertial Measurement Unit, an Optical Unit, and a computer. The Inertial Measurement Unit contains three gyros and three accelerometers. It measures position and velocity relative to one of two reference coordinate systems, one centered on the Earth and one centered on the Moon. Over long periods of operation, the Inertial Measurement Unit has a tendency to drift from its original orientation relative to one of those coordinate systems. The Optical Unit, a sextant, is used to update the alignment of the inertial unit by measuring angles between stars. The guidance computer integrates the information on position, velocity, and spacecraft attitude, the direction in which the nose of the vehicle is pointed, and uses it to develop engine-firing commands necessary to take the crew where they intend to go.

Service Propulsion System: The propulsion system is mounted in the Service Module. The system's rocket engine produces up to 20,500 pounds of thrust for insertion into and exit from lunar orbit and for midcourse corrections on the way to the

Moon. The engine uses hydrazine fuel and nitrogen tetroxide oxidizer, hypergolic substances that ignite when mixed together. Engineers mounted the engine's nozzle on gimbals that are used to point the engine's thrust in the required direction.

Reaction Control System: This system includes groups of small rocket engines and their fuel tanks. The engines can control the spacecraft's attitude. They can also impart small increments of velocity in any desired direction. They are used for maneuvering during docking procedures, station-keeping on orbit, and control during reentry. The Service Module Reaction Control System uses sixteen engines grouped into clusters of four, or quads. Each engine can generate up to one hundred pounds of thrust. The four quads are placed ninety degrees apart around the circumference of the Service Module. The Command Module has two systems with six engines, each of which can produce about ninety-three pounds of thrust.

Earth Landing System: Housed in the forward compartment around the docking tunnel, this system includes three pilot parachutes and three main parachutes designed to slow the spacecraft to a safe speed before it impacts the water during reentry.

Telecommunications System: Apollo mission control involves synergetic cooperation between flight crew and mission operations controllers in Houston. Without the communications system, there is no cooperative mission control. With it, flight controllers are able to augment the efforts of the flight crew by monitoring data on the performance of the spacecraft and the crew themselves, determining spacecraft position and velocity, sending commands and data to the spacecraft, and exchanging voice messages with the crew on the results of their evaluations. Four groups of onboard equipment groups make up the communications system:

Intercommunications Equipment

This equipment enables two-way voice communications between:
- Astronauts onboard the spacecraft.

- The Command Module and Launch Control Center during launchpad operations.
- The Command Module and the Manned Space Flight Network, the Command Module and the Lunar Module, or the Command Module and an extravehicular astronaut via very high frequency radio.
- The Command Module and the Manned Space Flight Network via Unified S-band.
- Rescue swimmers and the crew during recovery operations.

Data Equipment

The functions of the data equipment include:

- Collecting and encoding measurements (pressure, temperature, etc.) to monitor the status of both the spacecraft and its crew.
- Converting analogue measurements to digital form and incorporating them into the telemetry format that is used to transmit the data to the ground network.
- Decoding data uplinked by mission control and routing it to its destination.

Radio Frequency Equipment

This equipment mounted in the lower equipment bay of the Command Module generates and receives the signals that carry voice, telemetry, tracking, and television information between the space vehicles, and between the spacecraft and ground. The group includes:

- Two independent very high frequency transmitter-receivers that can operate in a simplex mode, transmitting and receiving voice only, or in the duplex mode, transmitting both voice and data. These radios also interface with the Unified S-band system to relay information to and from the Lunar Module through the Command Module to the ground network.
- Two Unified S-band transponders and an S-band frequency modulation transmitter.

- Primary and secondary power amplifiers that increase the power of S-band signals for transmission to the ground stations.
- A pre-modulation processor that provides the interface between the data equipment and the radio frequency electronics. It modulates, demodulates, and switches signals depending on the communication mode the spacecraft is using.

Antenna Equipment

The very high frequency radios use two omnidirectional antennas called scimitar antennas (because of their shape) that are located 180 degrees apart on the skin of the Service Module. Each antenna has a roughly hemispherical radiation pattern.

The S-band transponders can use either a directional high-gain antenna or omnidirectional antennas. The high-gain antenna is located at the aft end of the Service Module. It is in a stowed position until after translunar injection, when the Spacecraft Launch Adapter panels are opened. Once deployed, the antenna can be automatically or manually pointed toward a ground station to give sufficient gain for operations at lunar distance.

The four omnidirectional antennas are flush mounted around the circumference of the Command Module. They transmit and receive signals during the near-Earth phases of the mission and provide a backup to the high-gain antenna during lunar operations.

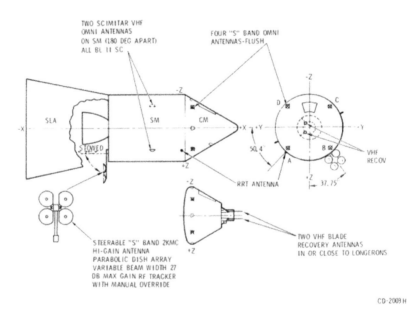

Figure C-3: Antenna locations. (NASA illustration)

APPENDIX D: LUNAR MODULE

One glance is enough to convince you that this is a machine that means business. The thing is squat and ugly, maybe even a little bit menacing. It is all legs, nozzles, and antennas. Form follows function without regard for the streamlining required by passage through the atmosphere. The objective is to land two crew members on the Moon and then return them to lunar orbit. Consistent with that objective, the machine is made up of two stages: a descent module and an ascent module.

The descent stage is an octagonal structure with four landing-gear struts. One of the struts supports a ladder used to descend to the surface. The Descent Propulsion System engine is mounted at the center of the stage. The engine produces just over ten thousand pounds of thrust. It can be throttled between 10 and 60 percent of full thrust to control the descent to the lunar surface. Compartments arranged around the periphery of the stage contain tanks of fuel and oxidizer for the engine, and consumables for the lunar stay such as batteries, oxygen, and water for drinking and cooling. Other compartments store a deployable S-band antenna, a surface television camera, surface tools, and lunar sample collection boxes. The astronauts set the antenna up on the surface early in their Moon walk to facilitate communications with the ground network. Batteries stored in the descent stage provide power for most of the landing mission duration. Smaller batteries in the ascent stage provide power for the short period of independent operation by that stage. The descent stage also houses the Lunar Module landing radar used to measure distance to the lunar surface during the landing approach.

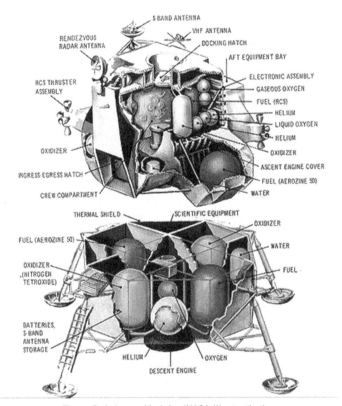

Figure D-1: Lunar Module. (NASA illustration)

The shape of the ascent stage defies description in simple geometric terms. It looks as though the designers piled up a bunch of different sized boxes and hoped for the best. A crew compartment equipped with two windows and display and controls panels occupies the center of the pile. Two crew members stand side-by-side with the docking port above their head and the Ascent Propulsion System engine below them. An environmental control system regulates oxygen supply and temperature.

A Primary Guidance and Navigation System and an Abort Guidance System provide data on position, velocity, and attitude. The primary system uses the same basic setup as the Command Module version. The abort system is a stripped-down version of the primary system. It is not meant to duplicate the full functioning of the primary system. Instead, it is just good enough to control the spacecraft if the primary system fails and the crew is forced to abort the lunar landing approach. To make sure that the abort system is up to the job, the Lunar Module Pilot monitors the agreement between the two systems during the descent. In the case of an abort during approach or the launch from the lunar surface, the crew depends on the Ascent Propulsion System engine to save their lives. If it fails, they die. With that thought very much in mind, engineers designed the system to be as simple and reliable as possible. In particular, it uses propellants that ignite on contact to avoid dependence on complex ignition circuitry. Sixteen Reaction Control System engines mounted in sets of four on the exterior surface of the ascent stage control vehicle attitude during both descent and ascent. At the top of the ascent stage pile there is an antenna for the rendezvous radar that provides range, bearing, and velocity relative to the Command and Service Module, as well as antennas for the S-band and very high frequency communications links.

The ascent and descent stages are joined together at four attach points. When the time comes to separate the stages, explosive bolts sever the attachments while explosive charges drive guillotine blades that cut through the bundles of wiring and the plumbing that connect the two stages. In the nominal, case separation takes place just as the ascent stage uses the descent stage for a launchpad to leave the lunar surface. Like the Saturn, the Lunar Module is a multistage vehicle that discards each stage as its job is done. In this case, the expended stage is left to sit forever on the lunar surface as a monument to those who dared to come there.

APPENDIX E: ABBREVIATIONS AND ACRONYMS

AGS—abort guidance system
AOS—acquisition of signal
ARIA—Apollo Range Instrumented Aircraft
CAPCOM—capsule communicator
CM—Command Module
CDH—constant delta height
COI—contingency orbit insertion
CP—communications processor
CSI—coelliptic sequence initiate
CSM—Command and Service Module
CSQ—Coastal Sentry Quebec
CVTS—space vehicle test supervisor
DOI—descent orbit insertion
ETR—Eastern Test Range
FM—frequency modulation
GET—ground elapsed time
HF—high frequency
IMU—inertial measurement unit
IU—instrumentation unit
LM—Lunar Module
LEM—Lunar Excursion Module
LES—Launch Escape System

LOI—lunar orbit insertion
LOS—loss of signal
MILA—Merritt Island Launch Annex
MOC—mission operations computer
MOCR—Mission Operations Control Room
MSFN—Manned Space Flight Network
NORAD—North American Air Defense Command
PAD—pre-advisory data
PDI—powered descent initiation
PGNS—primary guidance and navigation system
REFSMAT—reference to a stable member matrix
RFO—reason for outage
SM—Service Module
SPS—Service Propulsion System
SRO—supervisor of range operations
TIG—time of ignition
TLC—translunar coast
TLI—translunar injection
TPI—terminal phase initiate
VAB—Vertical Assembly Building
VHF—very high frequency

ABOUT THE AUTHOR

Richard Stachurski is a retired US Air Force colonel whose career was spent in aeronautic and astronautic development programs. His military service included six years on loan to NASA for the Apollo lunar landing program where he participated in the Apollo 5 and the Apollo 9-14 missions. Returning to civilian life, Stachurski worked as a satellite systems design manager for the Boeing Company. He is the author of *Longitude by Wire: Finding North America* and numerous articles on the history of geodesy, cartography, and exploration. He is a native New Yorker and currently lives near Seattle, Washington.

INDEX

Note: Page numbers in bold refer to photographs. Page numbers followed by an "f" indicate illustrations. Page numbers followed by an "n" indcate notes.

487th Tactile Missile Wing, 300

abbreviations and acronyms, 331–332
abort guidance system (AGS), 232, 280–281
abort mechanisms, 54–56, 58, 61, 156
accident on *Apollo-Saturn 204*, 125–126
aeronautical ratings, 155
Agena upper stage rocket, 117, 119, 123
air-to-ground communications, 29–31, 56, 265–266
Air-to-Ground Communications Technician (COMM TECH), 4, 31
Aldrin, Edwin E. "Buzz," 216, 220
Allen, Augustus Chapman, 73–74
Allen, John Kirby, 73–74

Anders, William, 223, 236
antenna
    blockage of, 259n8
    equipment on Command and Service Module, 325, 326f
    gain, 304, 325
    Mars antenna at Goldstone Tracking Station, 225–226, 245–246, **305**
Apollo 11
    backup crew, 223
    incidents during mission, 216–219, 224, 287, 290
    mission phases, six, 304–305
    Mission Report, 279n9, 281n10, 299
    pre-launch preparations, 133–140, 317
    T minus 2 hours-8 minutes, 156–164

T minus 3 minutes-liftoff, 167–170
T minus 27 hours-T minus 3 hours, 145–149
T minus 93 hours-T minus 28 hours, 144–145
team divisions, 44, 212
see also lunar landing; Saturn V
Apollo Program
Apollo 5-10 missions, 67, 130–135
Apollo-Saturn 204 accident, 125–126
Apollo-Saturn 501, 128–130
beginning of, 117–118
Apollo Range Instrumented Aircraft (ARIA), 179–180, 199, 309f
Apollo-Saturn V Countdown, Test and Checkout Procedure Number V-40300, 144
Armstrong, Neil Alden, 119–122, 137, 224, 261, 265
Ascension Island (Britain) Tracking Station, 310
Ascent Work Schedule General Ground Rules, 271
Assistant Flight Director (AFD), 3, 44
astronauts
see specific names
Atlas intercontinental ballistic missile, 82, 104, 123
Aurora 7, 84
azimuth variations, launch, 39, 171, 306–308

B-58 Hustler, 91, 93, 98–100
Baker, John, 217n5
Bales, Steve, 255
"barbecue mode," 209
Beach, Dean, 103, 105
Berry, Charles Alden, 135, 137
Blalock, John, 41
Boatman, Wayne, 30
Boeing Company, 299, 300, 317
Booster Systems Engineer (BOOSTER), 3, 41
Boyd, Major, 97–98
Brady, Bill, 41
Brantley, Chet, 31, 116, 124
Brenning, Orin, 299
Buffalo Bayou (Texas), 73–74
Bulls, Robert, 97
Bunker Hill Air Force Base, 93
Bunker Hill (Indiana), 92–93
Burckhardt, Jacob, 89
burns, orbital
see specific type

call signs, 3–6
Canary Island Tracking Station, 162–163, 165–167, 183–189, 308
Capsule Communicator (CAPCOM), 3, 43–45
Carnarvon (Australia) Tracking Station, 308
Carpenter, Malcolm Scott, 84
Carr, Earl, 128
casualties in U. S. space program, first, 125
Cernan, Eugene, 236
Chaffee, Roger B., 125
Chapman, Bob, 128

Charlesworth, Clifford E., 44–45
Chinese legends, ancient, 230
circuit quality descriptors, 26
The Civilization of the Renaissance in Italy (Burckhardt), 89
Clayton, Elden, 26–27, 33
Clements, Henry "Pete," 124, 126
clocks, countdown, 143–144, 155, 223
Coastal Sentry Quebec tracking ship, 121
coelliptic sequence initiate (CSI) burn, 269, 286–287
Collins, Michael, 17, 231, 290
Command and Service Module (CSM) *Columbia*
    coordination with Eagle, 233–234, 269–270, 286–289
    lunar orbit, 209–211
    return to Earth, 289–291
    simulator, 23–24, 54, 56
    spacecraft detail, 319–326, 319f, 321f
    see also Lunar Module (LM) *Eagle*
Command Module *Gumdrop*, 131–132
Commonwealth Scientific and Industrial Research Organization, 306
communication systems
    air-to-ground, 29–31, 56, 58, 195, 265–266
    Apollo 11 Mission Report on, 281n10
    equipment, 323–325
    between Houston and Cape Canaveral, 175
    for lunar landing, 236–237, 242–245
    pre-launch preparations, 157–163
    satellites, 191
    troubleshooting problems with, 217n5, 247, 287–288
    Unified S-band, 118, 157–158, 195, 302–304, 306
    see also Manned Space Flight Network; tracking stations
Communications Controller (COMM CONTROL), 4
Communications Processor Controller (CPC), 4
Compass Cope pilotless aircraft, 299–300
Computer Maintenance and Operations (M&O), 3
computer maintenance procedures, 274–276
Computer Supervisor (SUP), 3
Congressional speech by President John F. Kennedy, 79–80
Conrad, Charles "Pete," 113, 236
constant differential height maneuver, 287
contractors, NASA, 117, 217n5
control system of Command and Service Module, 321f, 322
Convair, 98
    see also B-58 Hustler
Cooper, Gordon, 104, 113

Countdown Demonstration Test (CDDT), 136
Crawler Transporter, 317
Cuban Missile Crisis, 93–95, 97

data functions on Command and Service Module, 324
data quality standards, 56
De Cosmo, Ronald, 153
debriefing of flight simulation exercise, 68–69
Debus, Kurt, 235
Deep Space Network stations, 209, 219, 268
defense readiness condition (DEFCON), 94
Degner, Augie, 245
descent orbit insertion (DOI) burn, 225, 231, 234–235, 241–242
display system
    failure of, 62–66, 216–217, 217n5
    transitions of, 221, 225, 273–274
Display Technician (DISPLAY), 4
Douglas Aircraft Company, 317
Duke, Charles Moss, 43, 231
Dumis, Charles L., 43
Dutch (nickname), 15–16, 153

Eagle
    see Lunar Module (LM) *Eagle*
"The *Eagle* has landed." (Armstrong), 261
Early Apollo Surface Experiment Package, 267

Earth landing system of Command and Service Module, 323
Earth orbit phase, 207
Egan, George, 37–38, 63, **154**
Electrical, Environmental, and Consumables Manager (EECOM), 4, 43
electrical power system of Command and Service Module, 322
electromagnetic spectrum, 240, 303
    see also Unified S-band communications system
electromagnetic spectrum bands, 54n2
Ellsworth Air Force Base, 103–104
Emergency War Order, 104–105
encapsulated environment, life in the, 208
environmental control system of Command and Service Module, 321f, 322
Evans, Ronald E., 229–230

Faith 7, 104
Fendell, Edward I., 67–68
flag-raising on the Moon, 266
Flight Activities Officer (FAO), 4
Flight Director (FLIGHT), 4, 45
Flight Dynamics Officer (FIDO), 4, 40–41
Flight Support Division, 123–124
Flippin, Don, 52

"For one priceless moment, in the whole history of man." (Nixon), 266
487th Tactile Missile Wing, 300
Frank, M. P. "Pete," **132**
Friendship 7, 82
Fucci, Jim, 121

Gagarin, Yuri, 77
Gemini Program
    beginning of, 117
    Gemini 3 (*Molly Brown*), 113
    Gemini 8 accident, 119–123
    Gemini 9-12, 123–124
    Gemini V, 113
    information exchange network on, 301–302
    plaques, 17
geologic samples of the Moon, 265, 267
Gilruth, Robert R., 45, 236, **295**
Glenn, John, 82, 236
Goddard, Robert, 223
Goddard Space Flight Center (Maryland), 58, 145, 311–312
Goddard Voice Control Technician (GODDARD VOICE), 5
Goldstone (California) Tracking Station, 196, 209–212, 224–226, 245–246, **305**, 308
Gonzales, Robert, **132**
Grand Bahama Tracking Station, 172
Green, Jay, 221
Greenwich Mean Time, 20
Grew, Harriet, 237–238
Griffin, Gerald D., 216

Grissom, Virgil I., 80, 113, 125
Ground Launched Cruise Missile Program, 300
"ground pounders," 155
ground tracking system
    see tracking stations
Guaymas (Mexico) Tracking Station, 196, 308
Guidance, Navigation, Control Officer (GNC), 5
Guidance Officer (GUIDO), 5, 41
Guidance Reference Release (GRR), 169
guidance system of Command and Service Module, 322

Haise, Fred, 223, 236
Haislip, Lee, 119
Hamel, Ray, 106–112
Henry IV (Shakespeare), 246
Hodge, John, 120, 122
Honeysuckle Creek (Aust) Tracking Station, 209–212, 218n6
Houston (Texas), 73–76, 115–116
Houston Telemetry Technician (TM), 5
Houston Zoo, 76
human reliability program, 105
Huntsville tracking ship, 310

IBM, 27, 117, 145, 216–217
incidents
    on Columbia, 216–217, 290

on Gemini 8, 119–123
at Minuteman Launch
  Facility, 106–113
at tracking stations, 218,
  218n6, 224, 287
see also accident on
  Apollo-Saturn 204
Inertial Measurement Unit
  of Command and Service
  Module, 322
Input Prediction data, 165
Instrumentation and
  Communications Systems
  Officer (INCO), 5, 62, 67
Instrumentation Support
  Team, 26

James, Lee, 135
Jet Propulsion Laboratory, 209,
  302, 305
John, Warren, 81
Johnson, William, 95, 99–101

Kennedy, John F., 79–80, 94
Kennedy Space Center, 143–144
Kepler, Johannes, 57, 223
Keyser, Larry, 44, 46–47
King, Jr., Martin Luther, 130
King, Ray, 108–110
Kokee (Kauai) Tracking Station,
  310
Kraft, Christopher C., 45, 124,
  217n5, 236, **295**
Kranz, Eugene F., 44, 120–122,
  135, **230**

Laser Ranging Retroreflector
  experiment, 267

launch azimuth variations, 39,
  171, 306–308
Launch Escape Assembly,
  319–320f
Launch Umbilical Tower, 317
Launch/Translunar Injection
  Work Schedule, 40
LeMay, Curtis, 124
Lima Launch Control Facility
  (South Dakota), 106–113
Llewellyn, John S., 47–49
Lopez, Bob, 108
Lovell, Jim, 223, 236
Low, George M., 135, 236, **295**
Luna Fifteen, 214
lunar ascent
  initial liftoff, 281–283
  launch velocity, 286
  phases of, 268–272
  propulsion system problem,
    276–279
  report during, 285
lunar dust warning, 237–238
lunar landing
  descent orbit insertion (DOI)
    burn, 225, 231, 234–235,
    241–242
  "The Eagle has landed"
    (Armstrong), 261
  lunar walk, 265–267
  manual guidance program
    (P66), 259–260
  phases of, 241–242
  preparation for, 225–227,
    231–233
  rest period report, 279n9
  see also powered descent
    initiation (PDI) burn

Lunar Module Guidance,
  Control, Propulsion Officer
  (CONTROL), 4
Lunar Module (LM) *Eagle*
  adapter, 315
  alarms on, 254–255, 258
  communication systems of,
    242–245
  coordination with *Columbia*,
    233–234, 269–270,
    286–289
  detail of, 327–329, 328f
  lunar orbit, 221–225,
    286–287
  see also Command and Service
    Module (CSM) *Columbia*
Lunar Module *Spider*, 131–132
Lunar Module Telemetry,
  Electrical, Extra Vehicular
  Activity Mobility Unit Officer
  (TELCOM), 6
lunar orbit insertion (LOI)
  burns, 221–225
Lunney, Glynn S., 44, 139

Macbeth (Shakespeare),
  155–156
Mackey, Ray, 117, 124
Maddux, Barbara, 116
Maddux, Orville, 116
Madrid (Spain) Tracking Station,
  214–215, 219
Manhattan College, 84
Manned Space Flight Network,
  69, 118, 304–312, 306f
Manned Spacecraft Center,
  10–12, 117, 118
Mariner Mars mission, 306

Mars antenna at Goldstone
  Tracking Station, 225–226,
  245–246, **305**
Mayflower Transit, 81–82
McCafferty, Riley, 24
McCandless, Bruce, 161–162, 220
McDivitt, James Alton, 236
Medical Officer (SURGEON), 6
Mercury Program, 69, 80, 84, 94,
  104, 117
Mercury tracking ship, 119–201,
  309
Merritt Island Launch Annex
  (Florida) Tracking Station
  (MILA), 52, 54, 128
Meyer, Larry, 212
Michoud Assembly Factory,
  317
Minuteman Missile program,
  103–113
Mission Control Center, 15f,
  17–19, 18f, 145, 217n5
Mission Control Center Houston
  Familiarization Manual
  (Philco-Ford), 118
Mission Rules Document, 38–39
Mobile Service Structure, 317,
  318
Monkvic, John, 154–155, **154**
Moon landing
  see lunar landing
moonquake experiment, 267
Moore, Wayne, 94
Mueller, George, 128

Naha Search One, 123
navigation system of Command
  and Service Module, 322

Network Controller
  (NETWORK), 5, 69
network validation testing, 58–59
news briefs, daily, 214, 220, 230
Newton, Isaac, 57
Nickerson, Russ, 117
Nixon, Richard, 137, 266
"no lone zone," 108
North American Air Defense
  Command (NORAD), 53–54
North American Aviation, 317

O'Brian, Hugh, 22–23
Ojalehto, George, 138, **230**, 239
Old Market Square (Houston,
  Texas), 74–75
Operations and Procedures
  Officer (O&P), 5
Optical Unit of Command and
  Service Module, 322
orbital chase of *Columbia* and
  Eagle, 269–270, 286
orbital ground track sequence,
  308–309

Paine, Thomas, 235
Parkes radio telescope, 306
Parr, Glenda, 93
Parr, O. C., 93
Pasadena (Texas), 73, 115–116
Passive Seismic Experiment, 267
Patrick Air Force Base (Florida),
  179
Petrone, Rocco, 135, 235
Philco-Ford, 117, 118, 216–217
Phillips, Samuel C., 135, 236
plaques, mission, 17, 296–298,
  297

position descriptions, 3–6
powered descent initiation (PDI)
  burn
  approach phase (P64),
    241, 257
  braking phase (P63), 241,
    250–256
  landing phase (P65), 242
  manual guidance program
    (P66), 259–260
Powers, Pauline, 82
pre-advisory data (PAD), 221n7
Presley, Will, 43, 47
primary guidance and navigation
  system (PGNS), 231–232
*Proceedings of the Apollo Unified
  S-Band Technical Conference*,
  118
Project Mercury, see *Mercury
  program*
Public Affairs Officer (PAO),
  5, 227
Puddy, Donald R., 240, 247

radio frequency equipment
  on Command and Service
    Module, 324–325
Randall, Ernie, 127, 146
Range Safety Officer (RSO),
  6, 314
Rapid City (South Dakota), 104
reaction control system of
  Command and Service
    Module, 321f, 323
Real-Time Command Controller
  (RTC), 6, 28–30
Redstone suborbital rocket,
  77, 80

Redstone tracking ship, 199–201, 203, 309
Reed, David, 40, 47, 268
Reining, Rod, 138–140
rendezvous radar navigation, 269, 270, 286
rest period report, lunar, 279n9
Retrofire Officer (RETRO), 5, 41
Richards, Steve, 22–23, 31
Ritchie, Charles, 146
Robledo (Spain) Tracking Station, 219
Roosa, Stuart Allen, **132**
Rose Knot Victor tracking ship, 121
RP-1 fuel, 148

Sanborn, Samuel D., 126, 133, 134, 138
satellites, communication, 191
Saturn rocket family
   Apollo-Saturn 204 accident, 125
   Saturn IB, 123
Saturn V
   overview, 313–318, 315f, 316f
   Apollo-Saturn 501, 128–130
   first stage (S-IC), 171–174
   second stage (S-II), 174–177
   third stage (S-IVB), 178–181
Saxon, John, 212
S-band communications system
   see Unified S-band communications system
Schirra, Jr., Walter M., 94
Schmidt, Egon, 91–92
Scott, David Randolph, 119–121
Seamans, Robert C., 236
seismic experiment, lunar, 267

Service Module (SM), 24, 132–133, 320–323
   see also Command and Service Module (CSM) *Columbia*
service propulsion system of Command and Service Module, 322–323
Shakespeare, William, 155–156, 246
Sheehan, Tom, 138
Shepard, Alan B., 77
side-lobes, 240
Sigma 7, 94
signal acquiring process, 310–311
signal masks, 189n4
Silverstein, Abe, 235
Simulation Supervisor (SIMSUP), 6, 24
Site Configuration Message, 29
Site Readiness Testing, 145, 148
Slayton, Donald K., 135, 223, 236
solar maximum period, 139–140
solar wind composition experiment, 266
Soviet Union space program, 77, 214
Space Task Group, 120
Space Vehicle Test Supervisor (CVTS), 4, 144
spacecraft detail, 314–317, 316f
Spears, Glenn, 28–30
Stachurski, Dale, 106
Stachurski, Mary Lou, 82, 84, 115, 300
Stachurski, Richard
   as Air Force Deputy Missile Combat Crew Commander, 103–106

as Air Force Flight
Commander, 93–95
childhood memories of, 85–89
early employment of, 80–82
marriage and family of,
82–84, 92, 106, 115, 300
as NASA Flight Operations
Scheduler, 116–117
as NASA Network Controller,
15n1, 69, 126–128, **132**,
133, **154**
post-NASA positions of,
299–300
Stachurski, Traci Ann, 84
Stafford, Thomas P., 236
Strategic Air Command, 94, 97,
103–105
see also Minuteman Missile
program
Supervisor of Range Operations
(SRO), 6
Support Count Handbook, 21
surface mobility evaluation,
lunar, 266
Sutton, Casey, 97

Tananarive (Madagascar)
Tracking Station, 308
team divisions, Apollo 11, 44, 212
telecommunications system
of Command and Service
Module, 323–325
Teledyne-Ryan Company, 299
Telemetry Instrumentation
Controller (TIC), 6
telescope, spacecraft, 215–216
television broadcasts
lunar walk, 265–266

from spacecraft, 208,
215–216, 220, 224, 290
temperature differentials,
spacecraft, 139–140, 209
terminal phase initiate (TPI)
burn, 270, 288
T/GET times, 20–21
"That's one small step for man."
(Armstrong), 265
Thompson, Floyd L., 125
Tidbinbilla (Australia) Tracking
Station, 209, 218n6
time descriptors, 20–21
Titan II rocket, 117
Tracking Controller (TRACK), 6
tracking frequencies, 54n2
tracking ships
see specific ships
tracking stations
handovers, 204, 207,
210–212, 214, 308–310
pre-launch preparations at,
54–55, 58, 148
signal masks, 189n4
see also Manned Space Flight
Network; specific stations
trajectory corrections, 208,
214–215, 254, 255
Tranquility Base landing, 261
trans-Earth injection burn,
289–290
translunar injection (TLI) burn,
193–204

U. S. Air Force
Easter Test Range, 306–307
manned-space program
support, 124, 126

U-2 aircraft, 94
Unified S-band communications system, 118, 157–158, 195, 302–304, 306
UNIVAC, 28, 117, 145, 217n5, 274, 311
USS *Mason*, 123

Vanguard tracking ship, 63–64, 148, 307
Vice, Joseph, 127, 267
Von Braun, Wernher, 70, 235

Wagner, Theodore, 95–96
weather report, space-based, 175, 215
Webb, Don, 31
White, Edward H., 113, 125
Whitehead, Jim, 91–92
Wilson, Doug, 216, 239
Windler, Milton L., 44

Young, David, 127, 134, 153
Young, John, 17, 24, 113

Made in the USA
Coppell, TX
27 August 2020